Truth, Trust, and Relationships

Healing Interventions in Contextual Therapy

Truth, Trust, and Relationships

Healing Interventions in Contextual Therapy

Barbara R. Krasner, Ph.D.

and

Austin J. Joyce, D.Min.

BRUNNER/MAZEL *Publishers* • New York

Krasner, Barbara.
    Truth, trust, and relationships: healing interventions in contextual therapy
by Barbara R. Krasner and Austin J. Joyce.
      p.   cm.
    Includes bibliographical references and index.
    ISBN 0-87630-755-1
    1. Contextual therapy.   I. Joyce, Austin J. II. Title.
RC488.55.K75 1995
616.89' 14–dc20

                                      95-8927
                                        CIP

Published by
BRUNNER/MAZEL, Inc.
19 Union Square West
New York, New York 10003
Manufactured in the United States of America

10   9   8   7   6   5   4   3   2   1

To Abraham, Sarah, and Isaac

"but Father, where is the lamb for the burnt offering?"

Gen. 22:7–8

CONTENTS

FOREWORD

Truth, Trust, and Relationships brings to contextual therapy a new emphasis on "direct address" as the cornerstone that helps to catalyze ethical imagination and initiate the process of dialogue. Krasner and Joyce build directly on Martin Buber's categories of injury to the common order: vital dissociation, the sickness and decay of organic forms of life; and "seeming," in Krasner and Joyce's words, that "form of collusion that protects people from having to know or having to be known, even in the midst of genuinely offered care." All these categories point, in turn, to the centrality of justice in relationship; for to the extent that withheld truth and fractured trust become the hallmarks of the interhuman, as they do in our age, the resistance to doing justice increases.

Like all contextual therapists, Krasner and Joyce point to the pressure of relevance to be found in the intergenerational family: "While Buber's notion of healing through meeting can occur any time that two people are fully present to each other, their capacity to be truly present is influenced in great measure by how each of them was addressed in their family of origin." Unfortunately, few of the adults coming into therapy have cohesive ground under their feet, as a result of which they adopt a basically reactive stance, blaming spouse, parents, children, employer, friends, or "the system."

In both family and nonfamily relationships, "dialogue is relationship's catalyzing tool, its fundamental conviction, its creative process, and its healing and redeeming way." Dialogue offers the option of merited trust while monologue imposes blame. Specifically, Krasner and Joyce look to "multidirected partiality, rejunction, therapeutic expectations, inclusiveness, timing, crediting, and eliciting" as "complex and catalyzing leverages for helping family members reengage."

Krasner and Joyce locate the keystone of the dialogic process and the chief resource of human relationships in "residual trust"—"the summation of a 'ledger sheet' that records the merit *between* people." Residual trust lies at the heart of every redemptive investment in the dialogic process and is "the sine qua non of fairness or justice *between* person and person." Trustworthiness evolves from mutual commitment and a multilateral stance, which can never be reduced to the psychological universe of one of the participants. As I define

xi

"existential trust" as "the courage to address and the courage to respond" (Friedman, 1972), Krasner and Joyce similarly point to "the courage to address someone who may withdraw from me, the courage to receive a word that is offered when that word may assault me." Realistically they see most relating as characterized by the pseudomutuality that arises from the tendency to withhold one's truth and the failure to credit the truth of another.

Like Ivan Boszormenyi-Nagy, Krasner and Joyce make Buber's concept of existential guilt central in their contextual therapy, and they add some important insights of their own as to how neurotic guilt feelings prevent both responsibility and the recognition of existential guilt. "A life devoted to compiling guilt feelings invariably obscures the way toward a stance of responsible response," they write and expound:

> Paradoxically, people often use guilt feelings to defend against a proper acceptance of guilt. Premature despair over one's own life situation, remorse over consideration intended but undelivered, the terror of unjust blame, and the indebtedness implied in receiving all converge to silence relating partners. Silenced over time, people retreat inward, live with stagnant guilt feelings, and abandon the healing options of facing and direct address. (Chapter 2)

They also distinguish between the anger and guilt feelings that arise on a psychological level when merit is unrecognized and the injury to the order of existence that results from uncredited merit on the ethical level.

Another central contribution that Krasner and Joyce make to the development of contextual therapy is their emphasis upon the elemental triad of mother, father, and child. Not only is a child's loyalty biologically based and triadically determined in the first instance, but also it rests in the child's unarticulated, self-preserving comparison of its parenting figures. When a child is ethically driven to disengage from one parent, that parent becomes a lost and nonreplaceable resource, which in turn engenders an intuitive guilt in the child arising from awareness of the profound injury to the common order of existence between the child and the other family members. This may lead to a habitual triangulation in which the child spends the rest of his or her life being for or against *any* relating partner, whether parent, mate, child, employer, or friend.

Nowhere, write Krasner and Joyce, is Martin Buber's philosophical anthropology "pursued more faithfully or implemented more rigorously than in the theory and practice of contextual therapy." They define contextual therapy as "a trust-based therapy whose strategies and interventions are powered by direct address."

What basically sets contextual therapy apart from other modalities are (1) *its determination to catalyze direct address. . . for the purpose of establishing just balances of give-and-take, (2) its refusal to collude with persons whose suffering tempts them to choose the false sanctuary of a therapeutic relationship over the dialogic imperative that exists between them and members of their entire world.* (Chapter 3)

The authors proclaim an "ontic connection" that is at the same time a very human one: "Multidirected partiality and direct address have become effective interventions just because they reflect the organic longing of each person present."

Krasner and Joyce remove themselves from the ordinary therapist and even the ordinary dialogic psychotherapist in asserting that "it is *the dialogic process* between people of significance to each other rather than the relationship between clinician and client that *is regarded as the primary agent of healing.*" The clinician's relationship to the client should be trust based and responsible, but it can never be ontically ethical since it is by definition accidental and substitutable. For this reason "*contextual therapists by definition remove themselves from competition with a client's parents, children, or mate.*" They also reject such current mental health buzzwords as "dysfunctional families," "toxic parents," "tough love," and "women who love too much" as diverting from healing through meeting. Furthermore, they attack the expediency that serves as a yardstick for many therapists:

> *Interpreting feelings as the basis of reality rather than as signals for unaddressed injustice is an example of emotional expediency.* It is a choice for isolation. Seeking a solution without surfacing unfaced injuries and crediting mutual contributions is an example of transactional expediency. (Chapter 5)

In place of the customary pathological categories, they give as their goal and that of the profession in general: "*guiding people toward balances of freedom and responsibility in themselves and between each other.*" This goal is grounded in their recognition that "*every human being is part of a multipersonal context whose members are ethically joined and dynamically mandated to help each other discover fairer balances of give-and-take.*"

Although the vertical dimension—the relation between and among generations—stands at the top of Krasner and Joyce's contextual therapy hierarchy, *Truth, Trust, and Relationships* also concerns itself with the give-and-take between mates, child and adult siblings, and friends. They point out that the connection between adult brothers and sisters is an anomalous one since structurally they are peers while dynamically they are more impacted by the third-party reality of their parents than by each other. What they wrote about friendship is so effective that I used it as the opening step in reinitiating direct address between my wife and myself and another couple who had become estranged. Although friendship is not as structured as other relations, "give-and-take with its primary questions of what is owed and what is deserved applies to friendship as well as to family." They also recognize most helpfully that *"the illusion that sexual passion, emotional intensity, and idealized compatibility are the basic building blocks of long-term relationships typically results in parentification between peers."* This parentification in turn "is characterized by chronically unspoken expectations, unacknowledged limits, and unilateral imposition, which, unfaced over time, destroy the fabric of just relating."

Their morality is not relative but neither is it abstract. They stress that sexual infidelity can become a resource when it surfaces stagnant balances of give-and-take that rob relationships of promise or hope, even as it can also be used for purposes of comparison, humiliation, self-exoneration, or the evasion of commitment.

The most moving statement of healing through meeting in *Truth, Trust, and Relationships* is found in its last paragraph:

> Therapists are entitled to witness to the holy ground of creation and connection. They are free to point the way to relational justice illumined by the burning bush whose branches are truth and trust. Epiphany, awe, and grace are the ineffable manifestations of healing through meeting. They are the outpouring of a still, small voice now breaking into a passionate cry for uncorrupted connection. They are the saving if unrecognized sacraments of all professional efforts at healing. (Epilogue)

In this final paragraph the religious undertone that one can sense throughout the book, particularly in the quotations from the Hebrew Bible and the New Testament, is made explicit.

What I have not touched on in this Foreword is the rich abundance of cases that the authors have interwoven with their presentation of concepts. These cases are more than illustrations of abstract ideas. They are the very stuff out of which such ideas have arisen. This fact makes *Truth, Trust, and Relationships* an effective clinical text for professionals and laypersons alike. Barbara Krasner and Austin Joyce's book is not only *about* mastering direct address. In its form, style, and clinical illustrations, it is itself a masterpiece of direct address.

Maurice Friedman, Ph.D.
Professor Emeritus
San Diego State University

REFERENCES

Boszormenyi-Nagy, I. (1987). *Foundations of contextual therapy: Collected papers of Ivan Boszormenyi-Nagy, M.D*. New York: Brunner/Mazel.

Boszormenyi-Nagy, I., & Krasner, B. R. (1986). *Between give and take: A clinical guide to contextual therapy*. New York: Brunner/Mazel.

Boszormenyi-Nagy, I., & Spark, G. (1973, 1984). *Invisible loyalties: Reciprocity in intergenerational family therapy*. New York: Harper & Row, Medical Division; Brunner/Mazel (reprint).

Buber, M. (1958). *I and thou* (2nd rev. ed. with postscript by author added). (Trans. R. G. Smith.) New York: Scribners.

Buber, M. (1985). *Between man and man* (Intro. by M. S. Friedman; trans. by R. G. Smith.) New York: Scribners.

Buber, M. (1988). *The knowledge of man: A philosophy of the interhuman*. (Ed. with an introductory essay by M. S. Friedman; trans. M. S. Friedman & R. G. Smith.) Atlantic Highlands, NJ: Humanities Press International.

Friedman, A. (1992). *Treating chronic pain: The healing partnership*. New York: Insight Books (Plenum).

Friedman, M. S. (1972). *Touchstones of reality: Existential trust and the community of peace*. New York: Dutton.

Friedman, M. S. (1985). *The Healing Dialogue in Psychotherapy*. New York: Jason Aronson. Paperback ed. 1994, Northvale, NJ: Jason Aronson.

Friedman, M. S. (1991). The worlds of existentialism: A critical reader. Atlantic Highlands, NJ: Humanities Press International.

ACKNOWLEDGMENTS

"Sing unto the Lord a new song."
—Ps. 33:3

These people were present to us as we struggled to put words to our reality and spirit to our song:

Michael Ruczinski and Karen Shirley, fellow sojourners, envisioned this book before we did. Maurice Friedman, teacher and friend, confirmed our quest for speech-with-meaning. Douglas Schoeninger, Jan Filing, Miriam McLeod, Siobhan McEnaney, Jane Buhl, and Lynn Vanderhoof, colleagues and friends, buoyed our hope as words took wing. Natalie Gilman, editor, lent subtlety and generosity to the writing process. David Krasner's unerring ear for words that "work" eased our path. Sue MacDonald's and Karen Krasner's intense investment in the text paralleled our own. Their probing questions, editorial eye, and assaultive humor commanded our attention with laughter and with tears. Karen's organizing prowess in producing the final product was surpassed only by her capacity to organize its authors.

Our families as family provided the bedrock and ongoing impetus on the journey to make our goal a reality.

The Joyce Family

Faith's passionate testing in her own life gave Austin heart to continue testing in his own. Jonathan and Rachel provided the crucible that lent Austin integrity and hope.

The Krasner Family

David's fierce devotion to her and his unparalleled confidence in the outcome of the book cushioned Barbara's way. Scott, Jill, and Karen's selective loyalties and their courage to be peers were infinitely sustaining. Donna's wit and enthusiasm for the project heightened motivation. And Zachary and Tate were and are the alpha and omega of Barbara's passion to point a way for coming generations.

INTRODUCTION

This book was born out of the authors' passion for direct address—that catalytic claim for connectedness, that will to test the possibility that in one's own
voice is the voice of a relating partner's suppressed longing. This work is a
unique distillation of Martin Buber's philosophical anthropology and of the
theory and practice of contextual therapy, a three-generational modality. Contextual therapy is essentially a dialogic stance set squarely on the conviction
that relational justice in the human order is most fully realized through turning
to face each member of one's elemental triad (father, mother, and offspring)
rather than fleeing them. In the first instance, this distillation points to the
dynamic connection between truth and trust and their efficacy inside and outside the therapy room. Few people disagree with truth and trust as ideal values. What confounds most of us is how to actualize and embody them. This
book then will focus on the mastery of direct address. It will examine the
clinical concepts and applications of the ethics of direct address. It will explore the facets of a trust-based, resource-oriented conviction that invites the
exchange of truth and trust in the service of justice. It will proceed from the
premises of contextual therapy, whose focus on merited trust offers practitio-
ners leverages for eliciting truth and fairness in context.

Our efforts are rooted in creative contributions of the past: Contextual therapy
was founded by I. Boszormenyi-Nagy, and developed and nuanced by
Boszormenyi-Nagy, G. Spark, B. Krasner, M. Cotroneo, and M. Friedman,
among many others. Martin Buber's massive body of work is drawn not only
from his overarching belief that the proper study of humanity is human beings
but from the rich storehouses of biblical faith and Jewish mysticism.

The cornerstone of contextual therapy is healing through meeting. To wit,
the fundamental longing of the human spirit is to be truly met: heard, considered, and addressed. The fundamental impulse toward true meeting with those
people to whom we are most powerfully connected is most often derailed by
the terror of mismeeting—the fear of being misheard, ill considered, and un-

fairly dismissed. *The possibilities of healing through meeting are made real when truth encounters trust, when trust elicits truth, and when the handmaiden of both is direct address.*

Each of us is born into a context whose members tend to invite each other's truth, or more likely, to dismiss it. In fact, it seems to us that children are taught to lie at an early age, however unintentionally. More often than not, the young are rewarded for keeping quiet, for withholding their truth. They are asked to conform and comply with the dictates of what their elders say, but they live with the truth of what their elders do. They are often at a loss to imagine how to bridge the gap between instruction and lived life. Cared for, but essentially unaddressed, members of the new generation themselves become parents and, unsuspecting, replay the cycle once more.

No wonder then, that parents are so repetitively declared toxic by limitless numbers of accusers, and become the targeted, if ill-considered, locus of their children's blame and disappointment. The terror that parents can strike in the hearts of their children is exemplified by a bank scandal in Mexico City, a failed pyramid scheme of $215 million recently devised by a 33-year-old woman. She was intent on keeping her lover from disclosing her pregnancies and subsequent abortions to her family. She capitulated to her partner's pressure to embezzle money from money market accounts that she handled at the bank (Uhlig, 1990). This situation may be an extreme example of the everyday deceptions that occur in ordinary life; it is also a measure of the lengths to which we will go to keep from disclosing ourselves to the people with whom we maintain significant connections.

Nowhere are hurts so hurtful or joys so joyful as they are in the ongoing contacts of enduring relationships. Each of the authors has sought for the balances between suffering and joy that are lost and found time and again in ordinary moments. Each of us has been buoyed by elation and submerged by despair over the peril and promise of relational life. And each of us has faced the risk of choosing for a path where truth meets trust. Why take this risk? Why the way of dialogue where trust elicits truth? After all, I know where I stand. We disagree. Why hurt each other? Why get hurt? Why bother? Why not just move on?

Truth and trust between the generations, frequently unimagined, untested, and inaccessible, lose their life energy and, attenuated, fall into disuse. Sapped of concreteness and vital meaning, they are transmuted into abstract values and beliefs from one generation to the next. Distorted patterns of relating and unintended imbalances result: The woman who uses her mother as a channel through whom to communicate to her father is likely to choose her daughter—over her husband—as confidante. The man who crumbles in the face of his wife's shouting will probably raise sons who are emotionally disengaged even when they are physically present. People are estranged typically because they do not know how to connect. Making relationships work always requires a dialogic stance. But the term "dialogue," like the term "communication," has been gutted of meaning. Without a stance in which truth is disclosed and invited, trust becomes a fantasy or a longing, but never a reliable reality. To regain their life force and healing capacities, truth and trust require a rebirth of dialogue with its key constituent of direct address.

The fundamental premise of dialogue is that merit exists in each person's side. I may disagree with you. I may feel injured by you. But I cannot eclipse your reality. You may react to my stance. You may feel rejected by me. But you cannot invalidate my reality. In any case we remain connected, unalterably linked. Direct address is the attempt to make these linkages palpable, to bring hidden resources into the open, to make relationships work.

Direct address is a tool, a method, and a stance, whether or not dialogue is its end result. Nothing can guarantee dialogue between two or more relating partners, but direct address is the cornerstone of dialogic possibilities. At some point in my life I have been addressed. In the primal unfolding of birth and of growth, I was named and I was given care. I was given to in my mother's womb, and I was provided for by the work of somebody's hands. And whatever my later interpretations are of what more my parents could have done, I survived and thrived because I received.

I received, therefore I owe. I also gave, therefore I deserve. "In the beginning a will to reciprocity is rooted in existential ties" (Krasner, 1986, p. 121). "Just as parents become responsible for the survival of their helpless infants, children soon become accountable to the people who alone among all others gave them life" (Krasner, 1986, p. 121). Loyalty is a hallmark of childhood (Boszormenyi-Nagy & Spark, 1973). Every child is driven to meet his or her family's expectations. Whether they are told directly or indirectly, children carry invisible loyalties, a primitive impulse that accompanies growing up. In fact, children tend to be captive to their parents' well-being. They earn merit from their efforts to please, whether or not their parents know it. Impending tragedy lies in the fact that parents may be or feel so wounded by their own parents that they are unable to see their child as giving, much less to acknowledge the gifts.

The existential burden of individual and relational maturity is not a one-sided revisionist history in which we simply critique what we did or did not get, but a bold facing of what is given and what is owed. We can attack parenting for its insufficiencies, but the fact is that, in one or another dimension, *parenting like all human relationships is deficient as well as benign*. What is more critical is the question of who my parents were or are. What were the forces with which they struggled? On what resources could they count? What did they do with what they had? How did they find meaning in their lives? Who nurtured them? What truths informed them? How did they ask for help if they did? Whose hand guided them? Whose voice addressed them? Whom did they trust? To whom could they speak their truth?

The problematic here is that if my parents failed to find their voice in a fair and reasoned way, what chance do I have to discover mine? In point of fact *there is a hole in the heart of the parenting process about which few questions are ever asked*: that is, the unexamined expectations and illusions that one generation holds of another. Indelibly marked by the consequences of parental legacies and decisions, members of each generation are obliged to find healing, freedom, and a capacity to teach the process of give-and-take to children yet unborn. The success of this task rests on a person's movement toward direct address. Whether or not my efforts evoke a reciprocal response, I alone must decide whether or not to raise my voice and speak my truth in the trust that I will strike a responsive chord in the heart and mind of another. In so doing, I can know at the very least that my choice to speak is an attempt to balance what I owe, to assert what I deserve.

It is our contention that dialogic psychotherapy, which occurs to some degree in every therapeutic process, is always served by truth and trust. Therapy is about transforming moments. People tell their stories; therapists respond. The stories that are told are always in process. The responses that are given are always impacted by the quest for meaning that has shaped a therapist's life. Therapy is about ordinary moments that are a prelude to healing ordinary lives.

In one form or another, healing occurs through genuinely trustworthy exchange. By accident or design, every mode of healing is based on the sacred foundation of trust. Trust is to committed relationship what food is to the sustenance of life. For

> what the problematic person wants is a being not only whom he can trust as a person trusts another, but a being that gives him now the certitude that "there is a soil, there is an existence. The world is not condemned to deprivation, degeneration, destruction. The world can be redeemed because there is trust." (Buber, 1965b, p. 186)

Therapist and client(s) commit themselves to a contract through which to explore and invest in the redeeming options of a trustworthy way. Therapeutic modalities are molded and informed by many factors: biology, psychology, family, and culture. Less immediately visible are the philosophical foundations that undergird a therapist's practice and conviction. The failure of direct address is rooted in long-term loyalty binds. Children withhold their truth as their parents did before them. Instructions in silence and deception abound in ordinary life: "Children should be seen and not heard." "Now look at what you've done!" "Your father works hard; don't bother him." "Don't talk to your mother that way." What is lost in these exchanges is the truth of each person's side. At one or another time in our lives, each of us has learned that our truths are inconvenient, that they are likely to cause trouble, that they tend to burden the very people whom we truly want to please.

The following premises are meant to orient the reader to the dynamic possibilities of relationship. They indicate a dialogic way. They penetrate the myth that *life between person and person is a problem to be solved rather than a moment to be addressed.* They point to a repository of interhuman resources that lie dormant in the realm of the between. They offer the reader the "high road" of speech-with-meaning, that is, the lived reality of the word born in tension and embodied in multiplicity that moves us toward each other to know and be known, and to love and be loved (Friedman, 1991, p. 126). *On this path from the "easy word" to the difficult one, contextual therapy embraces Buber's philosophy of the word that is spoken and of speech as event and event as speech, of the world as word and human existence as address and response* (Friedman, 1991). The following premises undergird the subject matter of the entire book:

- When people chronically give without taking or take without giving, injustices occur. Reworking injury to the common order of existence depends on the use of direct address.
- Direct address—a word, a tear, a touch, a look, a gift, a tone, a question posed—is the cornerstone of dialogic possibilities. It is a tool through which to catalyze ethical imagination and to attempt to initiate the process of dialogue. It is a way and a stance whether or not dialogue is its end result.
- In the long run, direct address is a healing intervention whose form is secondary to its substance, its context, and its goal of moving beyond interhuman stagnation and the destructive consequences of vital dissociation.
- A chronic inability to surface one's truth and to elicit the truth of another results in vital dissociation, the sickness and decay of organic forms of life (family, community, workplace) that enable people to live in direct relation to and security with one another.
- The intrinsic significance of direct address is rooted in an interhuman ethic whose dynamic reality is that people in relationship both owe and deserve, and require dialogue to right imbalances.
- Direct address between person and person is ordinarily a courageous and demanding choice. But direct address between person and person in the elemental triad is even more so, though latent resources and residual trust are likely to be greater between the generations than in accidental relations—terror notwithstanding.
- The absence of direct address results in "seeming," which can be viewed as a form of collusion that protects people from having to know or having to be known, even in the midst of genuinely offered care.

- Caretaking can be an embodiment of seeming, a diversion from dialogue, an expression that one caretakes because one's partner cannot take care of himself or herself.
- Seeming is an inevitable consequence of failed imagination. The dislocation that seeming produces in a person, and between person and person, usurps freedom and converts the balletic movements of truth and trust into clumsy attempts to climb onstage.
- Succumbing to a mandate to please, constrained by unreworked split and conflicting loyalties, and blindsided by the demands of felt or real unrelenting obligation, people take on a facade of seeming. Far from offering a safe haven, however, seeming corrodes being and corrupts the vision of healing through meeting.
- In the first instance, flight into seeming is rooted in one's family of origin where, bound to please at the expense of one's truth, children soon learn to avoid direct address.
- The choice for direct address, to surface one's truth and to elicit the truth of another, results in vital association between people who have a legacy of give-and-take in common.
- Movement toward vital association signals a willingness to own my contribution to injustice and estrangement—in desperate hope that you will be willing to own your part.
- The very move from seeming to being provides a counterpoint to the impulse to please. Turning to face the sources of injuries can level fear, free energy, open fresh options, and hallow the quality of day-to-day existence.
- The healing resources that lie dormant in the sphere of the interhuman are catalyzed by ethical imagination (the ability to conceive and dialogically test what one owes and what one deserves).
- Contrary to human longings, the freedom to be (in contrast to the constraint to seem) is an earned freedom, sometimes enlivened by grace, which comes of knowing one's truths and terms for relationship, embracing and disclosing them, and testing them in circumstances loaded with possibilities of many-sided injuries and potential retribution.
- Despite our distaste for the fray and our wish for an easier path, none exists. But what does exist is sufficient.
- It is only when we stand in the grace of sufficiency that ethical imagination can break loose and inspirit reality.

It is with these premises in mind that the authors proceeded to write for clinicians; educators; lawyers and court personnel; physicians, nurses, and hospital personnel; and, in fact, for anyone who recognizes the complexity of interfamilial relationships on the advent of the 21st century.

We are writing for people whose personal and professional lives interface and require them to reenter the realm of the between, where truth meets trust, and trust becomes the mainstay of commonplace exchange. It is especially meant for therapists whose work with families, couples, and individuals requires them to provide a way for others to gain meaning from the ethics of direct address. In sum, it is increasingly clear that chaos in relationship increases in direct proportion to the failure of "doing justice" between person and person (Micah 6:8). The resistance to doing justice in relationship increases in direct proportion to the degree to which withheld truth and fractured trust become the characteristics of the interhuman. The defining fact is that withheld truth and fractured trust have become the hallmark of the age.

This book is divided into two parts. Part I, "Roots of Relationship," identifies fundamental premises of interhuman connection and engagement. It places each individual in his or her ontic context and then proceeds to describe elements of commitment. Part II, "Ethical Tasks of a Contextual Therapist," moves from the underlying premises of contextual therapy, with its emphasis on balanced give-and-take, to clinical strategies, interventions, and practice. It points to how a contextual therapist elicits truth and trust in the service of relational justice. Janet I. Filing, Ph. D., friend and colleague, underscored the effort in Chapter 7, "Truth and Trust after Divorce: Dialogic Interventions," by lending her personal and professional acumen and experience.

In our journeys toward personal balance and professional maturity and competence, each of the authors has struggled with the painful consequences of not being heard. And we have lived with the regret of having failed to hear a loved one's still, small voice. Each of us has suffered from the limitations of our parents' lives and actions. Each of us has had occasion to stand helplessly by as our contributions to family members have been overlooked and have gone uncredited. Each of us has experienced withered self-esteem impaled on the jagged edge of disappointed parental expectations; and each of us has encountered marital, filial, and sibling anticipations and hopes that we have failed to meet. Each of us has children whom we have alternately loved, protected, hurt, and disappointed. But if this book is born of struggle, it is also born of joy. For it was inspirited by the courageous if sometimes unheralded gifts of our family members' lives and contributions. Each of us has been witness to hidden resources that have arisen out of the breach of interhuman injury, estrangement, and mistrust between us and our family members. From time to time, each of us has also bathed in the deep, pure waters of our family's adulation, and basked in the strong, bright light of their nurture, their love, and their care.

The struggle and joy in each of the authors' lives and contexts diverge in terms of particularity. Austin J. Joyce is a 45-year-old man, raised in the Irish Catholic tradition. The third of five children, he grew up in a housing project where the realities of the street and volatility between people became the foundation for his quest to find ways to repair fractured trust and fragmented connections. Sports, academia, marriage, two children, and the Presbyterian ministry became the constituent parts of his search for meaning. Barbara R. Krasner is a 61-year-old woman born to Russian-Jewish ghetto life in South Philadelphia. An only biological child, she grew up with the polar expressions of her grandfather's piety and her parents' secularity. The disparate dynamics between her family's immigrant experience and the Christian neighborhoods in which she was later raised became the foundation for her quest to find ways to integrate and embody her conflicting truths. Sports, academia, marriage, three children, two foster children, and Jewish mysticism became the constituent parts of her search for meaning.

The struggle and joy in each of the authors' lives and contexts converge in their mutual embrace of the covenantal realities of relational justice, the transgenerational legacy of loyalty, and the irreducible bedrock of trustworthiness in family and community. Their willingness to be informed by their respective religious traditions without being defined by them, their longing to be heard, their passion to be addressed, and their capacity to recognize the resources in their own limits as well as in the limits of others have become hallmarks of their personal and professional mandates and friendship. Their ability to write this book dialogically, word by word, sentence by sentence, and chapter by chapter, emerged from a decade of fair give-and-take between them. Address and response provided the fundamental bedrock for our common effort.

THIS ONE'S FOR ME

Soul, we need to talk.
Do you remember when, so long ago,
a thoughtless doctor mentioned in a casual tone
"You might have a mild case of MS?"
Remember what you did? You
numbly completed the interview,
took the referral card, and left.
Without a pause for shock or inquiry,
you sped directly into misbegotten heroism,
calm acceptance, one tear here and there,
"I'm ready to die."
(Dying prematurely seems my perverse talent.)

Do you remember when, even longer ago,
accepted without scholarship to the
high school students' summer writing camp
(your teacher worked so hard to get you in)
you turned down, on the telephone,
a last-minute offer of a partial grant.
"No, we can't afford it."
You didn't even take his name and number!
You didn't even turn to your parents and ask.
(What disbelief wells up now,
what rage at the casual neglect
that caused them then to let it stand
without any further comment!)
To get their approval, numb my pain,
I sought to prove I could die
without a fuss, without a claim on anyone.

Remember Patty Hearst? When the universe is small
one grows to love the captors, learn the lines,

enjoy the costume, even hold the gun.
Deprivation of the senses, isolation of the heart
work miracles on death's behalf (or life's?
like the flow of blood away from extremities
in shock and trauma? Partial death
in service of life, a desperate salvage?)

So here I am. Deciding once again about this
half-life, watching my self-protective leap
to self-destruction. Finding it natural
to die in advance so I control the killing,
spare myself the vision of some
beloved murderer doing me in.

New mother sees me dying and says, "Why?"
New mother says, claim your life, put up
your fight. Perhaps the early dying (now
and before) was to keep me from being the murderer.
My image of fight goes to destruction.
"Don't mess with a lioness."
I have more resembled a defeated dog.
Domesticated grief and self-destruction,
wasting away as she waits for someone to come.

Soul, you say, "No more" (but with a
gentle sickness of heart). Until you feel the
bite of what it is to hold accountable
(without hostility, no axe in hand --
no armor but self-respect, no
weapon but love) you'll not believe.
This missing piece is offered to me now
by grace again, despite my skill at fleeing.
I can finally trust this mothering
to seek my good, to prize my prizing,
teach me to fight like a woman
for life and love.

Alice Mann
August 15, 1990
(Reprinted with permission from Alice Mann).

PART I

Roots of Relationship

1

Here Am I

Let us consider the most elementary of all facts of our intercourse with one another. The word that is spoken is uttered here and heard there, but its spokenness has its place in "the between."

—Buber, *The Knowledge of Man*

THE REALM OF THE BETWEEN

In this chapter we mean to illuminate the ontic roots of relationship, trust, truth, loyalty, and justice. In the beginning infants are born into a context in which they require care and direct address. Eventually they are called upon to offer care and direct address to those who people their world. Loyalty to those people is generic, genetic, and binding. Justice between them is predicated on fair give-and-take. Trust is the basic requirement of justice. And speech-with-meaning creates truth that elicits trust. These ontic dynamics are at play in what Martin Buber has called the realm of "the between" and Paul Tillich has called "the really real."

Buber uses the term "dialogical" to describe how the sphere of the between unfolds. The psychological, he says, that which happens within each person's soul, is only the secret accompaniment of the dialogical. The meaning of dialogue is found not in either one or the other of the partners, nor in both added together, but rather in their interchange. Friedman writes that this distinction between the "dialogical" and the "psychological" constitutes a radical attack on the psychologism of our age. It makes manifest the fundamental ambiguity of psychologists who embrace dialogue as an ideal but tend to identify this dialogue as a function of a person's self-acceptance rather than as a value in itself (Friedman, 1985).

The dialogical unfolding of the between has its primal origins in the transgenerational realities of a person's dynamic family legacy. In that sense dialogue is never simply an interchange between two unrelated persons. While Buber's notion of healing through meeting can occur any time that two people are fully present to each other, their capacity to be truly present is influenced in great measure by how each of them was addressed in their family of origin. We mean to argue then that the philosophical anthropology undergirding contextual theory and therapy is founded not on esoteric concepts but on concrete, living moments that are the bedrock from which truth and trust evolve. How a person has been addressed or dismissed, heard or silenced, acknowledged or discredited, constitutes the cornerstone of his or her wholeness, uniqueness, and courage to face the world.

We mean to argue that at base committed relationship can prevail only between the unshakable poles of truth and trust. Commitment is rooted in a will and a call to dialogue that reverberates back to Adam himself—when he is asked, "Where art thou?" And however tentatively and with whatever fear and trepidation, Adam finds a way to respond, "Here am I." Here in the very genesis of the world as (wo)man encounters it, (s)he is faced with a mandate for dialogue. Dialogue is a reminder that something can happen not merely "to" us and "in" us but also "between" us (Buber, 1965b, p. 102). This then is the starting point for dialogue about dialogue.

The most common presenting problem of adults coming into therapy is their inability to say, "Here am I." In our experience, few people have cohesive ground under their feet. In general, people typically do not know what they want and do not want what they know. Their basic stance tends to be reactive, implicitly blaming of spouse, parents, children, employer, the "system," and friends. Anyone will do. Initially impelled by fear of pain, given or received, people actively opt, by omission and commission, for hurt withdrawal, imposition, and other well-entrenched barriers and dismissive defenses of monologue. "Adam, where art thou?" is never a question for monologic humans. "Here am I" is never their response to life's call and demands. But a choice for trust is inevitably a choice for dialogue, dialogue as method, process, and way.

A Fundamental Conviction

At base, dialogue is relationship's catalyzing tool, its fundamental conviction, its creative process, and its healing and redeeming way. As a method, dialogue, with all of the fear and trauma it inspires in family members, is empowered in the therapy room by the existence of residual resources in almost any given context. The therapist's capacity to catalyze dialogue is strictly mandated by the fact of a preexisting mutuality of commitment among family members who may or may not present themselves in the therapy room. Dialogue is endowed with a revelatory function that is wholly dependent on catalyzing its two stages: self-delineation and due consideration (see Boszormenyi-Nagy & Krasner, 1986, *Between Give and Take*, p. 75–81). Peoples' willingness to disclose their ground and to offer consideration to the truths of another can invariably be linked to the in-built human longing to hold and be held accountable for justice owed and deserved. *As a method, the therapist's use of dialogue is a pointer without context, a guide to an undisclosed way.*

Martin Buber put it this way: "I have no teaching," he wrote, "I only point to something. I point to something in reality that had not or had too little been seen. I take him who listens to me by the hand and lead him to the window and point to what is outside" (Friedman & Schilpp, 1967, p. 698). That, I think, is our mandate and our task. We too point to something. Contextual theory and therapy have followed Martin Buber's lead. Here the method points to the content that a client and his or her context bring. The therapist, impelled by courage, conviction, and repeated investments in dialogue, points to the signs of relational failure that underscore the absence of dialogue, relational failures that have been presented unilaterally. Methodologies that create options for ethical reengagement can be explored at many levels. Multidirected partiality, rejunction, therapeutic expectations, inclusiveness, timing, crediting, and eliciting are all complex and catalyzing leverages for helping family members reengage (Boszormenyi-Nagy & Krasner 1986).

MONOLOGUE

The "Norm" of Family Life

The fundamental premise of dialogue is that there is always some validity in every person's side. I may disagree with you. I may feel injured by you. But I cannot eclipse your reality. You may react to my stance. You may feel rejected by me. But you cannot use monologue to invalidate my reality.

Monologue is often the norm of family life. People talk at many levels, but deep loyalties typically silence family members from fairly raising hard questions with each other. The task of contextual therapy is to initiate dialogue. Dialogue offers the option of merited trust. Monologue imposes blame. Dialogue offers due consideration and acknowledgment. Monologue undercuts, discredits, and negates. Dialogue offers the option of multilateral truth and shared opportunities. Monologue is blinded by one-sided truth and forces people into unintended isolation.

The story of a father's ability to connect his truth with his son's truths powerfully embodies the living reality of truth and trust between the generations. Mark, a man of infinite sensitivity and loving concern, carries shame and regret over his impulse to be angry at Jeremy, 12, his only child. "Why couldn't you just get dressed?" Mark asks Jeremy in a family session. "You knew we were attending your cousin's First Communion." Turning to the therapist, Mark continues, "I was frustrated as hell at Jeremy's dawdling and refusal to get dressed. And his mother was so patient! She told him that sometimes you have to do things in a family that you don't want to do." "It occurs to me, Mark," said the therapist, "that what you describe as your wife's infinite patience is simply the opposite side of the coin of your knee-jerk annoyance. One of you is indulgent, the other dismissive. In neither case does anyone ask what's happening to Jeremy." "What does that mean?" asked Mark. "Jeremy," said the therapist, "can you tell your dad what kept you from getting dressed? What did you expect of this family event?" "It was going to be boring," he said, "and I'd have to stay indoors all day." The therapist asked, "If you could have stayed at home, what might your day have been like then?" "I would have played outside and hung out with my friends," replied Jeremy.

Mark sat there shaking his head. "When I was growing up, my father told me what to do and I did it—no discussion. Nobody ever asked me why." "Do you tell your father what's happening to you, Jeremy?" the therapist asked. "No," he replied. "But you're able to talk to your mom?" the therapist pressed. "Yes, it's easier," he replied shyly.

An indulgent mom, an angry dad, a silent child. *Truth withheld, trust untested, connections disrupted. Caring people trapped in monologue.* The move from monologue to dialogue offers family members new ears to hear, new eyes to see, and a new voice with which to speak and respond (Krasner & McCabe, 1987).

DIALOGUE

A Relational Paradigm

Dialogue stands at the heart of contextual therapy as it stands at the heart of life itself. The basic premises of contextual work, that is, the paradigm that informs us in all our complexity, are to be found everywhere under the surface of all kinds of historical, political, cultural, class, and religious realities and phenomena. It is our view that dynamically every entity is born or created in a given context:

- That all relationships, political, philosophical, and cultural, are shaped by loyalties to their origins and carry balances of freedom and responsibility
- That loyalty, inertia, stagnation, custom, and convenience operate to maintain these balances, even in the face of injustices, exploitation, injuries, and general dissatisfaction
- That when these injustices tip the scale intolerably, for even one person or simultaneously for a number of people, the ethical

dimension of existence is engaged and inevitably forces a reconsideration of the dynamic equilibrium by which the members of any system live out their day-to-day lives
- That the primary methodology for engaging the ethical dimension of existence begins with identifying the sources of one's own victimization, felt and real
- That utilizing the first stage of dialogue (self-delineation) has to do with disclosing particular grievances in either a radical (a revolutionary) or a conservative (an evolutionary) mode

To put it in other terms, a person's capacity for independence and interdependence essentially emerges from a premise that justifies individual freedom, interpersonal justice, and a reconsideration of ethical balances. These balances are weighed on the scales of merited trust. They contain the reasons why family members or members of any loyalty group revolt against self-isolation, cutoffs, impositions, and retribution. They motivate us to overthrow stagnant burdens in an effort to regain, again and again, fresh balances of give-and-take.

Doing Like Dad

To demonstrate our point, let's return to Mark, a caring father in active pursuit of his son. This is not an absentee parent, this is not a man of indifference, but a person invested in making sense of his own unreworked family legacy. Mark and Jeremy often play basketball after dinner. One particular evening they go outdoors, and after a few minutes a neighbor stops by and asks Mark to come over to see a newly acquired painting. He and his family are moving away soon, so there is some time pressure in the request. Mark hesitates, looks at Jeremy and says, "Sure, I'll come." "I'm going with David," he tells Jeremy. "I'll catch up with you later." He invites Jeremy to come along but the 12-year-old refuses.

Jeremy is dismayed. It is not the first time that he has been ranked second best to his father's outside demands. He goes inside and tells his mother. She consoles him, trying to justify his father's actions, and the issue seems closed. "Why didn't you talk to your father?" the therapist asked. The boy shrugged, "Grown-ups can do what they want to do. There wouldn't have been any point."

Mark recounted how caught he felt between his neighbor and his son. The therapist asked Jeremy if he were aware of his father's distress. He shook his head no. Mark repeated that in childhood, he was expected to do what his father required. The therapist asked Mark whether he might have deferred the visit to his neighbor. Might he have said, "Jeremy and I are playing basketball. I'd like to come over later. I'll call you after we are done"? "It seems too obvious when you put it that way," Mark replied. "But I rarely operate as if I have a choice."

Mark's father died suddenly several years ago and left him with a massive repository of anger and hurt. Still he missed his father and cried easily at any mention of his name. Over the past handful of years, he had tried to reconstruct where his anger belonged. Like many men in therapy, he wept easily at any mention of his father's name. Mark longed to know that he was cherished by his father. And Mark longed to cherish his son. The paradox here is that he was as quick to anger with his son as his father had been quick to anger with him. Mark had both idealized and stigmatized the father-son relationship. "When my son was born," he recounted, "I was in the delivery room. When I saw that the baby was a boy, I said, 'Jesus Christ, now the whole thing starts all over again.'" He carried an element of despair over whether he could address his son in a way that he himself had never been addressed. Still, Mark had increasing moments of awareness of what his father's struggles might have been. And as he was able to embrace his father's merit, he found himself increasingly free to embrace his son.

Constantly emerging declarations of independence characterize our personal journeys and pulsate in the loyalty groups called family. Our longing for autonomy addresses the fact that family members may attempt to overturn old balances, imbalances, abuses, injustices, and other destructive intermember behaviors and relational patterns through blatant or subtle unidentified activities. They may address the source of these patterns and behaviors, identify them as unreworked loyalties, and acknowledge that they are being dynamically informed. Paced by their own victimization, real and imagined, one or more family members may recognize the dilemma of destructive entitlement that characterizes their own existence and the existence of others. They may then choose, however tentatively and by whatever impetus, to grasp the methods of a trust-building way. That is, they may rejoin each other to establish and employ a dialogic form for the purposes of catalyzing new and untested options for equitable coexistence—the basic foundation of personal liberation and interpersonal responsibility.

POINTING THE WAY

Therapists may be intellectually convinced of the efficacy of dialogue. But they are often unable to catalyze dialogue in or out of the therapy room where ethics as well as psychology, commitment as well as emotion, are the loci of intervention. Intellectual affirmation of trust building is a far cry from the internalized conviction that frees a therapist to get out of the way of the client's context. Put differently, can a contextual therapist move beyond theory to differentiate clinically between the realm of psychology and the realm of "the between"?

In the face of a client's outrage and pain, can a therapist grasp the limits of empathy that excludes all family members but one? Most significantly, perhaps, can contextual therapists rework their own personal status and condition as a parentified child, mate, parent, or friend in order to free themselves from the clutches of the impulse toward pastoral care or toward simple, supportive therapy? Can we help people grasp the implications of an action dimension in therapy because we ourselves know how to take action? In yet other terms, has the therapist's own inability to self-delineate transformed him or her into a victim of one-sided giving, which, taken in isolation, is just another monologic form? Our challenge here is meant to inspire freedom, not to pose judgment, to point to an ever-evolving and -deepening methodology, process, and way.

Our challenge is intended to normalize shame over roots that each of us carries, to argue for incrementally realized trust as an alternative to prematurely forfeited hope. On the one hand, there is no perfect, fast, or final stage of family trust or balance. On the other hand, contextual therapists can never hope to be effective without periodic assessment of their own context with family, friends, and community. Periodic assessment of a therapist's own context is a sine qua non for contextual work. We can teach the stuff, we can preach it, we can practice it to some extent. But without our making it our own, it casts empty shadows on the lives of the people we meet.

FUNDAMENTAL QUESTIONS

A soul is never sick alone, but always a betweenness also, a situation between it and another existing being.

—Buber, *A Believing Humanism: Gleanings*

The family is a meeting place for the converging currents—genetic, personal, and interpersonal—of thousands of individuals and hundreds of generations. It is the fundamental forum for early human injuries and injustices, lost hope, deep disappointment, profound disillusionment, and even exploitation, hurtful estrangement, and relational stagnation. It is also the fundamental forum for receiving early nurture and care, sustained protection and consideration, life-giving interpersonal exchange, deep-rooted loyalty paradigms for learned patterns of give-and-take, investments of parenting that give birth to hope and energy to aspirations, a socialized basis for trustworthy response, and justifiable reason for risking trust. The very passion—positive and negative—with which people tend to view their "close" relationships is evidence enough to underscore the tenacity of the family's enduring hold and sustaining meaning for its members.

Disappointed family expectations themselves are expressions of meaning, albeit meaning that is presumed to be lost. The capacity to tap into a family's trust base has to begin with self-reflective questions (Krasner, 1983, p. 43):

- Who is trustworthy in my own family and life?
- When I think about family and community, do I think in terms of trustworthiness, fairness, and resources? Or do my thoughts and feelings dwell mainly on pathology, unfairness, and mistrust?
- Have I failed my family, or have they failed me? How?
- Can anything be done to transform these real and felt failures? To whom can I turn to assess and rework them?
- Are my expectations of myself and of others realistic?
- Do I test my assumptions or do they typically stay locked up within me? What will the costs of testing them be?
- When I'm unsure of what I want, can I say so? If not, why not?
- To what degree do I retreat to moralism and ideologies when I lack firm personal and relational ground?
- When people are violent, can I still hear their side?
- When people are judgmental, can I still say my side?
- What kinds of criticisms evoke shame in me?
- Who in my context knows and accepts me for who I really am?

By their very nature, family disappointments can blind people to the residual trust that still exists between them. One person's presumption that another person has actively "rejected" him or her is an untested premise at best. At worst, it obscures each person's potential to identify the resources that manage to endure beneath the traumas of estrangement.

Beyond Pathology

One of life's more painful paradoxes may be that it is generally easier for people to cite problems and pathology in relationships than to identify resources. This issue is compounded by a contextual definition of resources. Here what may be a resource to one person can also function as a stumbling block to another person. Intimacy, money, humor, status, and religious or moral values can all be described as two-edged swords. Fundamental religion, for example, may represent the only remaining "parenting" structure for a woman who has lost her entire family in the Holocaust. As such, it is a resource that may keep her from despair. Religion may also be a roadblock and a source of despair for the young if, for example, it converts free inquiry into a taboo (Krasner, 1981–1982). Or consider humor or money, whose effects can be salving or bruising, an invitation to easy exchanges or a wall against accessibility. It is precisely the two-edged nature of every relational commodity that makes it impossible to define a given offering as a resource per se.

It is only a commitment to mutuality conveyed through trust-based dialogue that might rightfully be defined as an ongoing resource. Here the process has no content except what clients and the members of their context bring. Conviction and courage are required instead. Therapists are obliged to direct their attention to signs of vulnerability, rejection, and evasion between a person and his or her significant relationships. To the frequent dismay of beginning therapists, interhuman resources have no specific descriptions, no *a priori* prescriptions. It is in the midst of these failures that a therapist can begin to identify the still, small voice of residual trust.

ASPECTS OF TRUST

"Phony Relating"

Trust worthiness resides *between* person and person rather than *in* either of them. It is the direct consequence of give-and-take in all its nuances and particularity. It has little to do with liking or disliking a person but flows from demonstrated reliability vested over countless experiences, encounters, and years. Trustworthiness is an end result of choices made with freedom and reluctance alike; choices may be dutiful or sacrificial—but for all of that are choices rather than collusion or capitulation. Trustworthiness is a palpable reality that, when known, emboldens, sustains, liberates, and redeems. Consider the argument given by a first-year student of contextual therapy.

> I had a simple premise I thought I'd work on: dislike and distrust my mother—totally. It didn't seem to me you needed a rocket scientist to figure out that I meant that I couldn't stand the woman, so why did Barbara act confused? My *silent* observation, in itself contextually significant, was interrupted by Barbara's translation of my "dilemma" into a foreign language that now meant (1) my feelings were merely potholes indicating repair was needed on this relational roadway and (2) "it is impossible to distrust a person, it is the relationship between yourself and your mother that you distrust." My ethical disengagement was such that I lacked both the imagination and the desire to consider terms other than my own. As I considered address, I swung precariously by the slimmest thread of felt connection like a spider whose web has been nearly washed away by continual storms. They told me this pain was loyalty being played out. I didn't believe it. Repeated admonitions to take a multilateral approach meant somehow getting calm enough to address my mother's side. How could I "inquire politely over tea" when I couldn't get five words out before

we were in yet another fight that would last until one of us walked out or hung up? I thought direct address of one's context meant voice control in confrontational family situations! *It never occurred to me that you don't get to trust by defining people (which I was expert at). You get to trust by saying "I".* "Keeping the peace" and "not upsetting people" in the family had long ago silenced me. The hostility of sarcastic "joking" remarks were the bubbles atop a pseudomutual brew that had been stewing for years. I literally couldn't believe it when I heard: "If you can't say I, you can't say Thou: you wind up telling people what they're doing wrong." It would have been exhilarating to know that what I called "our phony relating" really was the problem rather than me.

For so long now, pain and mom went together for me sort of like pixie dust and fairies. My fury concerned my perception that whenever she flew around the family it was me she sprinkled it on—leaving my half-brother his escape to suburbia and my sister hers to a bottle. Daddy was good but dead, and rapidly becoming good-and-dead to me as my refusal to think of him became a failure to remember him at all. (Clancy, 1991).

Jan's dislike of her mother in no way adhered to the fact that unresolved issues between them in the past remained clear and present burdens to her in her current life and context.

Residues of Trust

In great measure or small, residual trust is the keystone of the dialogic process—and hence the chief resource of human relationships. It is the result of the long-term consequences of one person's actual care for another person. It is the fuel that empowers people to risk relating after they have suffered injustices and estrangements. It is the summation of a "ledger sheet" that records the merit *between* people. It is the token of a once-warranted faith that witnesses to the fact that assets in relationship are at least as significant as debits. It is the recognition that one person's investments in another may be limited or marred but, for all of that, are still worthy of consideration. It is the understructure of relationship, that is, the rudimentary resource of individual and interpersonal growth. Residual trust is the sine qua non of fairness or justice *between* person and person. It is the dough in the bread of relationship, kneaded by the energy and efforts of visible and invisible hands. In sum, residual trust lies at the heart of every redemptive investment in the dialogic process.

In the beginning, trustworthiness takes root through parents' unilateral, perhaps unconditional, investment in their offspring. Eventually trustworthiness becomes multilateral through the filial capacity to *acknowledge* the merit of parental investments. Early on, from the time that they can read their parents' wishes, children enter the process of establishing their own ledgers of merit. They develop responsive actions, behaviors, and ways of warranting their mother's and father's trust. They also receive their parents' "feeding" in varying ways, rejecting and accepting what is offered without awareness of the impact. Even babies are active in building up or tearing down trust worthiness long before they can consciously acknowledge the merit of parental investments.

Children are born indebted. Whatever their words, dependent and adult children alike are intrinsically loyal and reactive to what they have been given. Who lives for them, who wants them, who is available to them, and who has made material, relational, and spiritual investments in them are fundamental factors in a youngster's attitude toward the world. Moreover, the presence or absence of parental contributions is irrevocable, irreplaceable, and nonsubstitutable for their children. These contributions are subject to interpretation and always benefit from dialogic exploration between parent and child. But whether or not they are ever addressed, their impact and consequences exist in the lives of untold, even yet unborn generations. The dynamic ties between the generations are established at birth, and outlast physical and geographical separations. Most significantly, perhaps, they influence the degree to which progeny can eventually be free to commit themselves to building trustworthy relationships outside of their original contexts (Boszormenyi-Nagy & Krasner, 1980, p. 768).

At base, then, trustworthiness evolves from a mutuality of commitment. It also evolves from a multilateral stance. It requires a capacity to stand up against the proposition that any one side, person, or group can ever function as a measure of the whole of any relational situation. It is always a product of at least two people, and can never be reduced to the psychological universe of either one of them. It is characteristic of mature, nonexploitative relations of any kind. It helps people control their exploitative tendencies in close relationships. It serves self-interest through retaining the resource of a given relationship, and through functioning as a resource for relationship. Caring for another person's needs can enhance personal satisfaction through establishing a basis for equitable balances of imagination and love.

Mutual Vested Interests

Retaining a trustworthy relationship is in the reality interests of all participants. A sustained capacity to consider and to respond to another person involves long-term balances of fair give-and-take. Trust-based relationships help people accept periods of transitory unfairness, and result from mutual commitment and actual exchange. On the other hand, a chronic failure of trustworthy relating reinforces the likelihood that people will be cynical, manipulative, exploitative, and unfair—if only to protect themselves. Without some manifestation of trustworthiness, there can be little will to risk investing in new relationships or in sustaining old relationships. And so there can be no further development and accrual of residual trust. Without the motivation that is nurtured by the resource of trust, there can be little justification for dialogue or for hope for the healing that comes of meeting (Friedman, 1985, pp. 262–263).

The ability to recognize and utilize trust resources requires an autonomous self as well as a will to reciprocity. It requires, even demands, the inner strength for self-assessment as well as the courage to hold accountable those people for whom we care. It requires a capacity to make personal claims and, when indicated, to hold to them in the face of hostile, opposing messages. It requires an ability to tolerate short-term injury and exploitation in the interests of continuing a merited relationship. It requires a decision to disclose hard-won convictions, and to run the risk of having them challenged and reshaped. It requires the will to test the possibilities of a given relationship, to identify its intrinsic limits, and to learn to differentiate a person's limits from his or her intentions to reject. It also requires the maturity to abandon the self-defeating game of comparative victimization. Hard questions characteristically yield healing answers. Trusting enough to test our truths with people from whom we are estranged may produce trauma. It is also likely to produce new degrees of freedom—whether or not we are well received by people whom we address.

Between Person and Person

Deep in the structure of being itself, there is a wellspring of residual trust that resources and catalyzes authentic commitment. From generation to generation across time, geography, class, and diverse loyalties, residual trust has provided the grace of sufficiency. It is the reservoir from which the process of exoneration and forgiveness is drawn. Residual trust functions as the primary restorative element of interhuman existence. Consider James as he sat facing his mother in the therapy—head bent, shoulders slumped, conveying his deepest longing, "that Mamma could just hold me." "James," his mother tearfully replied, "I love hugs." She reached toward him, tentatively touched his arm, and drew him into her embrace. At that moment the 40-year-old man and the 7-year-old child merged and reunited with "their" mother who had left "them."

Residual trust is a resource that presents itself at the outer limits of the human psyche when a person's longing to connect transports him or her to the realm of the "between" (Buber, 1970). It is here between person and person that trust and truth interplay in the service of just relationship. It is here in the arena of the interhuman that each human life is placed to address and help heal the injured order of existence. Take, for example, the 45-year-old man, professionally established, in an intact marriage, his children grown, a 10-

year bout of bulimia still ongoing. One of eight children, Mike defined his father as a devoted provider who was never present to him. He was terrified by the notion that he might ask his father to offer him parenting. "He's 89 years old," he protested, "half-deaf, half-blind, and diabetic. How can he help me?" A week later Mike and his father appeared at a therapy session together. "I asked him and he came," Mike explained. "Maybe he was always there." His father's reply: "I would do anything for my son." Residual trust cannot be objectified, psychologized, or theologized. It can be known only through genuine meeting between being and being.

Residual trust is the bedrock of committed relationship. It undergirds the fragile sanctuary of the word that is spoken and the word that is heard. The terms of committed relationship are not a hidden mystery but truth to be embraced and terms to be rebalanced. When a person maintains a dialogic stance, his or her trust base deepens: The courage to address someone who may withdraw from me, the courage to receive a word that is offered when that word may assault me are acts of confirmation and expressions of esteem. I care enough about you to risk my truth in full knowledge that I may wound or be wounded. You care enough about me to receive my truth in its own context and risk joining your truth to mine. Now relational reality displaces supposition. Moving out of the domain of psychological perceptions and untested assumptions, human truth takes on the assurance of things hoped for, the conviction of things not seen (Heb. 11:1).

TRUTH IN CONTEXT

The truth vouchsafed men opens itself to one just in one's existence as a person. This concrete person, the life space allotted to him, answers with his faithfulness for the word that is spoken by him.

—Buber, *Between Man and Man*

Barriers to Relationship

The bonding quality of connections notwithstanding, the tendency to withhold one's own truth and the failure to credit the truth of another are the dual barriers to redemptive relating. In fact, most relating is characterized by pseudomutuality. As often as not, human interchange is superficial, bound to form above substance, seeming above being, and pleasing above genuine meeting. Consider ordinary life in which people are normatively silenced and learn to withhold their truth:

> *I was being silenced by my tendency to make it okay for Mom* and didn't realize that I needed to make it alright for myself first or I'd

never be able to make it alright for her ... or anyone else. The idea seemed to be that you ask for what it is you want whether or not you can get it. This went against my background for I had been taught not to ask anybody for anything, never even to borrow anything, and don't tell anyone your [family] business. *My side never counted.* I was, even now, so involved with defending my position that I *had lost all ability to imagine another's side, let alone credit it* and allow them to have it. Universally, in all my relationships it was "my way or the highway." I began to understand where that entrenched attitude came from, but I had no reason to believe this time would be any different. I was scared I'd get hurt again, but Austin told us this was all "regardless of outcome." Barbara spoke of our inability to find ourselves by ourselves: I went back five generations to summon up the courage to address family and in my own way I reached out—to friends, to teachers, to other contextual therapists, to classmates.

I tried to consider what it cost my mother when Dad had his first heart attack at 34 and the doctor said she better count on being the breadwinner. What did it take to give up her dreams of little girls in starched dresses playing in the flower-filled garden? She had the little girls and the garden but needed full-time work and night school to obtain a career that would pay the mortgage. The gardening became yet another chore that needed doing. *I came to feel like a chore she had to attend to as well. As time went on neither of us spoke much to each other*—I'm not sure which of us couldn't and which of us wouldn't. Balancing due consideration for another against what I'm entitled to was a bizarre concept, we were both so massively unentitled. I remember being sort of embarrassed when I learned (years after it happened) that Dad had near fatal heart attacks or that there had been strikes and we were without money. I had gone on as usual during those times and when I said later I wished I had known and possibly helped somehow, Mom said it was none of my business and what did I think I could do? I came to feel peripheral in some way, not an important part of any group, family or otherwise. Austin spoke of parents' withholding information ostensibly to protect, but that what happens is the kid introjects the emotion and builds her internal scaffolding based on false information. Was it possible that my internal masterpiece was a fake, that God's signature on my life was a forgery? *My "ground" felt like quicksand.*

Ontic Roots of Relationship

To one or another degree, Jan's struggle is everyone's struggle. Whether or not she is aware of it, she is in a desperate quest for meaning. She is attuned to the struggle but not to the stakes. She knows that the trust base between her and her mother lies in fragments. What eludes Jan is that her willingness to risk her own truth against the chaos alone has the capacity to restore meaning to her world. The ontic roots of relationship go well beyond the question of good or bad parent or of liking or disliking a family member.

- Whether Jan likes or dislikes her mother, events have taken place between them that are unresolved in the first instance because they are *unaddressed*.
- Jan has psychologized the reality between her and her mother. "When events that take place between people are moved into the inwardness of a person, that is *psychologism*" (Friedman, 1990, p.10).
- Jan's concentration on her own pain and her apparent contempt for her mother have entrapped her in a situation with no exit. Paradoxically, freedom and growth are irrevocably linked to testing the very relationship she perceives has betrayed her.
- A great deal of psychopathology arises from too much distancing or too much relating (Friedman, 1990, p. 14). To this point Jan's distancing has neither resolved her enmity toward her mother nor ended their relating. She is no more free by refusing to face her mother than if she chose to reengage.
- Jan's true uniqueness is not a thing in her, like a vein of gold in a mountain. Her uniqueness is what comes into being precisely in the way she responds to others (Friedman, 1990, p. 16). Her silent withholding cripples her uniqueness and diminishes her relating.
- Jan is split between a longing to please her mother and an impulse to flee her. The outcome of either movement amounts to injury, loss, and a rupture of meaning. What is required instead is Jan's capacity to disclose her truth to her mother through presence, immediacy, and direct address.
- Jan's view of herself as victim precludes the possibility of imagining her mother's side. If she fails to establish a point of entry into her mother's reality, by what right can she continue to expect her mother to imagine a point of entry into Jan's reality?
- The relationship between Jan and her mother injured what was originally intact between them. Jan cannot get back to the original intactness, but she can move toward healing where one brings the very problem into process.
- In her effort to normalize life for her children, Jan's mother not only had to forego her own dreams but also tried to protect her children from realizing how demanding her life was. Where then does existential guilt lie here? Who has injured whom? Only in their communicating themselves to each other as what they are can their truths emerge and redeem.
- What after all is Jan hoping for in her despair but a presence that

says that, in spite of all, there is meaning? The opposing truths held by Jan and her mother are unjoined truths—untested, untried and monologic.

In a world in which image is so overriding, the healthy returns and rewards of a person's truth and the trust that evolve from words spoken with meaning are typically overlooked.

Direct Address

> *He who really knows how far our generation has lost the way of true*
> *freedom, of free giving between I and Thou, must himself ... practice*
> *directness—even if he were the only man on earth who did it—*
> *and not depart from it with fear, and hear in his voice the voice of their*
> *own suppressed longing.*

—Buber, *The Knowledge of Man*

Psychotherapy and the culture at large seem to forego the resources implicit in the ethics of direct address. Most of psychology tends to focus on pathology at the cost of crediting the loyalty ties that bond as well as bind. It seems safer to interpret a person's motives than to test one's truth against that person. It seems easier to take a victimized stance than to initiate action on one's own behalf. It seems less trouble to psychologize than to address someone of significance to us.

Psychological perceptions, however well informed, are still internalized constructs. The limit of an internalized construct is that it in no way obligates me to imagine or to test another person's reality. It in no way asks, to say nothing of answers, the questions: "What do I owe and to whom?" "What do I deserve and from whom?" "What relationships do I need or want?" "What relationships am I obliged to retain whether or not I need or want them?" These questions constitute the basis of the ethical dimension of relationship.

In the absence of direct address and ethical imagination, family members are unable to rely on the fact that commitment, devotion, and residual trust lie latent in their connectedness—waiting to be tapped and used for personal gain and growth as well as for fairly considering others. What few people seem able to do is to balance their passion for connection with their freedom to unfold. But without our having the courage to disclose our own terms and the ethical imagination to envision another's, relationships cannot be made to work. The reality of our lives is that we are connected to what already exists. Inarguably, "the species, generations and families which have brought me forth are carried in me and whatever new that I do, receives its characteristic meaning first from that fact" (Buber, 1963, p. 73).

In large measure, Jan's struggle in her family is every person's context. It reflects the commonalities that characterize family life:

- Passion to connect is always present.
- The dilemma at hand is what to do with interhuman connections as they currently stand. How does a person act on his or her own behalf and criteria as well as address other people and their life priorities?
- Split loyalties, that is, being caught between seemingly conflicting expectations, prevent family members from redeeming their connections.
- Split loyalties are directly connected to unfaced, unreworked family loyalties from generation to generation.
- Parents require the imagination to identify the residual indebtedness and rage that continued to bind them to their own parents.
- Parents typically believe they are accountable to their parents but cannot imagine that their parents are also accountable to them.
- Jan's mother probably tried to use the criteria by which she was raised (loyalty expectations) as a point of reference for her own children. That failed. Children have their own context and criteria.
- Young adult children typically want "something more" and look to a shifting society to redress their grievances.
- Relational injustices in the family were linked to societal and cultural upheaval in the 1960s, when John Kennedy was killed and the war in Vietnam escalated.
- Legitimate authority fell out of fashion. Rights became a rallying cry. Indebtedness, which constitutes one pole of the balance between rights and responsibility, was held in contempt. Fair give-and-take was bypassed or ignored: Policemen were defined as pigs; government as subversive; all manifestations of institutional life were seen as corrupt; and the family as an entity was viewed as irrelevant.
- External criteria like roles and structure, custom and ritual, had been questioned, impacted, and reshaped by personal longings that poured themselves into social movements opposing the status quo.
- Sources of meaning, grounded in history and legacy, in trust and reciprocity, were beclouded.
- The "me generation" began to unfold, more likely motivated by despair than by selfishness: If you cannot count on people to hear you or credit your side, if differences are so much more significant than commonality and trust, then better to withdraw and try to construct an artificial world—one that promises greater control and accessible nurturing.

The Living Stream of Tradition

In the first instance, meaning and the very reason for being is produced by what has gone before us. Members of each generation, when they shut themselves off from facing and addressing the influence of all that happened before their time and that in fact brought them forth, find themselves without moorings in the living stream of tradition. Their drive to give form to things no longer has any connectedness to the primary reality of being itself (Buber, 1963). Without connectedness to the primary reality of being itself, catalyzed by direct address from one family member to another, by one genuine friend to another, by a corporate mentor to the young in his or her charge, we have a world adrift—whatever its veneer. We have a world where personal passion is prostituted. We have a society in which despair at being heard deteriorates into a compulsive search for methods to narcotize the soul.

Ethical despair is a flight from direct address. Ethical imagination is a decision to build trust through disclosing my truth and intuiting and inviting yours.

Commitment is a dialectical and dialogic way, a caring stance whose consideration for the I holds parity with consideration for the You. Few of us can stand in the face of a loved one's needs and not feel responsible for them whether or not the responsibility is ours. To feel deeply and to offer help in the midst of a committed relationship may be a reasonable expression of compassion. Concern, imagination, and the longing to act on another person's behalf, whether invited to do so or not, may be a natural impulse. They are also a potential trap for acting against our own vested interests and obscuring the validity of the self's longing for pleasure; that is, the will to please you is easily pitted against my responsibility to identify what I want, to act on it, and to handle the consequences that come when our needs and wants collide.

People tend to confuse commitment with control. In fact, escalating efforts at control are essentially expressions of despair. The underlying premise is that I have lost all hope of receiving the consideration due me. As despair deepens, the option of direct address lessens, and efforts to control grow more frenzied. This frenzy usually masks a monitored rage at an unanticipated injury from a usually trustworthy source or situation. There are two injuries operating here: One is an internal reaction to the moment's disappointment; the other is the breach of trust that occurs in relationships. But internal reactions to a moment's disappointments and breaches of trust in relationships are ordinary phenomena and in themselves do not produce despair. They are, however, the building blocks and the natural outcome of the failure of direct address.

Despair as a condition builds up over time. It is comprised of assaults untempered by care; of one-sided giving untempered by the reprise of receiving; of ascribed blame untempered by crediting and confirmation. Despair is the end product of a life of obligation that eventually erodes the hope that who

I am and what I want is of any significance to anyone but me. It is the unyielding message that one more time my father is drunk; one more time my mother is angry; one more time I cannot have friends to my house; one more time my stomach is in knots; one more time I am expected to be silent to keep peace at any price. In more cases than not despair is the consequence of loyalty binds, which impose rather than elicit.

People rarely speak from their own suffering ground to the suffering ground of another. Each person speaks instead to the "problem," the manifestation of disengagement and dissociation. Here we speak of a subject-object split: I presume that you can hurt me but that I cannot hurt you. I fail to imagine that you carry the kind of pain that I carry. I am operating on a basis of almost nonexistent self-esteem. I do not imagine that I count. How could you be hurt by me? I think I am acting according to your expectations, and you think you are acting according to mine. Neither of us credits the other because, in fact, both of us are carrying the resentment and blame born of having silently surrendered our own side.

ILLUSIONS OF INTIMACY

Speech-with-Meaning

Genuine intimacy links our longing to connect with our freedom to unfold, and is always marked by speech-with-meaning (Buber, 1965b). It is steeped in a mutuality of commitment that requires trustworthy relating. Trustworthy relationships are the outcome of the fact that when I speak I mean what I say, I do what I mean, and I can rely on you to do the same. Genuine intimacy is neither a compulsion to please nor a thrust to manage information but a will to give-and-take that depends on the reliability of the spoken word. Facets of intimacy are carefully nuanced by Buber's description of how speech-with-meaning occurs:

> Whenever one shows the other something in the world in such a way that from then on he beg[ins] really to perceive it, whenever one gives another a sign in such a way that he could recognize the designated situation as he had not been able to before, whenever one communicate[s] to the other his own experience in such a way that it penetrates the other's circle of experience as from within so that from now on his perceptions [are] set within a world as they had not been before. (Buber, 1965b)

It is in the family that speech and meaning are first wed. It is also in the family that meaning and speech are first sundered. To be sure, even in the midst of mutual commitment, ruptures between speech and meaning and between truth and trust are inevitable. But what is retained in genuine intimacy is the conviction that, whatever the reasons for the rupture, whatever its consequences, there is a clear if reluctant willingness to address them. On the other hand, a failure to address and to be addressed, to speak and to mean, to hear and to act, is a sign of dissociative intimacy.

Fundamentally dissociative intimacy is a statement that I am essentially connected to you and you are essentially connected to me, but we cannot make the connection work. It is characterized by protectiveness of self and others, denial of pleasure, collusive silence, shame over individual creativity and achievement, and an exquisite sensitivity to the pain of others typically addressed by distancing and the refusal to take solace for oneself. It is also characterized by a subtle self-righteous stance that tolerates no criticism: "If I've expended so much of my existence to maintain family equilibrium, peace at any price in the midst of chaos and threat, how can I be viewed as doing anything wrong?" These attitudes and actions are signposts by which people indebt each other without being accountable for the consequences of their own actions.

The paradox here is that family members feel wronged and in fact are wronged. At the same time, each family member remains irrevocably and inextricably connected to each other one, whether they will it or not. How then does wrongdoing take place? Most parents, like their parents before them, feel trapped in an unending spiral of obligation. Imagination fails them. They are unaware of a way to move beyond their unexamined and binding ways of relating. There is no one to credit the merit of their suffering. They feel as if everyone wants something from them; no one is there to give, only to take. They know nothing of their *ethical right to act on their own behalf.* Given binding loyalties contracted by birth, people tend to be blindsided to the option of shaping their lives through the mechanism of choice. They tend either to settle for the fantasy of idealized relationship or to conform to the bleak prospects of relationships as they currently exist. Their stagnation is anchored in the inner construction of their psychology, that is, their own way of perceiving another person. We speak here of an inner dialogue that's kept within, blocks out the possibilities of testing or inquiring into another person's reality, thereby locking out a relational partner's truth.

The notion of acting on one's own behalf is conceptually foreign while dynamically compelling in family and culture alike—this despite the myths of the "me generation." Birth itself endows upon every human being the need to hear and be heard, to receive and be received. The act of hearing and being heard is a necessary and therefore ethical right. Hearing and being heard is never a monologic act. It always entails give-and-take. Balances between give-and-take are always in flux. The very act of hearing and being heard requires courage and conviction.

Schooled to Please

People are schooled to please. The mechanism of direct address poses a choice between pleasing relational partners or risking self-disclosure and eliciting another person's reality. Patriotism, religion, education, and the workplace, as well as the family, collectively mystify the imperative to make discreet and considered choices. The burden of their message is always weighted by the notion that it is better to give than to receive. But the fact is that one *has* to receive in order to continue to give. Sometimes though it seems easier to disengage than to risk the consequences of the spoken word.

Parent and offspring can misunderstand, wound, and undercut each other. They can tear down all visible evidence of trust between them, but their linkages remain. It is these linkages that function as the reservoir of residual trust. Liking, approving of, or agreeing with each other is not the primary basis of their invisible attachment. Rather it is caring, given and received—and documented in the predetermined facts of begetting, pregnancy, and survival—that provides the cornerstone for their mutuality of commitment, the mortar for building a sturdier foundation, and the basic potential for meaning between person and person. Fully turned and radically open to the other, the parent and the child who truly meet are strengthened by their course (justice) and lent courage by their source (residual trust).

Residual trust can never be confined, delimited, or reduced. It lies latent in the substream of enduring relationships, waiting to be tapped. It needs to be identified, however. It is most readily identified in the midst of the lingering devotion and of the amorphous commitments of family members who are irrevocably linked by ties of root and legacy. It is never to be found in some pure or idealized feeling state. To the contrary, residual trust is typically to be mined in the depths of volatile passions and in the midst of forbidding injustices, ethical disengagement, and mistrust (Krasner, 1986).

Periods of unbearable weight are part of everybody's life. How one addresses these periods determines whether cut-offs or trust will characterize a person's future of relating. Inexorably, though, and in their own time, people crash into the stone wall of unbearable weight and excessive limitations that are produced by life's ordinary demands: marriage, parenthood, filial concern for aging parents, profession and job, social expectations and economic realities, to say nothing of life crises like sickness, death, separation, and loss. It is at points of chronic overload that the inner gnawing of meaninglessness threatens to deteriorate into despair. It is at the moment when people intuit that they can give no more without getting in return. When we perceive ourselves as giving without sufficient return, the very fabric of day-to-day existence unravels, and meaning disappears.

It sometimes seems that it is only when life's apparent foundations crack and are laid bare that we can finally let go of the illusion of control and look for invisible resources. For in point of fact, all authentic commitment is finally resourced by residual trust, enabled by ethical imagination, and catalyzed by ongoing attempts at direct address—mounted in the face of anticipated rejection, dismissal, and rebuff.

A person's ability to identify, mobilize, and catalyze residual trust through direct address offers a counterweight to individual and relational limits, stagnation, and disengagement produced by suppurating blame of self as well as others, and massive rage linked to unexamined and untested family patterns, myths, and assumptions. Jan's eventual claim on her mother to hear and be heard has redemptive ramifications not only for the two of them but for their relationships with everyone in their past, present, and future contexts.

2

Elements of Commitment

FROM GENERATION TO GENERATION

In this chapter we mean to argue that deep in the structure of being itself, there is a wellspring of residual trust that resources and catalyzes commitment. Our premise here is that injustice in the human order can be rebalanced in the process of genuine address, in those brief moments of relationship where "deep calls to deep" (Buber, 1965a). One's address to the other may remain unanswered, and the dialogue may die in seed. Yet the very attempt at direct address satisfies an existing psychic need and fulfills an ethical mandate that enhances a person's personal merit and worth. Whatever the outcome of direct address, the self is made freer, more entitled, less burdened and neurotic. Because I have offered care I am "allowed" to make a claim. Our point here is that committed relationship exists between the poles of truth and trust.

Truth and trust draw from transgenerational and intergenerational facts, experience, transactions, and a mutuality of commitment evidenced by long-term due consideration (Boszormenyi-Nagy & Krasner, 1986). Invisible "records" of give-and-take, contributions, and injuries, and the distribution of burdens and benefits within a family system, develop into legacies, ledgers, and loyalties (Boszormenyi-Nagy & Spark, 1973). In turn, family legacies, ledgers, and loyalties form a repository of assurance that in small measure or large confirms the fact that a person's existence is enough. Who I am is sufficiently significant to elicit concern, attentiveness, and nurturance from those people to whom my life has been entrusted, even in the midst of disappointment and conflict.

Mutual Lacerations

On the other hand, injustices abound in relationships. The absence of truth and trust and the failure of direct address lead to what Dostoevsky calls "mutual lacerations" that no one intends.

Take 12-year-old Susan, for example, whose father died of cancer when she was 8. Her father's diagnosis came before Susan's birth. Susan, with her younger brother, lived as a bystander to her father's suffering. Her mother had been mandated with overresponsibility early in life. Now she was overspent again—tending her husband, finishing her college studies, and raising two children. She expected Susan to be good and cause no further stress. Susan's loyalty to her parents was such that she complied. She learned to say and do what was pleasing and withheld her own desires and pain. Her childhood needs and freedom to grieve were constrained by fear that her mother could not bear any more strain. Four years after her father's death, Susan and her mother were estranged and embattled. The precocious 8-year-old "pleaser" had become an embittered rival for her mother's energy and time. Mother had little left to offer of herself beyond functional caretaking of the family's daily needs. "We went through the motions," Susan said, "just like we did with Dad." Going through the motions characterizes stagnant relationships. Disclosing our own truth and imagining that truth of another, on the other hand, characterizes dynamic relationships where balanced give-and-take lends itself to enduring commitments. Were mother and daughter committed to each other? Yes. Had the elements of their commitment been reduced to structure? Yes.

I Am I, and You Are You

Nuanced and elusive, the characteristics of committed relating can be more readily pointed to than described:

- Commitment can be grasped only through testing, rather than through a monologic belief or stance.
- Commitment, or the impulse toward it, is motivated by a will to reciprocity (to give and take) beginning with birth itself. It is never simply a value, feeling, or principle but a relational dynamic having to do with existing in a condition of indebtedness without undue guilt.
- Commitment is an order of giving, in trust that what is received will be valued, redemptive, reciprocated, credited, or at least duly noted, considered, and in time returned in due measure.
- Dynamic commitment is the basis of "lived life" (Buber, 1965a). Its methodology is a honed capacity to delineate one's own terms and to validate the merit of another person's stance, however adversarial.
- Commitment between people is the primary dynamic measure of human meaning and the basis of interhuman ethics.
- The glue of any just order of human existence, commitment is a sacred trust. At another time in an arguably gentler world, commit-

ment was an assumed characteristic of personal, interpersonal, and intergenerational life. In generations past, a handshake may have sealed commitment. Today, in a world steeped in hype and a lust for "communication," a handshake may be a civil protocol or even convey a rush of feelings. The substance of commitment, not the feeling or ritual behind it, is what is in question in our time.

- The bread of just relationship, commitment is a long-term sequence of intended choices; a series of dedicated decisions to invest in a person or life circumstances with trust, freedom, and responsible response.
- A failure of commitment is signaled by words like abuse, abandonment, exploitation, and betrayal. Commitment requires a person to move out of the psychological realm of reading or interpreting feelings and into the arena of ethical awareness to rebuild trust between one another.
- A person's capacity to attempt to verify a relating partner's motives and justification constitutes the apex of personal freedom and interpersonal and interhuman justice.
- Religious rituals have long been used to incarnate the meaning of commitment. Rites such as Baptism, circumcision, Communion, Bar and Bas Mitzvah, betrothal, marriage, and the Sacrament of the Sick are embodiments of commitment. As such they are ethical statements that can yield value and meaning in and between the generations if people take responsibility for seeking their truth vis-à-vis the ritual.
- Commitment is a dialogic way, a caring stance whose consideration for the I holds parity with consideration for the You (Krasner & Joyce, 1989).
- Relational balance is predicated on the understanding that making a claim for oneself can be an expression of giving, a contribution to the well-being of relatives and friends instead of a selfish act (Krasner, 1986).

Consider Tom's relationship to his world. Seventeen years old, he swings between affability and disinterest whenever he visits his dad. His parents' hostile divorce converted him into his mother's consort and his father's wounded "child." The focus of bitterness between his psychiatrist father and his insecure stepmother, Tom is at best polite and noncommunicative, at worst truculent and glib. His parents "protected" him by withholding the facts of their divorce from their children. Tom soon became the designated recipient of his mother's unfinished contempt for his dad, and his father's chronic fear of Tom's mom. Tom's father is clearly devoted to his son but seems unable to respond to Tom's distress: "I'm not sure he's suffering any pain," the father says. "He is a narcissistic kid in many ways. He's masterful in sublimating. His problem is with intimacy." Unconsidered here is where Tom might have learned to be intimate. No one has chosen to speak about his or her truth. No one has known how to guide Tom toward due consideration. The consequences of their silence has left Tom isolated—with no adult to address. At his tender age, to whom can he turn in trust? Who will teach him that he has a side that suffers that is not heard? The ability to make connections work is linked to a person's will to delineate his or her own truth and terms; and in a parallel motion rooted in trust, to invite and elicit the truth of another. All of this while walking through fears and anxieties over being absorbed or abandoned. But still, in the words of Rebbe Menachem Mendel of Kotsk,

> I am I because I am I and you are you because you are you, then I am I and you are you. But if I am I because you are you and you are you because I am I, then I am not I and you are not you.

THE SURGE OF JUSTICE

The motto of life is 'give and take.' Everyone must be both a giver and receiver. He who is not both is as a barren tree.

—Rabbi Yitzhak Eisik

Balancing Give-and-Take

All human beings are periodically faced with the task of assessing and reassessing whether or not the balance of give-and-take in their world are serving them and others in a fair and trustworthy way. Direct address is the means by which such assessments can take place. These assessments may be demanding and unwelcome but their emotional alternatives are resentment and guilt. Their ethical alternatives are alienation and disengagement. In any case, just balances of give-and-take remain the dynamic foundation of viable, enduring close relationships. A person's ability to give freely and receive without fear of endless indebtedness is an endpoint of relational ethics.

Take Carol, for example, whose life is made volatile by a dead-end affair. She talks about her former, idealized relationship with her husband. Then she talks about her husband's impotence, and how distancing her husband is. Then she talks about a legacy in which her father was cold and judgmental, her mother clinging and depressed.

What quickly comes clear is that Carol is terrified of commitment. She cannot imagine that she can ever be addressed on her own terms. Her notion of relating requires her to give to the maximum, and then pull into herself to avoid not receiving. She would rather swing between idealized, if long-gone, memories of her husband, and her current passion and excitement with her lover, which may have more to do with titillation than attachment. What brings her into therapy is the increasing chaos and fragmentation in her day-to-day life. Neither husband, lover, friends, children, nor career—is long able to sustain hope or meaning. What also brings her in is a growing intuition that what she calls her life is truly not her own. The sum total of the people whom she knows and the work that she enjoys are no substitute for the breeches of trust born of one-sided giving in her family of origin. If she were bred to tender care and protection, by what measure can she expect to receive? On the other hand, to what degree has she explored how she has come to be who she is with all her personal assets as well as liabilities?

Unfaced Contributions and Injuries

Sooner or later Carol would have to make a choice about how to interpret his feelings. Would they eventually be used to validate only her injuries and pain? Or would they also be used as valid indicators of real and perceived injustices that exist between her and the people to whom she remains loyally attached?

- Will Carol use her feelings to justify her estrangement from her family, that is, to underwrite her disappointments in her relationships? Will her sense of being overwhelmed by her family's neediness (psychology) freeze into a permanent state of injury and injustice (relational ethics), and solidify into an inflexible rationale for ethical disengagement? Will she choose to protect herself from the sources of her injuries and, in so doing, cut herself off from the sources of her healing? Will she trap herself in the self-pitying confines of self-imposed monologue and so lose the validation she can have confirmed only in the dialogic process? Buffered from the merit of their valid truths and trust, will she unilaterally impute causes, motives, and blame to her husband and family—and victimize them as she feels they have victimized her? Will her self-protectiveness ultimately reify into the keystone of a lifetime's solipsistic stance?
- Can she move beyond her own psyche to inquire into other people's realities and life interests as they themselves define them? Can she move beyond her most reactive behavior to a point of surfacing her own terms for relating? Does she know her own terms, that is, what specifically she wants? Can she muster the courage to test the conclusions she has drawn about a relationship, or does she choose to proceed on untested monologic premises? Can she differentiate between when people are actively rejecting her, and when they are simply functioning within their own personal and interpersonal limits?

- How do past injustices, actual and perceived, affect the status of her current relationships? When last has she directly surfaced her regrets over the injuries and disappointments that estrange her from a close relative or friend? When last did she elicit or simply tolerate someone else's assessment of the causes of their estrangement from her? When last has she risked saying what she wants, and received a caring response? Can she identify the merit that still exists in a formerly significant relationship that is currently stagnant? Can she identify what still holds her to an estranged relationship? Does she draw a negative satisfaction from perceiving herself as victim? Is she using a relationship to avenge herself of injuries that belong to someone else (revolving slate) (Boszormenyi-Nagy & Spark, 1973, pp. 65–67)? Does she see a realistic pathway toward reclaiming a relationship that is still founded on pockets of residual trust?

The Risk of Receiving

The act of receiving in Carol's context is simply too threatening, too replete with risk for her to attempt to require a balance of give-and-take. For to receive implies indebtedness; and indebtedness opens up further possibilities of being exploited; and further exploitation threatens an even more disabling loss of trust. Put in terms of contextual family therapy, Carol's capacity to take pleasure from relationships is largely linked to the balances of fairness and unfairness, and trustworthiness and the lack of trustworthiness in her family of origin. Her current state of depression and depletion may have brought her to a crisis of maturity. In the long run, her felt estrangement from her sources of strength may be read as a gift, an opportunity for a careful reassessment of her context—done through a dialogic stance. Carol's freedom to risk receiving in peer and professional relationships can be most directly won through "going home" to test the relational premises by which she is shaping her future and life.

Unfaced family injuries, their implications and unintended consequences, and their replication in the workplace and community, are probably the most onerous, enervating, and demotivating forms of human bondage. The mistrust and injustice that emanate from interpersonal injuries—real and imagined—are probably the source of people's most intense intellectual, emotional, and spiritual pain. The pathology that results from containing conflict among caring people, that is, keeping it under wraps, is probably the single most formidable obstacle to attaining a genuine condition of forgiveness and the freedom that that implies. The slavish tendency to please people rather than to risk hurting them by saying what we need and want ranks among the most destructive and trust demolishing of any human tendencies.

Irreversible Influence

The foundations of truth and trust in family and community are subtle and profound, and carry unforeseen transgenerational and intergenerational consequences. In the beginning a will to reciprocity is rooted in existential ties. A parent cannot help but exert a lasting, irreversible influence—positive and negative—on a child, with all its attendant implications for posterity. A child cannot help but inherit the consequences of the past's endowments and be intrinsically loyal to them—for good or for ill—for every child is born into a family legacy where he or she is bound to experience disappointment and pain. Every parent has placed undue and unfair demands on a helpless child at one time or another.

Injury and exploitation are givens of every parent-child relationship. There is simply no way for people—in this or in any other significant relationship—to be cast into a long-term involvement without encountering conflict and collisions in their life priorities. It is not the fact of injustice, disappointment, and pain, then, that is intrinsically destructive between the generations. The question before us is whether family members can eventually choose to reassess the meaning of these facts in terms of maturity rather than from the long-internalized perspective of helpless and overpowered children. Is there anything new that people at age 36 can grasp about their parents' relational realities that were beyond them even at age 19? What fresh insights and freedom of options and action can be won when they readdress their parents' contexts and lives, this time with adult ears and eyes (1 Cor. 13:10–11)?

The process of reassessing the nature of our parents' positive and negative contributions to our existence raises demanding questions (Krasner, 1983, pp. 43–44):

- Can family members find the courage to grasp each other's reasons for what was given to them and for what was denied?
- Can adult children come to grips with their parents' potential and limits without finally being contained or defined by them?
- Can adult children find ways to tell their family members about their own relational perceptions without having to coat them with veneers of idealization or deprecation?
- Can people take the mass of their deep-held anger, resentment, and guilt and begin to reshape it by addressing its causes and sources?

- Can family members mobilize the residual trust that flows from the past into redemptive options for action for posterity? Or, by omission, will they choose for a peace that is no peace, and so repeat their parents' destructive transgressions?

In sum, most adults settle for a stagnant existence essentially defined by power tactics, timidity, and blame. In the midst of fears and disappointment, would it be possible for them to invest their truth in a process of identifying, mobilizing, and utilizing hidden resources that can turn their hearts and minds to trust (Malachi 3:24)?

Pointing to Justice

> *Justice, like trustworthiness, characterizes the underlying existential ledger of a relationship system. Both concepts lie beyond the realm of individual psychology, and both lead to a re-examination and redefinition of the theories of projection, reality-testing, fixation, displacement, transference, ego strength and autonomy.*

—Maurice Friedman, *The Healing Dialogue in Psychotherapy*

"The greatest cultural task of our age," say Boszormenyi-Nagy and Spark (1973), "might be the investigation of the role of relational justice, not merely economic justice, in contemporary society" (p.74). The term "justice" as used here is neither a philosophical abstraction nor a legal mandate. Nor, in the first instance, is it meant to convey the notion of distributive justice, like illness, race, or wealth, which hinge on the whim or coincidence of destiny; nor retributive justice, which is always a substitute for the failure of direct address and give-and-take in relationship. Relational justice, as we grasp it, is rooted in trust and catalyzed by truth. Heschel writes that the prophets discovered the holy dimension of living by which our right to live and to survive is measured. However, the holy dimension was not a mechanism, he says, measurable by the yardstick of deed and reward, of crime and punishment, by a cold law of justice. They did not proclaim a universal moral mechanism but a spiritual order in which justice was the course but not the source. To them justice was not a static principle but a surge sweeping from the inwardness of God, in which the deeds of man find, as it were, approval or disapproval, joy or sorrow (Heschel, 1949, p. 620). To us, justice is not a static principle but a surge sweeping across the generations, to hallow the every day, to soften the meanness of existence, and to redeem the cynicism of our age. The possibility of relational justice points to a healing dimension.

GUILT AND GUILT FEELINGS

Guilt and Relational Justice

If the healing dimension of relational justice is founded on trust and direct address, the destabilizing dimension of relational justice founders on unaddressed guilt and the ethical distortions of pervasive guilt feelings. Born into a context in which we are now entitled and now indebted, each of us faces the never-ending task of life in common: figuring out when to give and when to receive. The question of when to give and when to take, when to act for oneself and when to do for others, constitutes the central dilemma of relational justice. Guilt and guilt feelings are an intrinsic by-product of this dilemma.

Guilt

The primal fact of human beings as human beings is that they can become guilty and know it (Buber, 1965b). The resource side of guilt is that it performs the necessary function of leading a person to want to set relations straight (see Friedman, 1985). The pathology side of guilt is that it isolates, insulates, and forces people into unintended disengagement from lived life. Ann's situation is a ready demonstration of both the pathological and resource functions of guilt:

> Ann has just dropped out of college for the fourth time. This past semester she contracted a venereal disease, totaled her parents' car, put herself in serious danger by getting drunk and suffering attempted rape, and moved back to her mother's home to discover that she cannot live there anymore. She also cannot live without her mother. When Ann was at school she called home at least once a day. She is massively dependent on her mother and almost totally estranged from her. She knows that her behavior has been destructive to herself as well as to her family.
>
> There are many psychiatric categories to describe why Ann is doing what she is doing, but none of them capture the fact that she wants to atone for the misery she has caused—and cannot find a way. On the other hand, she is enraged at her mother's blame and allegations and has chosen "never" to disclose herself to her mother despite Ann's own deep longing to connect. "There are lots of things I want to tell her," Ann says, "but she always thinks she is right. She does it with everyone, not only me. She is not human, she's my mother. I know

it's not so, but sometimes I feel she never gets tired, she will never age, she will never die, she is always strong, she will never bruise." Ann knows that she is responsible to live another way. Intimidated and overshadowed by who she thinks her mother is and what she wants, Ann capitulates, and runs away from home emotionally or physically whenever she can. Friends remind her that she is 21 but acts 15 whenever it comes to her mother. "I spend my time trying to figure out what's right and what's wrong," she says, "but my mother is so sure of herself that I do everything her way. I could live my own life if I had money of my own." Disengaged from her mother's truth and withholding her own, Ann is aware of her part in the breakdown. She carries guilt and knows it.

True guilt has to do with a failure to respond to the legitimate claims and address of the world. It is linked to our actual stance in the world and how we choose to relate to the people around us. Real guilt has to do with an insular, monologic stance in which we either use ourselves as the sole reference point for events that occur between us and the people with whom we have to do; or totally abandon ourselves as a valid point of reference, and regard other people's expectations and feelings as more legitimate than our own. Friedman writes that the source of moral obligation is identical with the question of authentic dialogic existence. That translates into a way of living in the everyday in which a person consciously struggles toward balanced give-and-take. At one and the same time I risk the assault of hearing—even inviting your truth and of clinging to the charge to speak my own.

Response and Responsibility

Interhuman existential guilt is to be distinguished from intrapsychic guilt feelings—however intermingled the two may be (Friedman, 1985, "Paradoxes of Guilt"). People in relationship expect a response. One person's failure to respond to the other, his withholding response or her attacking response, has consequences whether intended or not. Short of suicide or psychoses that absent a person from the everyday world, every human being carries a responsibility to respond. When two relating partners routinely abandon their respective responsibility to respond, they injure the order of their existence in common. When truth is withheld, trust is diminished, justice is ruptured, and guilt is incurred. Sam and Katie are a case in point. Both of them *feel* guilty, that is, they feel discomfited, burdened, regretful, even somewhat responsible. But neither of them is inclined to be responsible for responding to their painful situation. Blaming one another for the guilt feelings that each suffers serves to deepen their already considerable estrangement.

Sam and Katie met after being involved in a string of other relationships. In their early thirties, they felt ready for marriage, enjoyed each other—especially sexually—and quickly were at war. Katie wanted to have a baby, Sam wasn't sure. The firstborn child of a Protestant, middle-class family, Sam felt burdened by past and present expectations of him. The only daughter of a traditional Italian, Roman Catholic family, Katie, a corporate lawyer, was mandated to success by her stay-at-home mother. Two years into their marriage, the two of them were at a dead end. Katie began therapy as a means toward getting pregnant, and Sam began therapy to find a sympathetic ear. Sam expected to be relegated to the status of sperm donor. Why would Katie need him once they had a child? Katie felt pressed by the passage of time and the demands of her biological clock. The death of her father heightened her commitment to produce a child.

Two years passed and they had a little boy. In a weak moment, Kate explained, "I got Sam to have sex with me. It's a miracle that I became pregnant. We haven't had sex since." Sam currently feels exploited, Katie feels rejected, and their toddler, Daniel, has already become the repository of his parents' broken trust. Sam's worst fears about what would occur between Katie and him once they had a child seem to be coming true. Bound by heavy financial obligations they both have full-time jobs. Katie blames Sam for "making" her go back to work. Sam resents how Katie dotes on Daniel and blatantly disregards him. He was used, he feels, to get Katie pregnant and then was discarded and dismissed. Katie feels unpursued, bereft of intimacy, ill considered. Neither of them can imagine their own contributions to what has broken down. Once overly responsible children, they are now depleted and vindictively entitled adults. Both of them are convinced that they have given far more than they have received. They are justified then to take what they can get however they can get it. Neither one of them is yet able to take the single step that might lift them out of an exhausting morass—to move beyond the realm of inner feelings, beyond the self's relation to self. Were they able to move from simply feeling guilt to use their feelings to prod them toward mitigating guilt, they could transform their almost automatic reactivity into response. Taking responsibility for response might close the distance between them. Taking initiative—whether or not it is reciprocated—can mitigate guilt and open up new options. In point of fact, Sam's and Katie's felt injuries are secondary to the guilt incurred by the fact that they do not address each other. Whether they withdraw into hurt silence or issue a barrage of blame is incidental to the fact that they are choosing to disengage. No responsibility here, only disappointment and a frightened thrust toward flight. Still, the threat of divorce has awakened them to the guilt of disengagement. And awareness of that guilt may yet catalyze their will to reconnect.

Guilt Feelings

Sam and Katie use guilt feelings to substitute for an ethical obligation to respond. Both of them deeply long to make their connection work. Failing the imagination to disclose their suffering without accompanying blame, they fall silent or attack. Whatever residual trust remains between them erodes under the onslaught of their hurt and judgmental words. Theirs is a never-ending spiral of bitter lamentation. Their feelings have become the overriding basis for how they treat each other. The more they react to their own guilt feelings, the further removed they are from identifying their personal portions of guilt in this particular situation. A life devoted to compiling guilt feelings invariably obscures the way toward a stance of responsible response.

Existential guilt is relieved by dialogue, whatever its outcome. Intrapsychic guilt (or guilt feelings) is deepened by monologue and predetermines outcome: If I don't respond I will never have to hear that I am not who you want me to be—even if I already know that in a given situation I was not who *I* want me to be.

Guilt feelings confine persons to the boundaries of their own psyche, and erode their freedom to take fresh soundings of trust. Even more, one person's guilt feelings make little room for another person's differentiated life. The bearer of constant guilt feelings is typically unable to allow for the independent existence of a bond between oneself and others, as Friedman suggests, that connection through which each of us again and again authenticates our existence. *A person's guilt feelings are a statement of hopelessness over never being able to do enough to earn merit.* Bereft of all hope of being addressed, people take refuge in categorical wrongs and rights and in the process lose each other even more.

Let's return to Ann, whose mother, bitterly disappointed in her daughter, is frightened and aghast. "I love you," her mother insists, "but you can't keep living this way. Your health is in danger, you've got to stop smoking, you need different friends, and you have to change the way you act with men." "I know you love me," Ann retorts, unable to look at her mother and trying to withstand the brunt of her mother's attack. "But nothing I ever do is right. When I was little you thought I was cute and neat, but look at the way you see me now. What happened to that little kid?" Ann's mother is so invested in what is right for her daughter, so intent on proving how Ann is wrong that she is blinded to the fact that Ann too thinks that something has gone askew.

Her mother feels like a failure. All three of her daughters have disrupted her image of what a good mother "should" be. In order to be a good mother, she needs children who act right. Ann knows how disappointed her mother is in Ann's older sisters. "I didn't want to hurt you like they did," she cries, "so I didn't tell you what was going on. I think that if we had talked, I wouldn't have gotten into the same mess. I still don't know much about men or sex. I didn't know what was right, and you could have told me. But if I had called, you would have made me even more confused." A mother feeling guilty for having failed her daughter, a daughter feeling guilty for having failed her mother, a relationship in which guilt feelings dominate and eclipse responsible response.

Paradoxically, people often use guilt feelings to defend against a proper acceptance of guilt. Premature despair over one's own life situation, remorse over consideration intended but undelivered, the terror of unjust blame, and the indebtedness implied in receiving all converge to silence relating partners. Silenced over time, people retreat inward, live with stagnant guilt feelings, and abandon the healing options of facing and direct address. Moreover, as Friedman (1985) notes, in our culture there is such a strong conditioning of guilt that most people are simply triggered by the term and *cannot* make the distinction between real and neurotic guilt. Under the circumstances neither Ann nor her mother can imagine a way of tapping "the riches of secret places" in their relationship, or of "making crooked places straight" (Isa. 45:2–3).

MULTILATERAL MERIT

People are indentured to their biological roots, to their family legacies, and to those who in some ways have given them life and invested in their well-being. An inability to credit the merit of family members or of relating partners whom we might want to set aside invariably results in stunted imagination and restricted freedom. Crooked places in relationship are made straight by the recognition of multilateral merit.

Relationships are characterized by two or more sides each of which has at least a grain of validity or merit. Relationships are also informed by the legacies and consequences of transgenerational and intergenerational predispositions and dynamics. Multilateral merit is a characteristic of relationship that goes beyond individual psychology, beyond a *focus* on the mental health or illness of one person at another person's expense. Whether a situation is significant, legal, accidental, or casual, people bring more to a moment of meeting than their own internalized view of themselves or another. They bring a longing and expectation of due consideration. Multilateral merit implies that *every* person in relationship deserves consideration and direct address by virtue of the fact that he or she is. My daughter may not do what I think is good for her. I may not act in ways she can appreciate. But neither our hurt nor our disappointment invalidates the fact that there is merit on each of our sides, merit that until this moment may have been obscured by a competitive press to be good or be right. Most of us are ingrained with one-sided views that imply that if I am right, you must be wrong. Dynamically, people tend to deny their partner's side, and try to constrict relationships on their own subjective, untested, unilateral terms.

"Merit" is a bilevel term that implies a condition of being, and an embodiment of action. In its noun form, "merit" can be understood in individual terms. A person's life and existence per se carry uniqueness, singular value, dueness, and entitlement. I am, therefore I deserve. In its verb form, "merit" can be understood in relational terms. How you and I address each other earns value and deserves consideration by virtue of the choices and actions each one of us takes. I relate, therefore I owe; I fulfill my indebtedness and merit consideration for having done so. At a psychological level, when the merit of one person's contribution to another goes unrecognized, anger and guilt feelings prevail. "An entitled if exploited person is likely to be angry; an indebted if ethically disengaged person is likely to feel guilt" (Boszormenyi-Nagy & Krasner, 1986, p. 164). At an ethical level, however, uncredited merit results in an injured order of existence, in skewed balances of give-and-take.

Merit as a Critical Mass

In seventh grade, for example, Susan was so upset by what occurred between her older sister and their parents that she vowed never to do anything to bring additional harm to them.

> The strain of trying to be her parents' good girl and their failure to credit her efforts on their behalf resulted in her demotivation and withdrawal from them. In high school Susan was an outstanding student. She graduated among the top 10 students of her class, was deeply involved in school activities, and received academic scholarships to a prestigious university. Her life seemed to be in order. It was not.
>
> Early in her senior year, she entered therapy to address her parents' concern over anorexia. Her father felt that everything would be alright if only she would eat. A medical assessment resulted in a weekly weigh-in and her mother's supervision of what she ate. After 6 months of this structure, Susan's weight remained basically unchanged. "Every conversation we have," Susan said, "ends up with questions about my weight. Am I hungry? Did I eat? What would I like for dinner? Nothing I do is ever enough. My parents are worried, the doctor is worried, the school nurse badgers me. Why won't everyone leave me alone?" "I just couldn't live with myself," Susan's mother rejoined, "if something happened to her because she wouldn't eat."

To be sure, Susan knows the wisdom of short-term medical intervention for anorexia. What she is grieving for is parental recognition of past and present merit. Here one person's pathology, Susan's anorexia, has become a focal point that has eclipsed the meaning of merit, and has skewed the relationship between Susan and other family members even further.

Merit: A Self-Motivating Factor

Merit is a self-motivating factor that addresses and transcends inevitable conflicting interests between a self and a significant other (Boszormenyi-Nagy & Krasner, 1985). But the motivational qualities of merit never reside in one person alone. If Susan was not credited for her contributions to her parents' well-being, her parents have not been credited for their ongoing investments in her, however distorted they may now seem.

> Mary, Susan's mother, expects both of her children to leave home soon. She would be putting her energy into a first-time teaching career if Susan weren't ill. There are also a lot of issues between her and her husband, Jim, in desperate need of address. Consigned to a caretaking she neither wanted nor liked, and feeling caught between Susan and Jim, Mary's life is not her own. Estrangement from his own parents from boyhood on has left Jim dutiful if bereft of the terms of intimate give-and-take. He handles "Susan's crisis" with silence and sarcasm. He feels confused by Mary when she allies with Susan against his recourse to authoritarian ways. He simply doesn't understand what's required of him. Won't somebody tell him what he's supposed to do?

No one has a blueprint in conflictual situations, but an acknowledgment of each partner's merit is usually the critical mass.

Over time Susan began to put on weight. As significantly she decided that her parents deserved to be told that something new had occurred. Susan's offer of consideration to them drew an equal and opposite response from her parents. Jim's sarcasm subsided in direct proportion to his relief; and the energy and worry that Mary had invested in Susan was now redirected to living her own life. Susan's movement from pathology to fair consideration can be linked to a growing freedom to act on her own behalf *as well as* to credit the merit of her parents' respective stances. These family members have begun the long process of reworking their expectations of each other and of themselves.

LOYALTY AND LOYALTY DYNAMICS

Family expectations are passed from generation to generation, and are reconstituted in each person's life through choices that are made in an elemental triad. An infant born to a particular father, to a particular mother, and to a particular context, however tranquil or troubled, clings to those who have given to him or her in name or word or deed. A baby's smile of recognition, out-stretched arms when a parent appears, or tears when a parent departs are all early embodiments of loyalty and loyalty dynamics. By definition, child, mother, and father are connected to each other. It is in the matrix of this connection that expectations of each other arise, develop, grow, reach impasses, are reworked—or not.

Bound by Blood, Bound by Merit

Early on, the burden of giving is asymmetrical and falls to parenting figures. Later on give-and-take takes on a greater symmetry. As children assume some responsibility for themselves and for their context, they begin to relieve the burden carried by their caretakers. There seems to be a genetic impulse to give back as well as to take. Fairness requires children to take on their portion of due consideration. In order to fight free of the threat of devouring indebtedness incurred from birth, youngsters are impelled to bring a balance to what has been given by giving in return. This giving can take several directions:

- *Investing in one's own life*—the right to creativity, success, and self-expression.
- *Direct repayment to parents*—attentiveness to a parent's physical, emotional, and spiritual needs as he or she grows older or infirm; and, as significant, the challenging task of maintaining a life in common through having the courage to share in each other's truth.
- *Investing in the next generation's well-being*—as a parent or as a mentor who conveys meaning and merit through the way he or she lives life.
- *Investing in the future through contributing to society and the world*—attending to the tasks of the survival of the planet through redemptive diplomacy among nations, and commitment to environmental health.

Balanced give-and-take between the generations is the long-term result of children learning to give to their parents *and* to take for themselves.

Ideally, a child tries to contribute to both parents. It is almost as if the primal stirrings within a child are geared to pleasing and making one's parents happy. What happens, though, when to please one parent is to displease the other?

The Elemental Triad

By definition, a person's life is always immediately linked to the lives of two other persons whether or not he or she knows or likes them. In the first instance, loyalty is biologically based and triadically determined. In that way, it differs from bonding that is implicitly dyadic and suggests a primary attachment between mother and child, or a sturdy connection between any two people in a long-term relationship. The definition of "loyalty," as we use the term, does not apply to one person's straightforward attachment to another person but to a situation in which a human being stands between two competing forces (Boszormenyi-Nagy & Krasner, 1986, p. 418).

- By definition, children are loyal to each of their parents, but feel caught when they collide. "I hide under the covers when they fight," says Matthew, age 13. "I yell at both of them and tell them to grow up," says Karen, 15. The young cry, confused by adult conflict.
- Two people who become parents are entitled to disagree with each other, to hold differing and conflictual views, some of them bound-up in unaddressed loyalties to their own families of origin. In any case, it is reasonable that parents disagree.
- Disagreement passes the bounds of reason when parenting figures are always in hard conflict or pick and snipe at each other much or most of the time. Even when parents chronically disagree, a child is impelled to reconcile them despite the potential enormity of the task. Torn between parents, youngsters may use many defensive reactions to counter the fact that they don't know what do to. Eventually, though, they may be defeated and have no recourse but to ally with one parent against the other, or to manipulate their relationship to them.
- Matters are made worse when one parent turns to a child for succor and support in explicit or implicit ways; or both parents set their child up as a tribunal or court of appeal to comment on each other's behavior. "Didn't Daddy walk out of the room, Danny? Tell him, didn't he?" and "Listen to your mother holler, Danny, she acts just like a bitch!" are demands that force a child into loyalty conflict. Clearly, this kind of splitting is rarely a parent's intent.
- The intensity of parental demands for a child's unquestioning loyalty is usually proportionate to the degree to which a person feels dismissed or uncredited by his or her own parents, siblings, grandparents, and mates.

In the first instance, loyalty is always a factor in the justice dynamics at play among father, mother, and child in the context of three or more generations.

Comparing Parental Figures

A child's loyalty rests in an unarticulated, self-preserving comparison of parenting figures. Suppose that a father scolds his son and then returns to explain the reasons why, whereas the mother scolds the child and then cuts off, leaving the youngster without an avenue through which to reconnect. Whatever the child does now, pleasing both parents has become an impossible task. Breaches of trust between parent and child are inevitable, and may even be growth producing. But should a gap widen in the ways that this child expects his parents to treat him, then the father will emerge as fairer, more accessible, and more reliable, and the youngster will choose him over the mother to satisfy his own search for safety and due consideration. The dilemma with this choice is that it ruptures a youngster's self-confidence, and leaves him in a constant state of siege and unresolve. From the father's side, he has bested his mate vis-à-vis their child. He may exploit the situation, basking in the satisfaction of their child's preference for him, or he may encourage his wife toward a less punishing mode of addressing their son. From the mother's side, her disappointments in their son make her treat him like a peer. Mother may need help to differentiate between past losses and current opportunities to establish a trust relationship with their son. In any case her reactive overkill has driven their youngster into the willing arms of his father.

Loyalty Conflict

Unaddressed loyalty dynamics frequently deteriorate into loyalty conflicts that are exacerbated by marital bickering, the alcohol misuse of one parent, or the failure of team parenting. What emerges are the seeds of future human suffering and even tragedy: Here a child, continually attempting to attend to both parents' well-being is forced by circumstances beyond his or her control to choose the love and safety of one parent at the cost of sacrificing those of the other (Boszormenyi-Nagy & Spark, 1973).

The consequences of this choice include (1) the metamorphosis of a child into a captive investor in father or mother, with all of the difficulties attendant on surrendering personal vested interests to respond to the wishes and demands of another, and (2) "vital dissociation" (Buber, 1963, p. 123) from the other parent, with all the difficulties attendant on disengaging from a life-giving organic connection. Under these circumstances, a child not only suffers a loss of security but also is deprived of the potential yield of living in direct relation.

A Wordless Void

A parent from whom a child is ethically driven to disengage is a lost resource and a nonsubstitutable one at that. That parent also becomes an inexorable producer of guilt. Forced ethical disengagement triggers *intuitive guilt* in youngsters, guilt induced when they sense a profound injury to the common order of existence between themselves and their family members. Later on in life, intuitive guilt develops into *collusive guilt,* which results from adult failure to reexamine the circumstances in which ethical disengagement came about. Consider Walter, a president of a corporation who for the past 5 years has reluctantly lived over two hundred miles away from his wife.

> Forty-five years ago, Walter's mother left his father to live with another man. He and his brother were raised by his maternal grandmother, who prohibited visits between the boys and their father. Walter's sister was raised by their paternal grandmother and had ready access to their father. Until he began therapy, Walter had no words for the intuitive guilt that he had carried. He sensed that his world had been cut asunder early in life. "I have no family," he says today. But now he has the option of considering his part in furthering disconnection. For the moment he is stuck. Walter's unaddressed loyalties to his mother and grandmother bind and depress him. He is no more free to embrace his father now than he was as a loyalty-torn child. Asked if he sees his father now, Walter replies, "Only once a year." "Can you tell your father how you are struggling?" the therapist asks. "He has other children now," Walter says. "Do you tell your father that you need him?" the therapist persists. Walter is certain that his father won't really care.

The developmental sanctuary that a 5-year-old needs and deserves was shattered by the logistics of his parents' divorce and their failure to address their children jointly. Without Buber's notion of speech-with-meaning from his parents into which he might later grow, Walter was left to preserve the wordless void of his childhood and to repeat the same pattern in marriage.

By unknowingly continuing to participate in the aftermath of his parents' choices, which they made for reasons of their own, the 5-year-old, now 50, has become an accessory to their facts. Walter's self-isolating behavior per se has become a choice that sustains early breaches of trust. He is currently faced with new options: to maintain collusive guilt by silence or lack of direction, or to find words to describe what he still deserves, what he owes, and how to *raise his voice to make himself known.*

The outcome of ethical disengagement is a distortion of truth and a breakdown of trust. For how is a child supposed to know what drives his mother's rage and disapproval unless she is able to tell him? How is he supposed to grasp the meaning of his father's silence in the face of his mother's attack, unless the father finds a way to advocate now for his wife and now for his son? Short of being taught how to imagine each other's side, these family members are in danger of perpetuating a triadic paradigm in which in all of their relationship's split loyalties prevail: the preferring one, the preferred one, and the one who is not preferred (Boszormenyi-Nagy & Krasner, 1986).

ETHICAL IMAGINATION

*This "seeing the other" is not ... a matter of "identification" or
"empathy" but a concrete imagining of the other side which does not at
the same time lose sight of one's own.*

—Friedman, *Martin Buber: The Life of Dialogue*

Ethical imagination is a creative process born of *the twofold imperative to be just and to be free.* It is grounded in the particularity of a specific context; it does not give way to generalizations. Ethical imagination is catalyzed by the ongoing recognition that merit never lies in one person alone but is always intrinsic to each relating partner. If children are taught that only one of their parents has merit, they lose the ability to imagine that everyone has a side that counts. Carrying this logic to its furthest extreme, the question may be asked that if one parent doesn't count, do I? Psychosexual reductionism like the impact of the Oedipus complex has hindered rightful exploration of children's entitlement to consider and be considered by their mother and father alike.

Children who are inextricably caught between their parents grow up with a number of deficits that they then replay in their world at large. Failing the option of establishing a discrete relationship with each parent (dual loyalties), they may spend the rest of their lives *being for or against any relating partner—* parent, mate, child, employer, friend, or cause. As they enter adulthood, such children are typically unable to recognize the legitimacy in each of two opposing sides. A pattern of embracing one parent while dismissing or cutting off the other deprives people of the knowledge that they themselves have a side that counts. It can also convert them into self-proclaimed victims or self-righteous know-it-alls who can tolerate no deviation from a one-sided stance (Murrow, 1991). Unprepared to wrestle with the inevitable ambiguities and paradoxes of day-to-day life, people flee into the seeming certainties of absolutes, ideologies, and zealotry. Parenting is none of these, but failed parenting produces all of these.

Straining the Imagination

There is no life situation more in need of ethical imagination than parenting. The demand put on first-time parents in a society that offers little structure for parents and makes many demands on them strains the resources of young people who themselves are trying to survive and thrive. Competing with their children for time, energy, and money, overburdened adults prepare to raise their young with little instruction other than the parenting they themselves received. They are left to guide their children, sustain their marriage, and earn a living surrounded by little available support. Isolated, unaddressed, and often depleted, parents cannot give what they do not receive. For how does a person continue to protect, nurture, teach, and enjoy a child when his or her own life has been reduced to function?

It is true that parenting requires competency. But competency is not to be reduced to function nor to be had at the cost of connection. Real competency includes a capacity to meet the ordinary demands of day-to-day life *and* retain an ability to imagine what is required for one's own nurture and joy. Parents who give without grasping their own limits or without assessing what they require or deserve in return will unwittingly transmit the burdens of a monologic stance: One-sided giving, untested assumptions, unspoken claims, and acts of retribution are the factors that obstruct the impulse toward connection and corrode the foundation of ethical imagination.

Parenting: A Dialogic Stance

Parenthood is a dialogic enterprise that ideally begins with personal ground and shared commitment. In the first instance, it contains a clear embrace of an ethic of caring give-and-take. But justice between the generations is held by a fragile thread woven into the fabric of imaginative questions: "My parents never call me." Have I conveyed that they're intrusive? "My mother feels I'm unstable." Can she learn to address honest difference? "My 16-year-old hates me." Have I ignored him for my new girlfriend? "My mother and father are always fighting." Can I tell them what their fights do to me? Like any other significant commission, parenting ultimately requires moments of quiet and direction wrested out of the stuff of ordinary existence. It requires parallel growth for parent and child. And most of all, it involves the ability to meet a child with the fear and trembling of one who has no ready-made answers to life (Friedman, 1960, p.136).

Parenting is a dialogic stance born of accessible authority, ethically engaged with latent trust and untested hope. At the time of an offspring's birth, parents and child enter into a covenantal relationship that obliges both, and cannot be dissolved by either party, their objections notwithstanding. Above all else parenting involves imagination that delivers meaning and vision to parent and child alike. When meaning and vision fade into function, they are replaced by regimentation, rigidity, and inaccessibility, which snuff out the spark of real connection. Failure of parental imagination quickly gives way to parental structure, which unhindered, results in recourse to moralisms, maxims, and categories. Then human life and interhuman justice lose their force as instruments of creation and quickly plummet into objects of despair.

Failed Imagination

> *The heart of man is not evil; only its imagination is so; that is to say what it produces and devises arbitrarily, separating itself from the goodness of creation ...*

—Buber, *For the Sake of Heaven*

Unless the imagination of the young is stimulated to recognize the legitimacy of opposing sides and views, particularly in "one" parent contexts, the young are predisposed to a victimized stance that lends itself to social pathology, with its manifold expression of behavioral problems in school, delinquency in adolescence, and criminal behavior in adulthood or at any time.

People can hardly be expected to imagine the full sweep of another person's reality if they cannot give terms or voice to their own reality. The paradox here emerges from an unspoken premise that someone else knows my mind and is bound to respond to it. But only an infant is so entitled. Still, I withdraw disappointed and absolve myself of further need to respond if my partner fails to offer me unsolicited consideration. Why does initiative have to lie with me? is a defensive if common lament, itself untouched by any hint of imagination. "Is what you want in your own vested interests?" Yes. "Can you imagine your partner's lack of imagination?" Yes. "Do you presume that you are being rejected rather than bumping against your partner's limits?" Yes. Blame and lack of imagination go hand in hand.

Blame is commonplace in every relationship. People have conflicting expectations. If you don't do it my way and things don't work out, then you are to blame. The notion of blame implies personal fault. Implied fault is a factor that sometimes has merit. A subway train crashes in New York. The driver is faulted for drinking. His actions are blamed by all concerned. Here blame is a communal expression of disapproval and an act of reproach, and can be justified as a demand for personal accountability. On the other hand, the uses of blame can be unfair, especially in relationships in which assumptions are typically unexamined by participating partners and therefore remain unclear.

Unfair Blame

Unfair blame results from your excluding my truth in order to reinforce your own truth. Here blame is a one-sided act, an objectification of my reality and an imposition of your reality, a failure to elicit my motives, my context, my terms, my side. Under these circumstances, blame is an arbitrary act in which my partner unilaterally exonerates himself or herself from any degree of culpability, and decides that fault for what is wrong between us essentially belongs to me. Out of this posture blame becomes an aggressive act.

Unfair blame is often used as a haven from responsible response. Here I can justify hurt feelings without having to assume responsibility for corrective action. Constantly repeated as a mode of day-to-day relating, the use of unfair blame predisposes its user to a paradoxical dilemma: I feel the limitless ways in which I "have been made a victim" by you. But I am blind to how I discount you, and how the consequences of my actions can make you feel like a victim. When the reliability of one's truth is chronically deemed invalid, breaches of trust occur. Left unaddressed, patterns of unfair blame rupture the imagination, puncture justice in the human order, and cripple human inclination toward fair give-and-take. Failed imagination is a proclamation of what *I* feel and what *I* want, with massive disregard for the terms of another person; or my compliance with what *you* feel or what *you* want, with massive disregard for my terms. Ethical imagination is conceiving what I owe and what I deserve in a given context, with equivalent regard for my terms *and* for the terms of a relating partner.

TRIADIC INCLUSION

The inclusive process that takes place among members of the elemental triad is the cornerstone of ethical imagination and due consideration. To wit, to what degree can child, father, and mother be present to each other, have access to each other, and be mutually accountable without one or more of them having to pay an undue or escalating cost? Can I credit my father's merit and ask him to recognize mine, without fearing my mother's competitive ire? Do I know how to guide my youngsters to address their dad when they feel safer talking to me? When I mourn their divorce, will my parents hear me without feeling hurt and blaming each other for my grief, or worse, blaming me? As an adopted child who carries a double triad, can I search out my birth parents without estranging my adoptive mother and father? Can I embrace my biological father without offending and being punished by my newly found biological mother?

Vital Dissociation

At base, triadic inclusion has to do with the willingness of three people who are inextricably linked to move beyond "vital dissociation" (Buber, 1957, p.102) to ethical reengagement. To Buber, vital dissociation is the sickness of organic forms of life (including family) that enable people to live in direct relation and security with each other. Despite the outward preservation of some of the old forms, he says, inward decay has resulted in an intensification of human loneliness. In consequence, "direct, frank dialogue is becoming ever more difficult and more rare; the abyss between man and man threatens ever more piteously to become unbridgeable" (Buber, 1957, p. 222). On the other hand, ethical reengagement is the outcome of two people's decision to honor the connection that is already there. It is often a timid and wavering movement past old and stagnant impasses toward "a coalescence of vital forces" (Boszormenyi-Nagy & Krasner, 1986) that, latent in the triad, are waiting to be mined.

Ethical Reengagement

Ethical reengagement involves a choice to repair the breach between people who have given and taken in vital association with one another. It is a signal of my willingness to own my contribution to estrangement in the desperate hope that you will be willing to own yours. My choice to reengage with you is clearly a self-serving act. It is also an act of contrition that contains at least a hint that you deserved something better from me than I was able or willing to give. Ethical reengagement between person and person is ordinarily a demanding and courageous task. Ethical reengagement between person and person in the elemental triad is even more so, though latent resources and residual trust are likely to be greater between the generations than in accidental relations, terror notwithstanding.

The move toward inclusion in the elemental triad provides the basic antidote to repeated patterns of unfair blame. It is also the action component of ethical imagination. Nowhere are the seeds of justice and injustice, freedom and bondage, truth and propaganda, and trustworthiness and deceit more powerfully created, developed, and experienced than in the primal matrix of the elemental triad.

The causes of cyclical intergenerational injuries are squarely rooted in the breakdown that takes place in this elemental triad. Therefore the success of efforts to heal cyclical intergenerational injuries without facing back into this triad is inevitably limited. Breaking transgenerational cycles of destructive and depleting patterns, which are precursors of emotional and physical violence and retribution, requires members of each elemental triad to find the imagination to turn to address each other—*whatever their limits* and *regardless of outcome*. Failing to do so reproduces and reintroduces the corrosive dynamics that undermine future attempts to participate fully in family, in the community, in the culture, or in the workplace.

SEEMING: THE ABSENCE OF DIRECT ADDRESS

The widespread tendency to live from the recurrent impression one makes instead of from the steadiness of one's being is not a "nature." It originates...in men's dependence upon one another. It is no light thing to be confirmed in one's being by others, and seeming deceptively offers itself as a help in this.

—Buber, *The Knowledge of Man*

Buber distinguishes between two different types of human existence: "The one proceeds from what one really is, the other from what one wishes to seem." He correctly describes the duality of being and seeming as the essential problem of the sphere of the interhuman. He carefully notes that all of us are subject to seeming and attempts to distinguish between people whose essential attitudes are more characterized by seeming or by being. *And he concludes that whatever else the meaning of the word "truth" may be in other realms, in the interhuman realm it means that human beings communicate themselves to one another as what they are.*

Bound to Please

Buber cites the tension between being and seeming, but the weight of his argument comes from the perspective of the individual rather than the interhuman, from the intrapsychic sphere in the service of relating. He seems to suggest that to yield to seeming or to resist it is a singular choice that arises out of a person's will to be. Undiscussed are the encumbrances of the hidden claims of *long-standing, implicit or explicit, familial, and communal expectations that one be bound to please.* A stance of unilateral pleasing, or displeasing, for that matter, takes root in a pathology of the soul and embodies the residue of truth and trust that have been repeatedly breached.

To be sure, seeming is an individual dilemma and a singular choice. From this perspective, it can be viewed as a dependency on, even an addiction to, external referents as the basis for one's internal terms. It is an abandonment of oneself as an equivalent referent in relating. *Pleasing becomes seeming when it leaves out my claim to be and my willingness to disclose it.*

A Form of Collusion

Seeming is also a form of collusion that protects people from having to know and being known even in the midst of genuinely offered care. Consider the case of the Draper family, with three adult children and their elderly parents. Mr. Draper, now 80, has lived an active, hard-driving life, deeply involved in and committed to his career, his community and his family, and seemingly beholden to no one. In the face of deteriorating health, he is contemplating discontinuing dialysis, treatments that happen three times a week and tie him to the distance between home and the hospital. Increasingly depressed by the limits of his life, and burdened by the constant bickering that goes on between him and his wife, he has informed two of his offspring of his intentions. But he has not told his favorite child.

Kristin, 50, learned of her father's wishes through her older and younger siblings. She adores her father and is frightened by the possibility of what she describes as suicide. Her father-in-law committed suicide several years ago, and family members have borne the consequences of that act ever since in profound and painful ways. Whether Mr. Draper's eventual decision to halt dialysis is suicide or not, Kristin opposes the option. In her press to be a loyal daughter, she faces the question of whether she is free enough to disclose to her father his meaning in her life; whether to risk telling him that his being still has its independent merit and that she is terrified to contemplate the degree of threat and loss she will suffer should her father volitionally choose to bring his life to an end.

Constituent Parts of Seeming

At the moment, it seems that Kristin's only alternative is seeming, whose constituent parts include (1) the decision to remain silent and act as if she were ignorant of what is actually going on, (2) the decision to avoid the risk of addressing her father and act as if she were without influence in his life, (3) the decision to collude with her father's protectiveness of her, and act as if she were indifferent to his pain as well as to her own, and (4) the decision to duck her mother's wrath and denial of the gravity of her father's illness, and act as if she were irreversibly caught between her parents without an alternate choice.

In the first instance, seeming as a way is always shaped in one's family of origin. Kristin learned to please her father at the cost of not addressing him. They enjoyed each other but never spoke deeply or disclosed themselves to each other substantively. They spent a lot of time sailing together, an interest that has an almost mystical quality for both of them. But they never risked sharing their joy with Kristin's mother, who might have felt jealous or excluded. Despite their mutual love and attachment, father and daughter have no paradigm with which to overcome the seeming that comes of suffering in silence, a seeming that inevitably forces a wedge between people who care for each other and even offer each other care.

Seeming is an inevitable consequence of failed imagination. The dislocation that seeming produces in a person, and between person and person, usurps freedom and converts the balletic movements of truth and trust into clumsy attempts to climb onstage. Seeming becomes the unauthentic stance of the authentic person who longs to connect but despairs of truly doing so. Succumbing to a mandate to please, constrained by unaddressed conflicting and split loyalties, blindsided by demands linked to unrelenting obligation, we take on a facade of seeming that permeates our being and distorts our vision of relational possibilities.

Looking for "Guarantees"

As would many people, what Kristin would like as prelude to addressing her father is a guarantee that he will welcome what she has to say, and that neither he nor she will be "hurt" in the exchange. What she discounts is the degree of injury that they are imposing on each other by dint of their silence. Like many of us, Kristin has become habituated to withholding her truth, and to operating out of untested premises of what other people really want. She has become anesthetized to the merit of her own authority, blinded to the trustworthiness that has been built between her and her family members in the midst of conflict and even harsh estrangements, and numbed to the latent resources that exist between person and person in her immediate world. She is also unfolding, becoming, being—resilient, resourceful, determined, devoted, intrinsically fair, imaginative, and longing to fight free.

Testing Premises

What would it look like for Kristin to test her untested premises against her closely held relationship with her father and mother? What answers might she hope to receive?

Q: Has Kristin told her dad how precious he is to her?

A: "No, I've told him how much fun it is when we talk about matters related to sailing."

Q: Can Kristin imagine the healing impact on her father if she tells him of her pain?

A: "Nobody in my family talks to each other like that. Why worry him about me when he already has so much to worry about?"

Q: Are Kristin's siblings and mother currently resources for her?

A: "My mother always gets in the way of this kind of thing. It scares her. My brother and sister are the ones who told me what Dad is thinking about. They didn't challenge him. They are inclined to believe that he has a right to do what he has to do."

Q: Can Kristin challenge her siblings to consider her differing point of view?

A: "Yes, they would receive me, but I don't know how they'd respond."

Other questions exist and have no answers yet:

- Will it occur to Kristin that she offers her father respect and dignity when she tells him her hard truth?
- Has Kristin given credence to her father's right to graceful resignation, enhanced by the balm of their lifelong connection and by her embrace of who her dad is and has been?
- Can Kristin receive her father's decision when it finally comes, without making it the basis for further silence and self-blame?

The Task of the Interhuman

The task of the interhuman requires each of us to face toward the fullness of being, to share our truth from the depths of ambivalence, and to imagine the resources that can emerge from efforts at dialogue however hostile or volatile they may seem time and time again—and then to act. This is the way that points to the living substance of healing through meeting. In Buber's words, it is the way in which real being staves off the necessity for seeming. It is a way that prefers the realities of despair to the hysteria of chaos. The human predisposition toward seeming can be overcome time and again through discovering the freedom to be. Contrary to our longings, the freedom to be is an earned freedom, sometimes enlivened by grace, which comes of knowing one's own truths and embracing them, and then testing them in circumstances loaded with possibilities of many-sided injuries and potential retribution. Despite our distaste for the fray and our wish for an easier path, none exists. But what does exist is sufficient. The healing dynamics that lie dormant in the sphere of the interhuman are brought forth by ethical imagination, and surge upward when truth encounters trust, when trust elicits truth, and when the handmaiden of both is direct address.

PART II

Ethical Tasks of a Contextual Therapist

3

Relational Ethics:
From Monologue
to Dialogue

CONTEXTUAL THERAPY: METHOD, PROCESS, AND WAY

In this chapter we mean to describe a contextual view of a therapist's ethical tasks and their implementation. We will join the premises of Martin Buber's philosophical anthropology with the theories of contextual therapy by raising clinical questions, by identifying clinical issues, and by demonstrating strategies and interventions.

The influence of Buber's philosophical anthropology on the field of psychotherapy is well established (Farber, 1966). But nowhere is it pursued more faithfully or implemented more rigorously than in the theory and practice of contextual therapy. In brief, contextual therapy is a complex and sophisticated modality based on a dialectical, multipersonal, transgenerational paradigm of give-and-take in significant relationships. *It is a trust-based therapy whose strategies and interventions are powered by direct address.* The crucial dimensions of the contextual approach incorporate the variables of the human condition and include (1) fact (destiny), (2) need (individual psychology), (3) power (communication, transactions, alliances), and (4) merited trust (self-delineation and due consideration).

Contextual therapy identifies and utilizes unrecognized resources between and among partners in relationship. In the process, the contextual practitioner acknowledges the pathology that results from breaches in relationship. But contextual therapy pushes beyond pathological interpretation to a multidirectional stance that catalyzes healing through meeting. Its development of the concept of merited trust, squarely anchored in Buber's philosophical anthropology, has been a major contribution to psychotherapeutic knowledge. *The dimension of merited trust embodies demonstrated consideration of self and*

55

other. Underdeveloped to this point is the critical dimension of direct address, which, along with multidirected partiality, represents contextual therapy's core methodologies and interventions.

What basically sets contextual therapy apart from other modalities is (1) *its determination to catalyze direct address* between a person and members of his or her immediate and extended context for the purpose of establishing just balances of give-and-take between them, (2) *its refusal to collude with a person whose suffering tempts him or her to choose the false sanctuary of a therapeutic relationship over the dialogic imperative that exists between him or her and members of his or her entire world*. Its insistence on a multi-directional therapeutic stance mirrors the ethics of give-and-take borne of ontic connections.

"Relational ethics are distinguished by the proposition that no one individual or group can ever function as the sole measure of the whole of any relational situation" (Cotroneo & Krasner, 1981, p. 116).

> Relational ethics are concerned with the equitable distribution of the benefits and burdens of all partners to a given situation. They simultaneously consider the terms and claims of each active and passive participant who is affected by the consequences of [another person's] actions. Given this measure of human behavior, a therapist can help clients address themselves to the matter of equity among all members of the relational context that (s)he is treating. In the process he is relieved of the task of trying to decide who or what is right or wrong. (Boszormenyi-Nagy & Krasner, 1986, p. 173)

A Life Force

The methods and processes of contextual therapy have a life force of their own. These methods and processes are either constrained or catalyzed by embodied conviction, or what Martin Buber called lived life, wrested out of the ground on which we stand, from the raw clay of day-to-day existence. Choosing for trust is never an intellectual exercise nor even a fine-tuned grasp of complex theory and concepts. The ethical dimension of existence can never be put aside at will without consequence. Testing options and identifying resources may be deferred in the face of waning courage, but repeated delay may evolve into the prospect of irretrievable loss. At one level, the methods and processes of contextual work may be analyzed and identified like any other body of knowledge or school of thought. Here one can argue for a free-standing therapeutic modality that focuses on the realm of the between and asserts that the ontological, intergenerational interface is the fundamental human wellspring and primary leverage for a just and trustworthy existence, that is, for balance in motion, for fair give-and-take between person and person.

At another level, choosing for trust is a way, a way that may be catalyzed in the clinical setting, but a way that stands on its own in everybody's life. A way that includes but transcends the clinical setting, it is, for us, *a covenantal way, a recognition of the fact that we are born into partnership with all its attendant burdens, benefits, and joys.* We are born into a life in which dialogue is a healing option that, in the words of Hans Trüb, unlocks the locked up person for the meeting with the world. *The truth we hold to be self-evident links us to therapy, but frees us for the promise of community.* Our twin struggles are always to be free and to connect. *Freedom and connectedness are the mature outgrowth of a creative, revelatory, and redemptive process.* A trust-building way leads toward a creative mastery of life without offering ourselves up for undue self-sacrifice. It requires revelatory encounter, which transforms the bare and brittle bone of communication into the flesh and blood of genuine communion. It provides the redemptive movement that frees us for a deepened capacity to care. *Creation, revelation, redemption are truths we hold to be self-evident.* Here we think we come to a crisis in words, to a crisis of how to catalyze resources in the midst of pathology. *For the call to dialogue implicit in a contextual stance is an invitation to live life at its fullest even when life is at its worst.* It is the I of self-disclosure and the Thou of invitation. It is never the It of theory or the Should of morality. *The tasks of a contextual therapist are guided by the specificity of relational ethics rather than by the norms of preset codes and moralistic judgments.*

AN ONTIC HIERARCHY

Dialogue is endowed with a revelatory function which is wholly dependent on the fact that its preexisting stages of self-delineation and due consideration can invariably be linked to the in-built human longing to hold and be held accountable for consideration owed and deserved.

—Krasner, *Choosing for Trust: Method, Process, Way*

Whether or not suffering finds voice and ear in the spoken word represents the difference between monologue and dialogue. One of the most basic tasks of a contextual therapist is to stand for dialogue between a client and the significant members of his or her family and extended context. Dialogue in contextual therapy has two separate and discrete forums: the one between therapist and client(s), whose sole purpose is to catalyze truth and trust between person and person in their elemental contexts, and the other between members of a primary context who are estranged, whose connections are stagnant, and whose ethical disengagement has become a source of injury and injustice.

Elements of a Therapeutic Contract

"The ledger between therapist and client is separate from a family ledger if sometimes analogous in intensity. But the one can never merge into the other" (Boszormenyi-Nagy & Krasner, 1986, p. 402). The contract between client and therapist has structural, clinical, and ethical elements. *Structurally,* a client calls to make an appointment for a specific time and day, and agrees to pay a specific fee in exchange for professional expertise of a typically undefined nature. Basically, the client is in pain and looking for help. In return, a clinician contracts for a three- or four-session assessment process, after which the clinician and client agree or fail to agree to work together. *Clinically,* the development of a therapeutic contract begins with an assessment in which a clinician uncovers previously unrecognized resources, contributions, benefits, and options as well as identifies areas of pathology, injury, stagnation, and injustice between person and person. The ethical element of a contextual contract obliges a therapist to point to the hierarchical nature of relational ethics that is most compelling, binding, and profound in the vertical dimension of existence. To wit, *the vertical dimension of existence stands at the top of the hierarchy of all human relationships.* Regardless of circumstances, those to whom we are born and who gave us sustenance and those to whom we give birth and offer sustenance impact us in ways denied in any other context—except, perhaps, for long-term marriage partners who have children in common.

It is precisely because the vertical dimension of existence is so profound, so binding, and so potentially freeing that contextual therapists invite their clients to pursue dialogue in the family as the most efficacious means of healing and being healed. The problematic here is that if parents fail to find their voice in a fair and reasoned way, what chance do offspring have to discover theirs? *In point of fact, there is a hole in the heart of the parenting process about which few questions are ever asked—the unexamined expectations and illusions that one generation holds of another.* Indelibly marked by the consequences of parental legacies and decisions, members of each generation are obliged to find healing freedom and a capacity to teach the process of give-and-take to children yet unborn. The success of this task rests on a person's movement toward direct address. Whether or not my efforts evoke a reciprocal response, I alone must decide whether or not to raise my voice and speak my truth in the trust that I will strike a responsive chord in the heart and mind of another. And at the very least, I can know that my choice to speak is an attempt to balance what I owe, to assert what I deserve.

A Bold Facing

The existential burden of individual and relational maturity is not a one-sided revisionist history in which we simply critique what we did or did not get, but a bold facing of what is given and what is owed. We can attack parenting for its insufficiencies, but the fact is that in one or another dimension, parenting like all human relationships *is* deficient as well as beneficent. What is more critical is the question of who my parents were or are. What were the forces with which they struggled? On what resources could they count? What did they do with what they had? How did they find meaning in their lives? Who nurtured them? What truths informed them? How did they ask for help, if they did? Whose hand guided them? Whose voice addressed them? Whom did they trust? To whom could they speak their truth?

In the beginning, a person's felt insufficiency and reluctance to disclose or delineate his or her truth and to elicit that of another are consequences of the misuse of parental authority (see parentification, Boszormenyi-Nagy & Krasner, 1985). The paradox here is that parents who tend to expect too much of their children are typically victims in their own right. When children become captive investors in their parents' well-being, what is dynamically played out between parent and child are the unfaced, unaddressed, and often unimagined injuries that, unseen, are transposed from one generation to the next. When children are parentified and when their parents are parentified, each generation learns to become more and more obligated to the previous generation's patterns of nondisclosure, self-withholding, and personal hopelessness. Misused children become overresponsible adults. Overobligated, we learn not to disclose our pain, not to take personal pleasure. Depleted and weary before we begin, we learn to duck mounting assaults on our being and resources. Then we learn not to make any claims for ourselves. Finally, bitterness and silence deepen into inevitable despair. Mistrust seeps into relationship and invades and infects it. The onset of mistrust is insidious. Unaddressed, its outcome is without resolution. Self-protective boundaries are misread as defensive and selfish. When other adults fail us, we turn to our children. Then a spiral of inverted parenting begins once again.

An Ethical Crossroad

"You know more about me than anyone else in my life" is a gift frequently tendered by clients to their therapist. This comment is typically a genuine acknowlegment of the therapist's skill and reliability. It is also an indication of the clients' awe at recognizing their own deprivation and learning how to address their world. But an ethical dilemma is embodied in this comment, and has to do with many factors:

- Ethically, a therapist can never successfully compete with a client's family members without transgressing basic loyalties. Fifty minutes a week in the therapy room may suffice to disclose intimate details of a person's life but can never substitute for *the knowing that takes place over years and decades* between ontically connected partners.
- Therapy offers *asymmetrical safety*. Clients purchase the right to disclose whatever they choose about themselves, to work as hard

as they want on themselves, and to be unencumbered by a demand for reciprocal consideration that is implicit or explicit in all intimate relationships.

- Parents, children, and sometimes mates have no substitutes. Therapeutic relationships may be intense and stir up longings for primal connectedness. But should a therapist offend a client in some significant or even insignificant way, another therapist is as close as the nearest book of yellow pages.

- Shielding clients from members of their own context by excluding or preempting the latter from fair consideration in the therapeutic process may indicate a therapist's unfinished business with his or her own family of origin and limit the therapist's ability to lead clients toward a dialogic stance.

- Temporary refuge from imbalances in familial relationships is a reasonable therapeutic intervention. It is an ethical breach, however, if a therapist encourages clients to resist or flee from engaging in fair give-and-take with people who have made significant investments in and contributions to their well-being.

- Regardless of caring feelings between therapist and client, the existential ledger between the two can never be ethically analogous to the ledger that exists among family members. An accidental relationship typically carries neither the weight nor the leverage to sustain a family's transgenerational and intergenerational mandate in common to safeguard present and future generations.

- A therapist's choice of profession requires a high level of knowledge, skill, courage, and conviction. But therapists' primary connections and commitments reside in their own ontic hierarchy, not in the clinical realm. Their relationship to clients may be devoted and invested with care but fail to provide the primary source of therapists' life meaning. Why then should it be otherwise for a client?

- Healing through meeting can and does occur between client and therapist. Over time strangers with a mission in common can and do till the soil of earned merit and mutual consideration. What will always be lacking between them, however, is that unbreakable ethical dimension of reality that withstands all manner of injuries, breaches, and disruptions.

- Even dialogic psychotherapists are ethically obliged to challenge the tendency to operate as though they were guarantors of safety for their clients against members of their clients' context.

Ours is an era in which terror of commitment and cynicism over institutional reliability infect every layer of society. It is a time when people are disoriented over a lack of reliable structure. Do therapists as agents of healing, then, really have the right to position family members in a status secondary to the therapist-client relationship? Can therapists or clients really afford to overlook or diminish the residual trust, the lingering devotion, the invisible attachments, the amorphous commitment, and the powerful longings of people who are irrevocably linked to each other by ties of roots and legacy from generation to generation?

MULTILATERAL CONTRACTING

How do clinicians establish a contract in which everyone's relational options receive due consideration—whether or not they are present in the therapy room?

A multilateral contract operates on the simple fact that everyone is involved in a network of relationships, past and present, that hold massive significance for them. To discount the vitality of connectedness is to

- deny the reality with which a client is forced to contend actively or passively,
- further distort the possibility of fair give-and-take between people who know that they are estranged but do not know how to make their relationship work,
- give a person psychological permission to reject ethical considerations,
- retard motivation,
- impoverish ethical imagination, and
- lose therapeutic leverage.

On the other hand, the ethical task of a contextual therapist is to confirm the legitimacy of important connections and to acknowledge the real or potential suffering of relating partners. *To point to a way in which clients can embrace their own truth and at the same time make room for the truths of others inevitably frees them to invest in their own well-being.*

A multilateral contract leads to a process that can *authenticate the merit of each relating partner* and *catalyze the healing possibilities of primal connectedness*. In contextual therapy, a multilateral contract is a living document that reestablishes a reliable framework for the disclosure of truth and the rebuilding of trust in covenantal relationships.

Consider Diane Randal, who entered therapy with Dr. K. in flight from a marriage therapist who allied with her husband Matt to blame her for the breakdown of their marriage. She was also in flight from the escalating demands on her life. Left with feelings of abandonment and rage, by her previous therapist, she was investigating his credentials with an eye toward legal action.

Given Diane's current mistrust of therapy and her expectation of being betrayed, Dr. K. offered the option of seeing her and her husband jointly, or seeing her alone and referring Matt to Dr. J., a colleague. Diane chose to work with separate therapists, and Matt reluctantly agreed. As it happened, over time Drs. K. and J. saw the Randals individually, as a couple, in sessions with each and both of their children, and in joint sessions with the couple and both therapists. Matt tentatively decided to examine disappointments outside the marriage, though he saw little value to therapy if he and his wife were not talking about their relationship. The therapists saw it differently. It was clear to them that neither of these people knew what they wanted but were caught in a cycle of constantly reacting to what they didn't like. The couple's reactivity to each other was so intense that it potentially blocked the path toward either personal or interpersonal healing for them. Both of them were estranged from their siblings and from their surviving parents. They felt competitive about their children and were often in combat over them. Douglas, 12, and William, 9, were caught in constant conflict over their parents' conflict and estrangement, and they drew their parents' fire onto themselves. William was silent, sullen, and struggling in school. Matt and Diane were sorely buffeted by the confusion and chaos of their lives and sought respite in other people's arms.

The initial phase of establishing a multilateral contract involved (1) each therapist's advocacy for their client's suffering and (2) a careful inquiry into both the lapses and contributions of the marital partners. It quickly became evident not only that there was a mass of unfaced issues between Diane and Matt, like money, time, felt slights, and quarrels over who was responsible for what, but that both of them were severely distressed about their relationships to their own parents and sibs, and about how their parents' expectations of them differed in kind and fairness from expectations of their siblings. They were also distressed at their memories about how their parents' marriages had affected them. In no time at all, *images of people crowded the therapy room,* each of them directly or indirectly impacting and influencing Diane's and Matt's interpretation of their current situation.

Marriage as Symptom

Ostensibly Matt and Diane came into therapy to repair their marriage or find a way out of it. The therapists regarded neither of these as a compelling or immediate goal. Matt wanted Diane to enjoy, embrace, and confirm him and to make him the primary object of her interest and devotion. Diane wanted Matt to take more responsibility in money matters and household chores, and to assure her of his sexual fidelity while she maintained her own distance and her own options to boot. Therapeutic interventions here were not initially focused on repairing the broken structure of a stagnant, undeveloped marriage. They were geared instead to a multipersonal examination of the unformed and unexplored personal ground and operating premises of these two people who were no longer bound to each other—if ever they were—in a mature and active choice to build a life together. At this moment, at least, their ties to each other were held together by the intensity of their mutual disappointments, the existence of their two young sons, and their longing for something more—though not necessarily from each other. Both of them had no direction for their own lives although they had a lot to say about how the other person had failed them. Matt and Diane lived at the mercy of *unidentified forces in their families of origin* that constrained them from regarding themselves as legitimate objects of their own investment. To wit, "I have no permission to act on my own behalf. Therefore you owe it to me to take care of me. If you fail me as I've failed myself, I will take that as a punitive act, and I will respond to you as I have responded to my parents or as they have responded to each other."

The kudos linked to achievement, wealth, and success are no longer adequate to balance the felt and real deprivation suffered by two bright, handsome, articulate, and apparently sophisticated human beings. They can no longer force their myths about marriage to do the work of real relating. They can no longer use their *illusions of what marriage should be* to fuel day-to-day involvement with each other. Like most people entering marriage, the Randals initially walked down the aisle deaf, dumb, and blind, and counted on making their marriage "better" than their parents' without having the foggiest notion of what that meant or how to proceed. Now they have gone through their respective bags of assumptions—and nothing seems to work. Essentially the question faced by the couple and by the therapist alike is: *"How do you work on a structure like marriage when you are bereft of any notion of how to live your own life?"*

Puncturing Illusions

In this situation, or in any other, for that matter, it is not the therapists' task to maintain an ideological stance for or against marriage. It is their task to help Matt and Diane:

- *Assess the resources and options* that may still exist between them, and between each of them and other significant people in their context;
- *Provide continuity of parenting* to Doug and William and teach them how to think and speak about the consequences for them of their parents' struggle;
- *Begin to unburden their marriage by acknowledging its natural limitations,* as marriage as an institution is simply unable to sustain the full range and weight of people's romantic fantasies and longings; and

- *Investigate the legitimacy of their expectations* and demands of life on themselves as well as on each other.

Here as elsewhere, the therapists are facing two people who are drawing premature conclusions about the durability of a relationship between them without self-knowledge about what they want, who they are, how they got that way, and what they want to do about it. *In the first instance, then, the therapeutic task is to help Diane and Matt puncture defunct illusions.*

Initial interventions include efforts to do the following:

- Credit each person's suffering.
  Question: Is there anyone to turn to to help you with your pain?
- Assure them that they are entitled to be heard.
  Question: Can you identify what you want to say, and to whom you want to say it?
- Clarify that they have the right and even the obligation to speak on their own behalves.
  Question: If you withhold what you mean, why are you so resentful that nobody knows what you want?
- Underscore the fact that if people fail to speak out of the depths of their own hard-won conviction, there is no one to speak for them with *the same degree of vested interest* that they have in their own well-being.
  Question: When you were growing up, what did your family do with differences, and how did they help you say your side?
- Differentiate between the will to relate and the impulse to please.
  Question: If you lay out your terms, they will be upset. If you refuse to tell them what you think is fair, you will be enraged. What are your options then?
- Indicate a willingness to hear despite the unlikely prospect of being heard.
  Question: What would it mean to your father and mother if you chose to listen to them instead of defending against them and then asked them to do the same?
- Identify the inevitability of ruptured trust and mutual exploitation as an existential given, even in committed relationships.
  Question: What if in fact you can't get what you want? Do you mean to continue condemning her?
- Differentiate a partner's individual and relational limits from his or her choice to be unfair.
  Question: What will you do if he *can't* express his feelings?
- Surface the rationale for taking initiative even when it isn't reciprocated.

> *Question*: If you both want the same thing, but you want him to
> initiate, and he doesn't, can you still act on your own behalf?

There are many different ways to ask the questions that we've cited. The point here is to illustrate steps toward multilateral contracting, and to transcend the limits of an individual approach.

The initial phase of helping the Randals delineate their own terms and offer due consideration led them to making interim choices and life plans. The couple agreed to separate, but maintain joint responsibility for parenting their sons. Matt moved in with his brother, while Diane stayed in the house. This early arrangement broke down very quickly and led them to decide to alternate weeks for staying with the boys in the family home. This too eventually changed when Matt got his own apartment and Diane decided that she wanted to stay in their home. It should be noted that with each shift, at least one of the therapists saw the entire family and helped the parents explain what they were doing and why, and helped the children surface their confusion, anxieties, and needs to be assured. Money issues remained a point of massive conflict. So did their unrealistic expectations of each other.

Going "Home"

Once Matt and Diane emerged from the battlefield of shattered expectations, and lent what comfort they could to their children in their grief and blame, they were more focused if still volatile. *Now the question before them was "why?"* They saw themselves as streetwise—how could they have let themselves be so blindsided? Gradually the parallels between injuries sustained in their families of origin, injuries in their marriage, and even injuries between them and each of their children began to emerge. Their initial resistance to examining these parallels had been strong and clear: "What does my mother's treatment of me have to do with an inability to stay faithful to Diane?" "How does my father's preference for me over my mother have anything to do with overloaded expectations of Matt?" Eventually, mounting evidence linked past imbalances to current consequences. And Matt and Diane each decided to "go home." Reluctant and frightened but wanting to know, they began to imagine *what it would be like to find answers to questions unasked of their parents and sibs.*

Even as a child Matt saw himself as self-sufficient, independent, and mistrustful of the adult world. The third of four brothers, he struggled with an early breakup of his parents and sibs. His father, a prominent physician, now dead, was born to parents who were medical missionaries in China. Early on, his father learned that ministry was giving, and his mother apparently surrendered her own life view to whatever her husband said. Matt relates that his dad was raised by a native woman, rather than by his parents, who were preoccupied with the task of a medical and spiritual ministry to the unsaved. It is not surprising then that Matt's father felt more attached to the people with whom his parents worked than to his parents themselves. It is equally unsurprising that when he became a physician, he too lost himself in other people's needs. Adored by patients, worshipped by his residents, and esteemed by his colleagues, he knew little of his children and allowed them to know nothing of him. Hard work and inaccessibility came to characterize what it meant to be a man in Matt's family.

Matt's mother, a graduate of an elite woman's college, was her husband's intellectual equal, but little intimacy existed between the two. They were divorced by the time Matt was in first grade. It was about then that his mother was born again at an evangelical crusade. An overburdened mother of four boys and bereft of familial or communal resources, she clung to religion as surrogate parent and mate. Matt's contempt for religion is rooted in her unrelenting insistence that he and his brothers conform to her ideal of what a Christian boy should be. His contempt for women is rooted in a distorted belief that his mother always had it her way. "I can't handle how fragile I feel when I try to say what I mean," Matt relates. "Diane wants someone to take care of her. I want to be taken care of too. But it's tough to keep the focus on me. When I feel trapped, I make promises I don't keep. Then there's no negotiation, no follow-through. Diane gets crazy and I get lost." Matt feels as though he's the one who always has to compromise with Diane. But giving up his ground is characteristic of his entire life. He has had virtually no practice in surfacing his own terms or in conveying them. What other people want is his basis for response. What he wants goes underground and further reinforces his felt invisibility.

Matt became increasingly aware of how invisible he still was in his family of origin and began to wonder what might happen if he could face them. The therapist seemed convinced that Matt's freedom lay in his directly addressing them. Maybe he wasn't so off the wall after all. Dr. J. pressed Matt forward. The multilateral contract was now at play. Did his mother have a side? What was it? How was it that Matt could recognize his father's limits and vulnerabilities but not his mother's? Did he know what it meant for his mother to have to relate to all these men? Did she ever wish for a daughter? Why did he let his father off the hook? What happened to Matt when his eldest brother, Jim, was killed by a car? How did family members grieve Jim's death? Did they offer each other consolation? Matt and his elder brother, Ian, spent time in Vietnam together. Did they share their struggles with each other then? What does Matt do with Ian's drinking and his sarcastic humor? Is he jealous of Steven, who turned out to be his mother's idealized, "Christian" son?

Together and one by one Matt's family members agreed to come into therapy to start a process that they were unable to do by themselves. "Friday, I stopped by to ask Mom to come to a session with me," Matt reported. "She quickly said yes and I began to talk about me. She was surprised at my hesitation to ask her and startled that I felt so estranged from her." The invitation to therapy in itself began the process. The therapist began to help Matt imagine what he wanted of each family member. For the task here was not to confront them but *to engage them*; not to blame them but *to figure out their side*; not to protect them but *to inform them of his burdens and regrets—and to inquire into theirs*; not to diminish his truth but *to draw on residual trust*; not to stay stuck in the past but *to see if they could find a new way.*

Multidirectional Partiality

If a multilateral contract reflects the many-sided complexities of relational reality, multidirectional partiality provides the means by which people are helped to act on those complexities.

> Methodologically multidirectional partiality takes the form of sequential siding with (and eventually against) member after family member....If a therapist cannot credit a person for his or her stance in a current issue, e.g., child abuse, (s)he can at least credit a person in terms of past childhood victimization. (Boszormenyi-Nagy & Krasner, 1986, p. 419)

In any case the therapist has to mindfully set out guidelines that provide structure and allay fear. For example:

- To welcome people at the outset and credit everyone's courage in being present to each other.
- To assure newcomers that they are free to speak or be silent, to join a specific issue or to decline if it feels too threatening or too hard. The task here is to avoid trapping people.
- To help everyone act on the care that *exists* in this family whether or not it is openly displayed or discussed.
- To open the initial exchange in the therapy room by inviting the clients already involved in the therapeutic process to explain what they said in asking others to attend the session.
- In cases in which an entire family is present at an initial session, to place the responsibility for exchange on the adults; and to enlist their help in inviting adolescents or children to speak.
- To remind the original client of his or her earlier agreement to carry the weight of the initial exchanges in order to give newcomers room to orient themselves.
- To credit everyone's anxiety or reluctance about being there and to lend them the courage of the therapist's conviction about healing in the dialogic process.

- To establish reasonable expectations for both the process and the goals of an initial session.
- To slow down participants who, out of nervousness or need, try to take over the session; and to make whatever effort possible to incorporate those who are slow to speak.

With some exceptions, dialogue is likely to take over at this point. The therapist does well to use modified humor, self-disclosure, and plain common sense to catalyze the dialogic process. The give-and-take between family members will typically open a way, whatever the accompanying emotions. All of this is likely to take place in the first 10 or 15 minutes of an initial session but, sometimes, it takes longer.

At this point, conviction and technique have merged. Multidirected partiality and direct address have become effective interventions just because they reflect the organic longing of each person present. The therapist can act with conviction just because truth and trust serve the vested interests of people who, however long ago, were impacted by each other's lives and actions for better and for worse.

The impulse to know and be known is nowhere more gripping than between family members. The impediments to knowing and being known are nowhere more exaggerated than by the absence of dialogue between the generations. In the first instance, then, a therapist's use of multidirectional partiality is permission giving. It lends courage to each family member to say what he or she has lost and to envision what might yet be regained. It points a way by conviction, word, and stance to how family members, still connected by the threads of residual trust, might yet speak the truths that can help them ethically reengage. The bridges toward ethical reengagement may well be defended by coils of barbed wire and unanticipated land mines. Despite these obstacles, multidirectional partiality functions as a signpost marking a path through the barriers of terror, isolation, resentment, guilt, and shame.

To be sure, the person who initiates a process of facing when evasion has been a family's standard operating procedure feels placed at risk. When the option of facing his mother was first introduced to Matt, for example, it provoked extreme anxiety in him. Boyhood images of helplessness in the face of his mother's depression and his father's absences still had the force to silence him. But other forces were also at work. The silence that had been a refuge in his past had now become a weapon that threatened to shatter his future.

To hear him tell it, Matt seems to have been more at ease sitting on a mountain top halfway across the world from home, supported by the foreign faces and loyal hearts of his Montagnard compatriots and surrounded by hostile enemies, than he was at the notion of disclosing himself to his mother. In retrospect, the threat of physical death in war seemed to place him in less jeopardy than inquiring into his mother's truth. But his courage held in his current fight for survival. His choice to address an alien mother, a deceased father, faceless siblings, and children whose distance from him reflected his own childhood isolation was born of the same desperation that drove him to survive on the battlefield.

Despite the fear that multidirected partiality and direct address may initially evoke, the ethical task of a contextual therapist is:

- To move clients away from *the fantasy of unconditional acceptance* to the reality of colliding entitlements;
- *To move beyond the pathological yardstick of psychological interpretations* like rejection or castration, for example, to identify the latent resources that reside in the elemental triad;
- To move away from the *helplessness induced by real or imagined victimization* to an action dimension that can energize, catalyze, and actualize; and
- *To move beyond the primacy of the individual in his or her surroundings as the sole object of therapeutic intervention* to the ethics of the relational options of several interrelated people at a time.

SELF-DELINEATION

What is the process by which clinicians help clients embrace their own authority?

Self-delineation is the first of two phases of the dialogic process, and is best understood as existing in permanent tension with due consideration, dialogue's second phase. The task of self-delineation is a sine qua non of maturity and an inescapable ethical mandate. "Somewhere between birth and death people have to come to terms with the delineation of a unique self that is set apart from the world and from others" (Boszormenyi-Nagy & Krasner, 1986, p. 75). The failure to assume personal responsibility for portraying one's own truth in words, and for describing and outlining one's own side or claims with precision, automatically results in the immediate infantilization of the self and the eventual parentification of the world. *The intrinsic promise of trust-based relationship hinges on the capacity of relating partners to know themselves and to accept their own authority.* Diane, for example, appeared to be more than a match for Matt, so why was she so easily stampeded by him? Could it be that long ago she forfeited her own authority in exchange for the fantasy of placing herself in the safety of somebody else's care? Could it be that over time she came to dislike his mode of caring for her, and began to punish him for not caring for her in the way she might have preferred? Could it be that Matt became confused by her anger? After all, he was only caring for Diane the same way he had cared for himself.

At the point at which Diane entered therapy, she was a dutiful if distant daughter, an embattled and disappointed wife, an attentive and overprotective mother, and a woman desperate for consideration that she could find only outside her marriage. Her agenda for change included many factors—all of them based on what Matt had done wrong. "The more I give," Diane said early on, "the less Matt gives. The more I do, the less he does." Money, sex, child care, and management of domestic responsibility were all representative of Matt's dereliction of duty to Diane. "I needed my husband to be there, not out five nights a week. I suspect there were other women from the beginning. And then there was the Army reserve. Even when Matt was home," Diane continued, "he didn't connect with the boys. He always resented that I have more money: I kept assuming responsibility because Matt kept finding ways to ignore them."

Wrestling for Authority

"I know where I've been," Diane comments, "but not where I am." In point of fact, Diane knows little about either. While her litany of losses accurately reflects her disappointment in Matt, nowhere do her words specify Diane's lack of self-knowledge and/or just how much she has abandoned herself. Diane presents as physically beautiful, intellectually astute, socially sophisticated, and powerfully articulate. How then was she reduced to reactive and collusive behavior that blindsided her to the merit of her own authority? Men and women alike are given to yielding *intrinsic authority* to other people and then blaming the people to whom they've yielded it.

By definition, human beings are engaged in a lifelong mandate *to discover balances of freedom and responsibility for themselves and toward their world*— again and again. The capacity to wrestle meaning from the ordinary stuff of existence is directly linked to the degree to which a person takes responsibility for an ever-developing mastery of self-knowledge, due consideration, and direct address. At this point of the therapeutic process, the ethical task of the contextual therapist is to help Diane identify some of the barriers that have led her to submit to the presumed authority of others—an act that more often than not means to submit to chaos and illusion. Diane's failure to act on her own authority has many roots:

- Untested interpretations of childhood reality
  Question: Does Diane link the fact that her father had the final say in the family—undiscussed—with the fact that her mother refused to give her opinion or advice about anything?
- Misplaced indebtedness

Question: Did Diane feel she had to take over the family business when her father died because of her mother's indecisiveness and her own unexamined loyalties to her father?

- Failure to identify one's own contributions
  Question: Can Diane credit the degree to which she was expected to be her father's companion and able employee, her mother's buffer and go-between with other family members, and her brother's parentlike older sister?
- Undue deference
  Question: To what degree did her father's apparent lack of respect for her mother's practice of law teach Diane to be deferential instead of claiming professional competence and fair consideration?
- Pleasing transformed to pathology
  Question: Was pleasing without claiming Diane's only option for recognition from parents who also learned to survive by pleasing without making claims?
- Unrecognized exploitation in using other people to evade direct address
  Question: To what degree does Diane encourage her husband into a caretaking role with her mother in order to avoid working on an intimate relationship with either of them?
- The monologic use of empathy
  Question: To what degree does Diane's empathy for her children in their struggle with their father deprive them of her help in teaching them how to hold their father accountable?
- Confusion of feelings with fairness
  Question: To what degree have feelings of guilt and resentment provided a comfortable and familiar psychological haven to Diane that she has *chosen* as an alternative to fighting for fairness for herself and for people on whom her life impacts?
- Failure to distinguish between personal authority and misgivings at acting on one's own behalf
  Question: Does Diane's fear of being viewed as selfish undercut her right to her own terms? Does her flight from personal authority cloud her imagination and, paradoxically perhaps, drive her into a selfish stance born of the impulse to protect herself as well as her relating partners?
- The use of silence as justification for ethical disengagement
  Question: Does Diane regard her still undiminished preference for her dead father an insurmountable barrier to direct address with her mother?

Diane's willingness to face the imbalances and injustices between her and members of her context allowed her to begin to grasp the differences between mandated authority and intrinsic authority.

Mandated Authority

Mandated authority is a form of parentification that, within limits, has creative implications. Every child carries the onus of having to grow into parental expectations, and derives some authority from successfully doing so. Early enlistment into her father's business served a variety of functions for Diane. Both of her parents did everything well in the business side of their lives. Diane also learned to do things well in the construction business, in which she developed technical and management skills. She gained confidence from holding her own in a man's world and accepted every task that came her way without expecting special privileges. But work in her family business also had its downside. She did what her father wanted: It was his way or no way. She endured her father's volatile outbursts. And her mother's giving up her law practice to work in her husband's business reinforced Diane's presumption that you did what you were told, not what you deemed best. Diane had little difficulty fulfilling her father's wishes. She knew how lonely he was. Besides, she enjoyed his company. They talked about a lot of things but never about how close they were. What was missing then? To hear Diane tell it, whether at work or at home, no one ever elicited her opinion, her view, her terms, her preferences. In fact, she couldn't imagine that she was free ever to act on her own behalf in a way that was contrary to what either of her parents might want.

The destructive nature of mandated authority emerged from the degree to which Diane was rendered basically incapable of self-delineation. A youngster who develops a habitual disinclination to differentiate between her own terms and preferences on the one hand, and those of each of her parents, on the other, carries mandated authority that may be rescinded at any time. Or worse: *The young person who knows her own terms but never learns to act on them is caught in a mode of ethical disengagement whose primary outcome can be a lifelong loss of intrinsic authority.*

Part of Diane's mandated authority evolved from how her parents used her, however unintentionally, to compensate themselves for the rupture of their marital intimacy, which of course was rooted in their own families of origin. Diane's mother saw silence as a friend. She had heard her own mother voice an objection only once in her lifetime. "I would never have taken adverse steps with my parents," she said. "I can be belligerent. I would do what they thought best. I did the same thing with my husband. I prefer the weak path of least resistance." Diane's father took the opposite tack. "My grandmother always laid so much blame on my father," Diane recalled. "He fought his parents all of the way but never knew how to get what he wanted. When we got older, he always made my brothers and me run our grandmother around."

Diane's father was so embattled in his own family of origin that he felt he had the right to have the final say over his children and his wife.

What is a youngster to do when her parents' upbringing led them to empower her to act on their behalf when they themselves were unable to do so? "My father had to have it his way and my mother was never there. I didn't mind my mother working; I resented her absence when she was supposed to be present." "I always felt Diane preferred my husband to me," Diane's mother retorted. "He was characteristically outgoing and warm. I am not. There will be no children for me in my next life; I'm going to love them and leave them." The fact that Diane never had a parent to talk to is linked to the fact that her parents never had parents to talk to; that their relationships with their own parents were also based on mandated authority; and that Diane, like her parents before her, knew nothing of the intrinsic authority that can be won from self-knowledge, fairness, and direct address.

Psychotherapeutic literature is filled with language that describes the right of people to live lives of their own. Striving for autonomy, individuation, differentiation, and self-mastery involves freeing oneself from other people's control. But the term "control" *per se* assigns an adversarial quality to relationship. The perception of Diane's mother, husband, and children was that here was a woman in control of her life. If other people saw Diane in control of life, why did she feel so out of control? And what was she going to do about it? Where was the fairness in choosing for yourself? Where was the fairness in continuing to give herself away? Diane's choice to separate, her affair, her decision to move out of the house early on in the separation were all attempts to clarify what she wanted. Her struggle to limit what she gave to the kids and did in the house were early efforts to delineate herself. Wealth, travel, and beauty in themselves were of little help to Diane's quest for direction and meaning.

The therapist's exploration of what Diane wanted for herself was initially met by uncomprehending stares. Diane was making progress in her negotiations with Matt. She offered, "We've both come a long way in cooling off and we've even begun to negotiate. Maybe that is an inkling of what might be possible for our marriage later on." Diane could think structurally, but dynamically she was dead in the water. She could talk about marriage and motherhood, but she had no clue about what balanced give-and-take might look like with anybody. In psychological terms, she was defended, confused, and enraged. In ethical terms, she remained unaddressed—and she was unaddressed—by anyone of significance to her including the children. Their primary goal continued to be having both of their parents together again. For the people around her, Diane's appearance of well-being was a substitute for her reality. She felt that people not only misread her but consistently crossed her boundaries. For example, Matt was helping her mother arrange business affairs. Why did her mother choose him to help her instead of Diane?

Taking Ethical Action

For a long time, Diane used therapy as a psychological support and as a motivational personal prop. She tried to enter into dialogue even when she felt she had no personal ground from which to speak. She brought her frustration into the therapy room and left with options to test in her context. Sometimes she simply asked questions and became sharply aware of how seldom in her life did anyone risk addressing her directly. The therapist used *self-disclosure* to expand Diane's ability to reexamine her world. As a commonality between them became more apparent, Diane's imagination for what life could yet be began to move into gear. The therapist encouraged Diane to press against her own assumptions. Eliciting as well as self-disclosure began to undercut Diane's long-held patterns of acting and being. Why was Diane so distant from her brothers? How had they responded to their parents? Did her mother really prefer Matt to her? Why would that be? Maybe she frightened her mother. Had she ever asked? What had her mother lost when her father died? And what was missing for Diane that she had enjoyed when her father was still alive? Diane initially saw the therapist as a sounding board, a teacher, a parent, and a friend. But only when she began to imagine, identify, and register how much she had actually given to the people around her could she begin to conceive of the possibility that she deserved another level of consideration from family members and from friends. But to get it she would have to ask! Only when she could move away from psychologizing people could she begin to consider what it might mean to be fair to them and to ask them to be fair to her. Only when she could recognize her own terror at making herself known could she begin to imagine how withholding she herself had been. Only when she could grasp the depth of her own fragility and accept it as a legitimate given of life could she begin to tolerate the facades and defenses that other people used to cover their own fragility and even to try to penetrate them. Diane had been incapable of putting herself and her own terms on a par with others. Her tendency to yield her terms and "disappear" is a common phenomenon for almost everyone, including people who seem to be controlling.

Go and Tell This People...(Isa. 6:9)

A catalytic turning point for Diane occurred in her second year of therapy, at age 43. A precancerous condition required surgery and intensified her isolation and longing to make her connections work. Her physical recovery was accompanied by a quickening of her spirit and *a decision to make life count.*

- She had suddenly come to grasp life as a resource. In the face of threatened loss or even potential annihilation, she was tentatively able to let go of disappointment as a way of life.
- She was clear about having to act on her own behalf. She was no longer willing to settle for psychological self-victimization.
- Inspirited with the vision that she had a right and a way to fight for herself, she was prepared to yield the safety of a therapeutic harbor for the rough seas of ethically reengaging.
- She was newly invested in differentiating from her therapist, who had become secondary to Diane's passion to act on her intrinsic authority with members of her own context.
- She continued to feel the impact of her father's broken "mini-promises" long ago, her mother's caustic comments during her recent illness, and even Matt's increasingly kind and gentle presence. But she could now discern the difference between self-delineation and a definition of self imposed by others—however unintentionally.
- She began to assess what counted: what she deserved, what she owed, where she would put her emphasis, and how she would take action.

Out of newfound freedom and direction, Diane hired a new manager for the family business. She decided that any future marital work would be predicated on successfully negotiating a fair postnuptial agreement. She decided to pursue a postnuptial agreement outside of the courtroom unless the process deteriorated. She began to work on estate planning with her mother in lieu of Matt. She decided to invite her mother back into therapy and ask one of her brothers to join them. She ended her relationship with her paramour and deepened existing friendships. She helped Matt understand the boys' resistance to turning to him, and fought for them to have more one-on-one time together. She bought herself a grand piano, and actively began to wonder what she would do with her life. Diane's personal transformation was cast and molded in the tension between self-delineation (the grace of sufficiency) and due consideration (the grace of ethical imagination). And in the process, perception, conviction, and practice alike had changed. *In the therapeutic process, Diane had taken hold of an enduring truth: Reciprocity cannot be willed, confirmation cannot be demanded, and dialogue cannot be ensured. But she could always embrace intrinsic authority, always test the options before her, and always act on her own behalf.*

DUE CONSIDERATION

*How do clinicians catalyze trust among people who have colliding
vested interests?*

The imperative to do unto others as we would have them do unto us (Deut.,
Matt.) is dynamically irrefutable and stands at the heart of reciprocity and
meaning. It implies knowledge of the self, a life in common with the other,
and justice between the two. Every human being deserves due consideration.
Less clear is the question of who is to give it. In the face of real and felt injury
and hurt indignation, there is a cost to holding ground as well as to yielding it.
There is an impulse to withdraw and a longing to rejoin. There is an internal
demand to be heard and a nagging urge to hear even amidst fears of being
dismissed.

The paradox of fair give-and-take may well reside in the fact that the freedom to self-delineate is inextricably bound to the human will to offer due
consideration. What does it do to persons to have lingering doubts about the
validity of their own position—if they aren't able to test it? What does it mean
to insist on one's rights if one denies those rights to others? What are the
consequences, present and future, of unilaterally withdrawing from relating
partners and settling for stagnation and estrangement?

*Relating parties are dynamically released to live according to their own
terms—freely, creatively, and productively—in direct proportion to the degree
to which they can offer due consideration in situations of colliding vested
interests.* The constituent parts of covenantal relationship, to love mercy and
do justice (Mic. 6:8), are signposts of antiquity that still apply to the postnuclear
age. There is no escaping the costs implicit in the tension that always exists
between delineating my side and offering due consideration to you who stand
over against me. Temporary pain and distress are inevitable factors in situations of colliding vested interests in any case. But the consequences of self-
delineation (autonomy, rights, individuation) *without* due consideration are
distortions of everybody's truth and breaches of everybody's trust. On the
other hand, the consequences of due consideration *in tandem with* self-delineation are a less fragile, more reliable relational world and a heightened commitment to transform isolation into new creation for oneself and for posterity.

Diane had broken free and Matt was on his way. Though the shape of their
future together was increasingly unclear, they both knew that they were
irrevocably linked by the existence of their two sons. Diane and Matt were
still on friendly terms, though she had filed for divorce and was currently
involved with another man. On the surface of things the boys accepted Gabe.
They were polite, if dutifully distant, but his presence in their mother's life
seemed to make little difference to them. They saw their father regularly, were
acclimated to their new routine, and had a reasonable degree of independence

as the summer wore on. Then one day Diane brought Doug into a therapy session.

> He has been acting up, she complained. He brings friends to the house uninvited. They slop up the kitchen every time they are in it and insist on leaving their towels on the ground whenever they use the pool. "I'm responsible for their safety even when I'm not at home," Diane complained, "and Doug needs to act responsibly too. What's more, Doug takes off with them whenever he feels like it. I don't know what's happened to him. I need to know where you are, Doug. What if something happened?"

Doug was in tears and angry but was clearly reluctant to speak. The therapist asked Diane to give Doug permission to say what was on his mind. She also reminded Doug that his words were a contribution to everyone's well-being. Pointing to his mother's increased involvement with Gabe, Doug spoke to his mother in the midst of his tears. "It used to be that you'd tell me where *you'd* be. Now I have to ask where and when before you leave the house. I think we need to intertwine our plans. You're not living out what you're asking of me." Doug's unexpected outburst served to shatter Diane's focus on her son's household misdemeanors and apparent lack of responsibility. The merit of his words transformed a mother–adolescent difference into an ethically rooted dialogue. "I'm entitled to have a life of my own," she said and repeated her earlier disappointment in how Doug left the house. The therapist asked Doug to make his point again and tried to slow Diane down.

"Doug misses you," the therapist said. "He's going to boarding school soon and doesn't know where he stands with you. You and Doug's father have been the primary adults in Doug's life, and now he has to make a place for Gabe." But Diane was stunned and stung by Doug's words. She knew that something significant was going on but was unable to get the point. Was this one more male who, like her father and husband, was telling her what to do? Or was her son the first male in her life to trust her enough to address her? She stared at Doug trying desperately to penetrate the meaning of his words. She retrenched for a moment and picked up where she had left off. "I'm responsible for you in a way you're not responsible for me, Doug! Why can't you understand?" It may have been the first time that Doug was trying to make himself known. A reticent if straightforward boy, he watched his mother's every move. Buoyed by the climate of multidirectional concern, Doug responded to the therapist's encouragement to address his mother with his truth. The main thrust of his words was as follows:

- He had become invisible to his mother.
- She owed him more than she was offering.
- He was no longer motivated to be good.

- He was asking her to be fair, to ask of herself what she expected of him.

Diane struggled against being defensive. Was she now a failed mother as well as a failed daughter and wife? No, something more was happening here. There was a ring of truth to what Doug was pleading for, a willingness to acknowledge his own culpability. He was not asking her to do something more or even to be more than she already was. *He was asking for due consideration*, for his mother to imagine his side and respond to the truth in it. Diane managed to cut through her initial complaints and to hear what Doug was trying to say. "I love you, Doug," she told him. "There will always be room for you no matter who else is in my life." She then asked him to come back for another session so they could talk more directly about Gabe. They left the session shaken but came back with resolve. They had tested the trust between them and could afford to test it again.

"Why don't you tell Dr. K. about the incident with Gabe?" Diane asked in the following session. "I will," Doug said, "but first I want to talk about you and Dad. The last session was the first I heard that you had filed for divorce. This is the end of July and you filed in the beginning of May. Our entire family situation is like that. Will and I are always in the middle. We keep getting pulled into things we know nothing about." Diane and Matt had been faced with a common dilemma of parenthood, heightened by impending divorce. They wanted to protect their children from hard and assaultive facts, yet help them face what was real. But protection was not enough; the children needed direction.

Now Doug was prepared to return to the topic of Gabe. "Gabe pushed me and my friend into the swimming pool. Mom had asked me to make sure the dog was in the pen. He got out, but we didn't know that. It was late. Gabe and Mom had just come back from being out. Mom was mad when she couldn't find the dog, and she decided it was my fault without talking to me. She complained to Gabe and he offered to help. He charged down to the pool and insulted my friend. I thought that was wrong and I told him so. He pushed me, and my friend and I argued back. Then Gabe pushed again and we both landed in the swimming pool." Doug got out of the pool embarrassed and enraged. He ran to his room and placed a midnight call to his father.

Doug turned to his mother in the therapy room. "I don't like the way you treated Dad," he said. "It wasn't fair." "I don't know what that means," Diane responded. "We had just gotten back from dinner, it was late, and the dog wasn't there. It just seemed like you were being irresponsible again. I was upset and Gabe knew it. He asked if he could help and I said yes. That's when he went down to talk to you. Things just got out of hand, and the next thing I knew your father drove up to the house." Dr. K. turned to Doug at this point. "What happened when you called your dad?" she asked. "I was upset," Doug replied. "I was crying hard when I got him and told him that Gabe was push-ing me around. My father said to stay in my room; he'd be right there to get me. Dad got there, and my parents started to argue." Apparently, Matt had gotten judgmental and Diane indignant. "Was it your fault that they argued?" the therapist asked. "Yes it was," Doug replied. "How is that?" she probed. "Did you overstate what Gabe had done when you talked to your dad?" "I was really embarrassed that Gabe had manhandled my friend, and I didn't know what to do. I guess I made it sound worse than it really had been." "What happens now?" Dr. K. asked Doug and Diane. "Have you told Gabe how angry you were, Doug?"

Diane had a plan. "Maybe we all need to straighten this out. I don't like the way that Matt talked to me, and I want to tell him so." "If you had gotten a call from your son at midnight and thought that he was being mistreated," the therapist challenged, "how would you have been?" Diane gave the point some thought. She could credit Doug's panic and Matt's protectiveness even if she still felt unfairly treated. "What do we do next then?" she asked. "How has it been up till now between you and Gabe?" the therapist asked Doug. "We get along okay." "Would it help you to talk to Gabe to tell him your side and ask him his?" Doug was asked. "I think so," he said. "I just want to tell him he shouldn't have pushed my friend." "Can you do that yourself or do you need your mom to help?" "No," he replied, "I want to do it myself." "Can you let that happen between Doug and Gabe?" Diane was asked. Diane hesitated, silently removed herself from the function of go-between for Doug and for Gabe, and slowly nodded her assent.

Diane's initial entry into therapy consisted of complaints about her mar-riage. Paradoxically, she saw herself as *intolerably overresponsible for others and massively helpless to take forceful action on her own behalf.* Under the circumstances, the therapist's major ethical task was to guide Diane in shift-ing her center of gravity. Diane's best use of therapy was to move away from an automatic dependency on doing for others, a tendency rooted in unexamined and untested premises about what was expected of her. Her dependency here was based not so much on the reality of other people's needs and wants as on Diane's *need to be needed*, on her *impulse to ingratiate herself* so that *no one could see her as lacking,* and on a *long-held terror of anger.* These elements can all be identified as *psychological and monologic. Her means to freedom, though, were ethical and dialogic.* Her immediate task was to grasp the ele-ments of multilateral complexity in which:

- She considered herself as significant a referent for fairness as her relating partners;
- She could offer them consideration because she could act on her own behalf—with and without reciprocity; and
- She could act on her own behalf *because* she offered due con-

sideration to people of significance—regardless of their response to her offer.

Shifting Centers of Gravity

Over a 2-year time span the centers of gravity in this family's context shifted:

- *Injuries* were still present in and among them, but now they *were no longer festering*.
- *Family members* were still timid and sometimes apprehensive, but they *could now anticipate the option of direct address*.
- Disappointments still existed among them, but *they had now learned to transform their disappointments into claims*.
- *The children* still longed for their parents to live together, but they *could now rely on individual and joint accessibility to both their father and their mother*.
- *The boys* were still predisposed to use anger at their parents against each other, but they *could now horse around with each other*.
- *The "good boy,"* Doug, no longer had to be "perfect" to compensate his parents for their distress.
- *The "bad boy,"* Will, no longer had to resort to tantrums to provide a diversion for his parents' anger at each other. *He could now channel his anger in creative projects like skiing, drums, karate, and even school*.
- Diane and Matt still tended to parentify each other and infantilize, themselves but they *could now imagine making use of their respective intrinsic authority*.
- Financial discussions remained a point of contention between them, but because each of them could self-delineate, *they could now afford to tolerate each other's inquiries and preferences with less reactivity and more equanimity*.
- *Diane's* pursuit of a partner was no longer an act of rebellion against a legacy of "victimizing males." She *could now identify male limits, vulnerability, and terror* and still act on her own behalf.
- Matt's continued pursuit of Diane was no longer a childlike clinging or an unfair demand for her to do things his way. *He could now act out of desire for her, knowing full well that she was disinclined to respond*.
- Diane and Matt no longer had fantasies of replacing each other in their children's lives—if ever they did. *Whoever their future partners, they now knew that their futures were joined together forever by the bond of parental care*.

Contextual therapy, intergenerationally linked, triadically based, and resource oriented, rests upon *the fundamental conviction that healing through meeting is the eventual outcome of the dynamic joining of truth and trust.* The will to dialogue, with its stages of self-delineation and due consideration, is the means to this end. It is the ethical task of a contextual therapist to identify and credit the merit of every member of any given context. It is through the therapist's capacity to know and live a dialogic reality in his or her own life that the fundamental conviction of healing through meeting can be achieved, maintained, and conveyed to future generations.

4

Therapist as Cornerstone: Acting on Conviction

How does a clinician sustain the tension between interhuman parity and professional credibility?

A PARALLEL JOURNEY

This chapter means to examine the implications and consequences of therapeutic conviction as the cornerstone that unites two people and their contexts, at a pivotal if accidental intersection. Therapeutic conviction provides the basis of clinical function and is an accurate representation of a modality's theories and applications. It is an aggregate of a person's orientation, training and degree of experience—and more. Therapeutic conviction is a faithful reflection of clinicians' personal journeys: who they are and what they practice. Part of why students usually enter the field is to acquire a professional overlay to fit over and eclipse their unformed ground and insecure reality. Few students are prepared for the shock of recognition that arises when they come face to face with human tragedy, and technique is not enough. It is the rare student who can identify the dialectic between professional competence and personal presence. Personal presence is less an offshoot of professional training than it is "the secret of the bond between spirit and spirit. The help of the therapist is not, in the first instance, a matter of finding the right words, still less techniques of communication. It is a matter of the healing through meeting coming into being between one who cannot reach out and one who can" (Friedman, 1985, p. 217).

Constantly assaulted by other people's struggles, contextual therapists are faced with daily reminders of the loyalty binds and imbalances in their own personal contexts. How they address, interpret, and rework the relational shortfalls in their own lives is the critical measure of their personal integrity and of the scope of their professional capacity to envision and apply dialogic interventions. Professional ground gained by credentials and licensing in no way protects a clinician against the hazards of meaninglessness and situationlessness that are common to everyone. No acquired skill or technique manipulated on behalf of a client's well-being can ever supplant the basic fact that the therapeutic venture is a parallel search for meaning for clinician and client alike. *The differentiating factors between them are the points at which they stand in their journeys, the particularities of their contexts, and the asymmetry of their contract.*

Most clinicians are driven to the field by the contingencies and consequences of their own contexts. "I became a psychiatrist to make my mother well" is essentially a paradigmatic statement for mental health professionals of every kind. The child's impulse to mend a parent's situation is easily transplanted to a successful career in the helping professions. So too is a person's vision and despair over what makes families work. When I become judgmental of a withholding client, am I reacting to how my father once treated me? When I am silenced by a mother screaming at her adolescent son, do I fall hopeless at the prospect of my mother ever hearing me? When I am put off by a couple's mutual blame and constant bickering, am I still swept up by my parents' disappointments? A primitive commonality exists between clinician and client. Each of them draws meaning from relating to the members of their context. Each of them has specific issues in their respective contexts. One of them, the client, is confounded by these issues. One of them, the therapist, knows how to identify those issues and how to address them dialogically, if not solve them. Clinicians can point to a healing way just because they have a firm grasp of therapeutic intuition wrested from the ground of his personal and professional struggle. "Subjective and undefinable though it may be, therapeutic intuition is a product of comprehensive knowledge. In fact it may be the end result of a personal, hence professional integration of complex psychotherapeutic and behavioral phenomena" (Boszormenyi-Nagy & Krasner, 1986, p.45). It is a therapist's grasp of the human condition informed by his of her own existence and relationships that paces the direction of any given intervention. "Technology helps of course—but only in balance with an intuition of where meaning lies" (Boszormenyi-Nagy & Krasner, 1986, p. 45).

Contextual therapists may practice in a variety of ways with a variety of emphases. But they proceed from *an unshakable baseline* that emerges from a quest for meaning. *They owe and they deserve!* Therefore they are mandated to do the following:

- Mine multidirectional crediting out of the pathologies of existence
- Hold to account people who seem too timid or too hostile or too fragile to imagine the options that may still exist in a context marked by conflict and estrangement

- Proceed with a tenacity that allows time to do its work on the seeds of growth and healing that therapy sows
- Identify apparent limits and impermeability that may exist in the client and/or in the client's context without being delimited by them
- Recognize a person's resistances and defenses, and help transform them into a mandate for ethical reengagement between the client and the members of his or her context
- Operate out of regard for the healing consequences of genuine repentance (*Tshuvah*), a process of turning, facing, addressing, retesting, exonerating, forgiving, and reinvesting
- Convey the fact that none of us can will reciprocity but all of us can act on our own behalf

These convictions are grounded in the fact that a therapist has tested them in the fire of his or her own context. Only so has a therapist earned the merit to ask other people to test them as well.

Parity in the Therapy Room

The fact that a clinician may have preceded a client in a parallel search for meaning in no way diminishes the parity that exists between them. The client's preferences, predilections, inclinations, criteria, intuition, and choice of a life direction are as inviolable inside the therapy room as they are outside of it. Clients always deserve direct address, even in the midst of potential danger to themselves or others. At no point is a therapist entitled to objectify, psychologize, or set aside a client's context, merit, dignity or intrinsic authority as secondary to the therapeutic process. The task for therapists is to impose neither their methods nor their ideologies of what is good for the client. Strategies, techniques, and skills all have a place in the therapy room but not without the informed consent of the client. Insofar as it is humanly possible, *everyone in search of healing deserves to walk a path of parity within the perimeters of an asymmetrical contract*. At the level of mutual respect, client and clinician are peers in their common humanity.

The clinician is ostensibly in the process of witnessing to reality in tandem with clients who seek healing through meeting. Here the clinician's primary offering is conviction, not caretaking, a dialogic stance that witnesses to the fact that *"the way is there in order that one may walk on it"* (Buber, in Rome & Rome, 1970, p.70). The issue at hand is not a request for clients to give clinicians permission to use their professional knowledge and tools. *The issue here is that although they may know more than their clients, clinicians are existentially not more than their clients*. In the immediacy of first meeting, the therapist, like the client, is deeply impacted by the depth and breadth of human suffering for which there is *no immediate solution*. Like the client, the therapist is finely tuned to the potential that chaos will strangle hope and *kill the desire to readdress life*. Like the client, the therapist is faced with the threat of defeat, the possibility that this moment between them will be insufficient to stave off despair.

Professional Credibility

Unlike the client, what the clinician can bring to bear in the immediacy of the first meeting is the existence of ground from which the spirit can be reborn and justice can be renewed. For the contextual therapist, professional credibility is invested in the knowledge that the covenant between person and person is finally not a tether or a chain, in Heschel's words, but living intercourse.

> A woman comes into the therapy room in great distress. Megan, 42, has undergone two mastectomies. Her husband, Dale, 61, is a good and decent man, but "the marriage was a mistake." They have two small boys. Blake, 7, struggling with ADD (attention deficit disorder), seems irremediable. Brian is an angel. Megan's mother is fragile, skittish, and unreliable. "She didn't even visit me when I was ill," Megan reports. "She doesn't know how to be a grandmother to the boys." Megan is stuck in memories of a father who was caring when he wasn't drunk. She is ethically disengaged from both of her brothers. But outside of her family, she has good friends. She is highly educated, well regarded in her profession, and hates her career path. Her childhood image, as she tells it, is one of being cut off and isolated, burrowed in her room, shielded from her father's outbursts and her mother's inability to protect her from them.
>
> Megan enters therapy with the longing for someone to make it okay. The therapist comes well recommended, but soon into the first session, Megan balked, "How far back do I have to go to make my life livable now?" Her pain and depletion will soon lead her into deepened depression. Her long-held assessment is that she is essentially selfish and needs to do more. "Blake taps into my inadequacies as a mother," she goes on. "My first surgery took place immediately after his birth. I don't think we ever bonded." "I hear your faults and shortcomings, Megan," the therapist says, "but doesn't anybody owe anything to you?" "No one," she replies. "Other people make it in difficult circumstances," she insists. "What's wrong with me?"

In the immediacy of first meeting, *the issue of professional credibility has been joined*. Megan is desperate for answers *now*. Any delay seems like a diversion. The therapist wants answers now too, but to her delay is inevitable. Pivotal to this potentially transforming moment is the clinician's ability to offer a counterassessment from a multidirectional stance and, at the same time, credit Megan's suffering and offer what guidance she can.

Here, *the mettle of professional credibility and competence, in Karl Menninger's terms, is dependent* not upon the rule of expediency, success, or technological triumph but *on the moral integrity of the therapeutic stance* (Menninger, 1973). To this point, Megan's life has been lived according to other people's criteria and standards. When she didn't like them, Megan judged them and cut herself off. Now words are spoken about the merit of her own intrinsic authority: about her own standards and criteria, about her freedom to act on her own behalf through a dialogic process of self-delineation and due consideration. Can she break free of the assumption that she is the sole cause of her felt oppression? Can she imagine the daunting possibility that the oppression she suffers is more than intrapsychic? Can she do battle with the fact that she deserves as much as she owes? Can she finally take recourse in her own intrinsic authority? "I hear your words," she tells the therapist, "but I don't know what they mean." Megan is struggling to trust the therapist, to consider her words, to imagine a way. But she is tentative and doubtful.

At this instant, time cannot be telescoped to rush a healing process or ameliorate a client's pain. Circumstances cannot be substantially alleviated to relieve a client's rage. Therapists can offer hope but not immediate motivation. They may function as a guide but refuse to be an authority. They may act *in loco parentis* but not as an ethical substitute for family members. They may point a way but must stand helplessly by as clients weigh their own truths in their original and generated contexts. They are left to elicit their client's terms *but firmly remain on their own side of the dialogue.* They are obliged to stand over against the maxims and pseudomutuality of their clients' ethical disengagement. To do so, however, they lean on the tried truths and passionate convictions of the personal victories and defeats that have buoyed and sustained them in their own context.

The current mental health buzzwords are off-putting to a dialogic psychotherapist. The matter of healing has little to do with "dysfunctional families," "toxic parents," "tough love," "codependency," "abusive men," or "women who love too much." *The profession's passion for naming human suffering in pathological terms and categories tends to divert the very mission to which it is bound: guiding people toward balances of freedom and responsibility in themselves and between each other.* To wit, can dialogic psychotherapists point to what is essential in a client's context, because they know what is essential in their own? Can clinicians help clients make sense of their own reality and embrace that reality without shame, as the therapists have more or less done for themselves? Can clinicians lend clients courage to grasp their own uniqueness and the uniqueness of the roots from which they have sprung—because the therapists have done that too? It is the task of every psychotherapist to identify hidden resources and unseen options that lead toward balance and healing. It is the compelling task of the dialogic psychotherapist to act on the fact that *every human being is part of a multipersonal context whose members are ethically joined and dynamically mandated to help each other discover fairer balances of give-and-take.*

A contextual therapist is sustained in this process by drawing strength and solace from his or her own intrinsic authority. That authority can be wrested only from the bowels of particular human existence, and earned from wrestling with one's own particular angel (Gen. 32). Only so can tempered truth and trust arise. Only so can the wings of an angel touch the ethics of connection *to transform the name of reality into a blessing.* Only so can those who have risked the encounter walk away limping but knowing they have prevailed.

The Pressure of Relevance

Therapists can only point the way toward angels with which a client must wrestle, without deluding themselves with the presumption that they are that angel. In a world characterized by a disorienting loss of meaning, therapists are obliged to point a way but not to create false meaning. To wit, they are obliged to recognize a client's investment in them. Clients whose words or actions convey that their therapist is "the most important person in their life" deserve to be received with compassion but disabused via therapeutic conviction. For in the long run, there is no substitute for the healing confirmation that members of a client's context can produce.

Over the years in the field of psychotherapy, people like Hans Trüb and Victor Frankl have argued that the human relationship between the clinician and client has been more determinative than applied methodology and technique. Contextual theory credits the useful if limited nature of methodology and technique. It acknowledges the effects and consequences of the human relationship between clinician and client. But the determinative factor for contextual therapists is the ethical bond between the generations and how people act on it. *The relationship between client and clinician has a transitional primacy that, even at its moment of greatest impact, is always secondary to what has been given and taken between a client and members of his or her context.*

The traditional psychological concept of transference lacks "the pressure of relevance" (Boszormenyi-Nagy & Spark, 1973), that is, the massive leverage generated by roots and primal connections. The psychological implications of transference differ from ethical implications. "Freud could speak of the patient's self-deception concerning the nature of the patient-doctor relationship as a cognitive error, a distortion in perception and attitudes" (Friedman, 1985, p. 15). Self-deception is an individually oriented concept, however, that *describes a person's attitude but eclipses relational consequences.* In major part, contextual therapy regards self-deception not only as a defense but as the result of an absence of dialogue between clients and their relating partners, a loss that automatically produces ethical imbalances and unjust blame.

In sum:

- Contextual clinicians are catalytic agents for self-delineation and due consideration among clients and members of their context. Their focus on relational ethics in context moves the field of therapeutic endeavor from individuals in their environment to a client's ontic context.
- Contextual theory's emphasis on the realm of the between shifts the immediate direction of therapy from the psychological to the ethical.
- Ethical interventions have intrapsychic consequences. Psychological interventions may or may not lead to relational ethics.
- The four dimensions of contextual therapy incorporate individual psychology. But it is the dimension of merited trust between members of a three-generational context that is held to be most instrumental in impacting intrapsychic dynamics.
- Aggrieved feelings are seen as indicators of imbalances and injustices, as consequences of mistrust, and of the failure of direct address rather than as the singular focus of therapy.
- It is *the dialogic process* between people of significance to each other rather than the relationship between clinician and client that *is regarded as the primary agent of healing.*
- The field of psychology has maintained a persistent bias against the significance of parents and family as a psychological and ethical resource.
- Little significant attention has been offered to the possibility that family members—regardless of conflict and estrangement—may be a more enduring repository of healing to the client and his or her posterity than any professional therapist.
- *The movement from an individual to a multiindividual point of reference mitigates or alters the dynamics of transference and countertransference,* a clinical concern of traditional psychotherapy.
- A therapist's leverage for healing exists by virtue of vision, contract, presence, and earned merit in the therapeutic process.
- A family's leverages for healing come by virtue of long-term investment: and earned merit:
  —a parent's will that a child have more consideration, options, and justice than the parent has had in life,
  —an adult's will to balance his or her ledgers with parents, and move beyond the confines and constrictions of split loyalties to the liberating dynamics and freedom of dual loyalties,
  —a person's will to reciprocity with a mate or friend, eventually activated by one partner's choice to act on his or her own behalf and invite the other partner to do the same.

- A *clinician's relationship to a client* is accidental and substitutable. It is presumably trust based and responsible, but it *can never be ontically ethical.*
- Merit may be earned by reliability, consideration, and interventions with successful consequences for a client. Meritorious dialogue between clinician and client may be short-circuited by a therapist's power alliance with a client against members of the client's context.
- Power alliances of this nature can manifest themselves in differing ways, including consistent focus on parental failures, confusion of limits with rejection, and a one-sided advocacy for a client's right to an unencumbered life.
- In their attempts to help a client address the triadic basis of interhuman justice in a multiindividual context, *contextual therapists by definition remove themselves from competition with a client's parents, children, or mate.* They cannot, of course, remove a family member's sense of competition.

If a therapist advocates for the primacy of contextual relationships over the significance of the client-clinician relationship, the function of transference and countertransference becomes a diminished force. If righting the imbalances of unfair give-and-take in context is the method and goal of therapy, clients' preference for their therapist over their parents is likely to diminish as well. If a degree of mutuality between clinician and client becomes an independent force (Friedman, 1985), the corrective to both transference and the possibilities of countertransference lies in an ongoing focus on relationships with members of each person's context. The parallel journeys of clinician and client are rooted in their respective contexts joined in the therapy room, hallowed by their recognition of human parity, linked by their quest for moral integrity, and catalyzed through professional credibility that witnesses to truth and trust in the therapeutic process.

MULTIDIRECTED CREDITING

How does a clinician gain the courage to credit clients even when they are locked in mortal combat with each other?

People come into the therapy room talking about pain. They want a solution to their problems and direction from the therapist. The therapist acknowledges their suffering and pain, and points to the fact that the root of their despair lies in their disengagement from members of their context. Clients are typically overwhelmed by the prospect of returning to a context from which they basically long to escape. The therapeutic task then is to help them identify points of loss in their lives and contexts and to surface options for restoration. Whether or not clients are able to move toward members of their context at a particular moment in time, *the very fact of facing its realities and complexities restores them to their roots as a proper subject of address*. The therapist's conviction is initially received in trust by clients who are motivated by the starkness and unacceptability of meaninglessness and situationlessness in their lives and their desperation for a fresh way. That way is initially pried open by multidirected crediting.

Simply put, multidirected crediting is a clinician's open recognition of the merit earned by every member of a given context. It is a therapeutic intervention and life-giving resource that identifies the merit of each person's side as he or she risks the disclosures of self-delineation and offer due consideration to people of significance to them. *To acknowledge the merit of each relating partner in collision is not to dilute one person's responsibility for injuring another. Nor is it to offer false compassion or a more comforting reframing of an ugly situation.* Multidirectional crediting is a means of rebalancing injuries that are a consequence of not speaking and of not being heard. It is a catalytic agent that serves a variety of clinical purposes.

- To confirm each person's truth and provide a channel through which to disclose it
- To peel back the layers of misconceptions that are a consequence of monologic interpretations
- To surface the legitimacy and inevitability of opposing or colliding stances
- To help people embrace the fact of their own injuries and suffering
- To free people to imagine that another person's suffering holds parity with their own
- To dispel malice and waylay the need for retribution
- To demonstrate that in every context, contributions and resources stand side by side with injury and deprivation—from generation to generation
- To point a way from reactivity to acting on intrinsic authority
- To help people break free of a life stance of monologic overresponsibility in exchange for dialogically testing the balances of ongoing give-and-take
- To enhance the trust base that gives people permission to speak their truths
- To ease people out of the silence of victimization into the language of direct address

Multidirected crediting is a technical expression of Rilke's words that *praise is the whole thing!* "A man who can praise comes towards us like ore out of the silences of rock. His heart that dies, presses out for others a wine that is fresh forever" (Rilke, 1981, sec. vii). The absence of praise, on the other hand, results in a stale bouquet.

The Silences of Rock

A chronic lack of crediting between people results is massive stagnation. Meg's entrance into therapy, discussed earlier, was linked to her bitter comment that other people make it—what's wrong with me? Meg feels ill attended and unacknowledged. Her father, now deceased, used to go into alcoholic rages. But when he was sober, she remembers him as a very caring man. Her mother never defended her against her father's outbursts. He never struck Meg as he did her brothers, but he frightened all of them. "My mother never did anything to protect us. My image of childhood," she goes on, "is slinking into my room, closing the door, and lying in bed." Meg sees her mother as frail and withdrawn to the point of indifference. When Meg was hospitalized, her mother did not visit. Nor has she chosen to be an active grandparent to Meg and Dale's two sons.

Meg feels she has nothing to offer her husband. Dinner times can be tense if Blake acts up. But his parents don't like conflict. They don't argue with each other. They don't address each other either. Dale and Meg typically remain courteous to but distant from each other. She has a superficial relationship with one of her brothers although she feels close to her sister-in-law. And she has lost contact with her older brother. Except for having a handful of friends, Meg feels alone, unassisted, and despairing. Divorce is not an option for her, and she feels more hopeless as days go on. "I don't trust anyone," Meg reports, "and I quickly resort to judgement and blame."

By the second session, it is apparent that Meg is directionless. She is unable to identify her own depletion and reluctant to hold Dale accountable for his part in their situation. She has not even told Dale that she is coming to therapy. "He doesn't believe in psychologists," she says. "It's all on me." It seems safer for Meg to interpret Dale than to address him. The therapist is assaulted by the pathos of the situation, and by Meg's press to know how long "this is going to take." He is also convinced that Meg's efforts to change things by sheer force of will is countertherapeutic. He recognizes the constraints on her imagination and sets out to help her extricate herself from the rock-hard silences in which everyday life is lived. He begins by simply acknowledging her side and in the process lets her know that her side counts.

He credits her in the following ways:

- The complexity of her situation;
- Her decision to seek therapy, and her willingness to take responsibility for the family's situation;

- Her persistence with Blake, and her conflictual legacy with men;
- The ease with which she parents Brian and how Brian's sweetness adds to her confusion with Blake;
- Her efforts to run the house and take care of the boys in the face of increasing depletion; and
- Her depletion.

Crediting is offered in a dialogic exchange, and usually elicits surprise, relief, and gratitude. It can also elicit denial and defensiveness. The therapist walks a very thin line in identifying a multidirectional ethic.

Crediting can backfire if it suggests that Meg is the only person who has really made a contribution to her context: if it focuses on her responsibility to others at the cost of ignoring her obligation to act on her own behalf; if it diminishes the efforts of others, however limited, who try to acknowledge her. Unilateral crediting may be emotionally consoling but it can also lead to felt victimization and is ethically unsound. Unlike unilateral crediting in which a therapist may ally with a client against members of her context, multi-directional crediting ipso facto recognizes that balances exist, that give-and-take has occurred, that contributions have been bestowed as well as injuries incurred.

The therapist observes that if Meg is reluctant to take credit for doing much that is right, she is also hampered in her ability to see, beyond pathology, to the merit of other people's actions. Her father's drinking has injured her. Her mother can never understand. Her brother is superficial. Her husband is inevitably distant. Her inability to credit is especially strong with Blake, who seems to be the repository of all that has gone wrong for her. The therapist's effort in crediting Blake to Meg initially takes place in an atmosphere of disbelief. Even when Blake is in the therapy room and disclosing concern for his mother, Meg is hard put to believe him. Over time though, Brian begins to have tantrums and Blake comes to his mother's aid. He offers solace and direction to his brother, and Meg is startled and amazed. But even earlier she had found some relief in the therapist's crediting Blake. Slowly she began to trust in his advocacy of her. It was not in Meg's vested interests to condemn her son, anymore than it was in her vested interests to maintain an unduly judgmental and blameful stance toward her mother, father, brothers, or husband.

It was never the therapist's intention to invalidate the reality of Meg's injuries and suffering. It was to suggest that Blake and Dale and other members of Meg's family have suffered with injuries too. In fact, it is the common ground of the fact that they've suffered that provides the bedrock from which mutual healing can take place. The therapist's ability to credit Meg's suffering in her context is given freely but also is conditional. What Meg owes in return is a willingness to credit the suffering of the people around her, and their merit as well as her own. In contextual theory, the therapeutic contract rests upon the willingness of clinicians to be accountable to their clients *in return* for the clients' willingness to be accountable to members of their own context over time. Crediting is the first step toward mutual accountability. It is a wedge that cuts into a monologic stance, and introduces a dialogic way.

Mutual accountability emerges as a possibility even if a client is reluctant to bring family members into the therapy room. Meg is looking for alternatives to her present situation. She takes what she learns in the therapy room and tentatively tries to apply it. At the first sign of resistance from her family she may back away. She may complain to the therapist that she tried, but it didn't work. Her mate may protest that what she is doing is the therapist's idea rather than her own. Or she may triangulate the therapist, using his words without taking responsibility for her own unique position in the exchange. On the other hand, the mere fact that she is testing dialogic possibilities begins to break the cycle of monologic blame, resentment, and guilt. Her exploratory efforts may have an immediate impact on how her family members perceive her, and they may find ways of responding in kind. They may be openly grateful for the change in her attitude and tone, and relieved that she is turning for help to someone other than them.

It is often more comfortable for the therapist to maintain a one-on-one relationship with a client. He may subtly ally with Meg's disinclination to bring her mother, husband or son into the therapeutic process. A clinician may betray his dialogic mandate with a client out of still unresolved issues in his own family. Or he may simply have to remind himself (or have his supervisor remind him) that the ease that may exist between clinician and client is secondary to the primacy of ethical balances between a client and member of his or her family. Breaking through his own vulnerability, ethical and emotional, a contextual therapist will continue to invite his client to include family members in some of his therapy sessions. His imagination for dialogue is more developed than hers. He can anticipate that when Blake comes into the therapy room, he may seek implicit permission to talk about his longing to be heard. When Dale comes into the therapy room, his dislike of psychology may dissipate when he can make himself known. In fact, when Blake comes into the therapy room, he describes himself as a victimized boy: His mother always scolds him; his father always cuffs him; his teachers don't understand him; his classmates are indifferent and dumb. Now the therapist faces a next step. He is no longer in dialogue with the mother *about* her son. Mother is no longer making occasional forays into her family to see if they can talk. The therapist and mother alike are in the process of ethically intervening for a new generation. In trying to catalyze residual resources between a mother and son, the therapist is asking them to be accountable for fairness to each other. He is incorporating Dale as if he were also present as husband and father. He is fighting against people's long-held proclivities to objectify each other.

TURNING

The dynamic leverage for healing through meeting is generated by turning, a movement variously known as conversion or repentance in religious terminology. Turning is an end point accompanied by "an assessment of the soul". This assessment includes the following elements:

- A periodic review of past contributions and injuries given and received;
- A reclaimed vision for the present that cuts through stagnation and frees hidden resources;
- A passion for truth and trust; and
- A reignited energy for life that transcends past consequences, transforms current imbalances, and offers solace and direction to future generations.

When turning finally takes place, it is usually in the aftermath of a dark night of despair in which a person comes to grips with the weightiness of life's limitations one more time. It is a moment when evasion, denial, and flight are no longer useful avenues of behavior. It is a moment when compensatory defenses that have evolved out of breaches of trust no longer serve to elicit even a modicum of return. It is a moment when, if for only a moment, sham ends and lucidity prevails (Krasner & Shapiro, 1979).

> "My father had pancreatic cancer," one man relates. "Its survival rate is 1%. For us he was going to be among the 1% who got better. We never managed to talk about the fact that he was dying. And we certainly never talked to him. I was 18 then. He had had a terrible day, and I lay in bed waiting for the hospital to call. I got a call, but it was my father. 'I'm dying,' he said. 'Come to the hospital right away.' I told my mother and she went. I couldn't bring myself to go. In our family we were struck by terror about loss. We didn't learn how to go; we learned how to flee. My mother went by herself. My father died that night. I was mortally wounded."

Paradoxically, perhaps, it is just such mortal wounds that slice through the barriers to an examined life. They offer a chance to turn toward a redemptive process that begins with facing, involves assessing and turning, leads to exonerating and forgiving, and concludes with repairing, restoring, and rebalancing. Such is the methodological paradigm that informs therapists as they are invited into a family's context. Multidirected partiality and direct address are the instruments of this process. The recognition of mortal wounds offers us a chance to rework blame and transform it into substantive ground.

EXONERATION

The recognition of mortal wounds involves a choice: to exonerate or not to exonerate people to whom we ascribe blame. One's capacity to assess where one has been, is, and wants to go is the prologue to exoneration. The next step is to pick one's way through the debris left behind by those who have used protectiveness and judgment as substitutes for fairness and intimacy. Exoneration is a recognition that there is no exculpation of the self without exculpation of the other (Boszormenyi-Nagy & Spark, 1973). It literally means *lifting the burden of culpability that crushes and fragments life in common.*

Exoneration may be a one-sided movement. It may or may not involve the participation of the object of exoneration. It may eventually result in a renewal of a relationship. Or it may simply free the agent of exoneration to more fully comprehend the motives of another person.

"Why exoneration?" a therapist is asked by Andrew, a 50-year-old man whose stepfather consistently refused to speak to him from the time he married Andrew's mother when Andrew was 8. Until Andrew left home, if Andrew and his stepfather *did* speak, his stepfather went into sudden rages. Then he acted as if nothing had happened. Andrew is now a competent, contributing member of society. He is also self-isolated, disinclined to intimacy, and apparently bereft of trustworthy relations, with the sole exception of his elderly mother. "That man destroyed my childhood." Andrew goes on, "I deserved consideration from my stepfather. It's true, though, that his own kids didn't get any more consideration than me."

> "Did your mother try to protect you?" the therapist wondered. "She couldn't do any better," was Andrew's quick reply. "In those days a single woman raising a child did not have many choices. Besides her life was ruined too. When I was 3-months old, my father came home one night. He seemed so satisfied with life according to my mother's reports. 'I have a brand-new 3-month-old baby,' my mother later told me. 'I have a brand-new 2-month-old house, and I have a brand-new one-month-old car. Life cannot be better.' Supposedly my mother told my dad not to talk like that. 'Something might go wrong if anyone hears you say those things,' she said. That night my father had a heart attack and died at 29. My mother and I went to live with her mother, sister, and brother. We were treated well there. Eight years later she remarried. While he was courting her, he brought her gifts and treated me well. What a scam! It all changed once we lived under the same roof.'"

Physical, psychological, spiritual, and intellectual injury in relationship is often labeled as abuse these days. The apparent dichotomy between victim and victimizer makes life neat but belies its complex realities. It is superficially safer to draw premature conclusions out of palpable injury and attribute blame than to elicit the massive complexity and justifiable limitations that are part and parcel of any human situation, including punishing ones. Language of abuse may be the current mainstay of youth services and courts of law. *But relational justice is never served by reductionistic compassion that can identify external contusions in one member of a context but refuse to look for internal injuries among other members who may also be suffering grievously.* In a just society, perpetrators have to be held to account. Fifty years later Andrew still bears the scars of his mother's remarriage. Fifty years later his stepfather is remembered not as a hopeful bearer of gifts but as a monster member of the family who devoured Andrew's youth. At some primal level, Andrew remains an 8-year-old boy still longing for the biological father he never knew, still stunned by the blows and indifference of the man his mother married, still grieving the sudden loss of his maternal grandmother, uncle, and aunt who helped raise him for 7 years—all of whom died within the year that Andrew's mother remarried. During his stepfather's life, Andrew was singularly unsuccessful in finding ways to make him responsible for the consequences of his destructive behavior. Since his stepfather's death, Andrew has remained locked into bitter and disabling memories. What options can a therapist offer in the fact of this ordinary tragedy?

Drawing on the outcomes of her own efforts at exoneration, a dialogic psychotherapist can readily identify with Andrew's despair over his life's losses and limits. She is also radically predisposed to help Andrew reexamine his context for still unidentified resources. What the therapist has heard throughout Andrew's litany of woe is that opportunities for relationship still exist in his context but he has automatically turned away from them. For to choose alternatives to ethical disengagement is to destroy the foundation of Andrew's world, which is so firmly ensconced in his perception of permanent victimization. His loyalty to his dead father, his idealized relationship with his mother, and his fantasies about what his life might have been, if only his grandmother, aunt, and uncle had survived overload the already weighted burden of contempt that Andrew holds for his stepfather. The therapist is now obliged to point to the goal of exoneration, and to inquire about Andrew's vision of relational justice in the future.

Andrew seems inconsolable over his lack of blood relatives. But he has cousins. Does their knowledge of who his father was help draw him closer to who he and his father might have been to each other had they had time together? Can his cousins themselves help restore a shared context of their parents' world, and in so doing bond them to each other? Andrew also had a relationship with his stepfather's son, Ira, now dead. Andrew's mother be-friended Ira and sent him parcels during the war. She also defended Ira against his father's rages. In gratitude Ira's wife and daughters have befriended Andrew, who wants nothing of it. "I don't feel toward them the way they feel toward me," Andrew says. Can it be that here Andrew feels second best again, victimized by the replay of his mother's choice for a second marriage over his well-being? Are his stepfather's children choosing for his mother above him? Or can it be that they are using his mother's good will in order to reach him? Do his longings for blood relatives have to exclude the offers of other people who want to embrace him? And what about his stepfather's older children? They all shared something of a life in common even if it was primarily the consequence of their father's violent outbursts.

Andrew recalled that his stepfather had suffered a severe head injury in a fall from a ladder at work. The story was that he had a "plate" in his head, Andrew reports. That was 50 years ago. Was his stepfather's explosive behavior a consequence of undiagnosed brain injury? Andrew doesn't know. But the therapist's questions touch him. *The therapist knows Andrew's longing to connect and begins to push him, guide him toward it.* She presses him toward his mother. What has he asked about her attempts to protect him in the face of his stepfather's behavior? What happened to her when these scenes took place? Might she have done something more for herself and her son? To whom could she turn for help? How was she affected when her second husband died? Was she relieved or did she miss him? Does she see him as the monster member of the family as Andrew does? What are her regrets? Can answers to these questions more fairly distribute the burdens and benefits of Andrew's difficult life? Can his ability to grasp the complexities of other people's suffering serve to free him just because he has managed to exonerate them?

Seeing with adult eyes and hearing with adult ears lead people to ethical imagination, and free them to envision the circumstances in which a victim-izer was once a victim. For a moment at least, exoneration can enliven the possibility that *persons held responsible for injustices done were also done injustice.* A contextual therapist's conviction underscores the reality that one person who feels despised and forsaken; who suffers pain and knows the si-lence of grief; who is discounted and bereft of esteem; and who is wounded, chastised, and cutoff is now obliged to acknowledge the self-same realities in the one whom that person has come to call oppressor (Isa. 53:3–10). When exoneration has successfully taken place, two things occur: (1) *Everything* that happens in a given relationship *is no longer filtered through the prism of personal pain and felt rejection*; and (2) *the person* who offers exoneration *is dynamically freed to enter into new levels of trustworthy relationship* in other aspects of his life, with lessened fear of being held captive to a future encumbered by a mortgaged legacy.

LIMITS AND IMPERMEABILITY

*Son: I would crawl through mud, struggle through brambles, stand
in a field with artillery shells dropping to find a way to reconnect
with my father.*

*Father: I'm simply tired of my children asking me for things.
I'm no longer willing to take initiative toward them. It's their turn to
come after me.*

Exoneration as intervention is applicable in any relationship whose long-term legacies are constricted by loyalty binds, and freighted with destructive and unrealistic expectations that eclipse the validity of genuine limits. It is true that the weight of transgenerational and intergenerational loyalties creates conditions in present and future generations that result in a revolving slate: Here adults play out unfinished family business against their marriage partners and the world at large (Boszormenyi-Nagy, Grunebaum, & Ullrich, 1991, pp. 226–227). It is also true that parents may benefit from exonerating their adult children, and that partners in relationship marked by considerable investment and continuity may benefit by finding ways to exonerate each other. Moreover, the positive consequences of exoneration are nowhere more powerfully manifested than between former marriage partners with children in common.

Consider Alex, a 69-year-old physician who has survived serious heart surgery, and his son Anton, 35, whose delight in his own two small children has stirred a primal longing for him to be parented anew. But his father seems impermeable to his pleas. Both of them are present in the therapy room. Neither of them knows how to proceed. Alex is operating out of the assumption that his bitter divorce from Anton's mother has sealed off real relating between him and all but one of his their adult children. Anton, the *de facto* eldest child of his family, is operating out of the fact that he has had to act *in loco parentis* in the care and decision making of his elder and younger brothers. "It would have been comforting to have had you at my side when Dimitri was so ill," Anton tells his dad. "It would have been respectful if you had let me have a say about what school Leo was to attend," his father shoots back. "Your choice was a total waste of my money."

This was a family that the therapist had seen 6 years earlier. During that time, most members of the family had attended sessions focused on the problems of Leo, the youngest child. Some meetings took place between Alex and Katherine, his former wife, but these were always marked by crackling tension and barely concealed rage. Eventually Katherine came into therapy to examine her own future and life. Anton, who lives far away, did manage to come into therapy a couple of times. Alex and Anton decided to return to the therapist on the basis of her knowledge of the family. At the point of her last contact with the family, Anton was struggling to decide whether or not to marry his pregnant partner. And the father was struggling with his new wife's feelings of being overburdened by the demands of Alex's children.

Alex, an only child, carried the legacy of having parents who had divorced when he was very young, of having his father reconnect with him when he was 8, and at 13 of losing his father in a WWI battlefield. He also lost his mother when he was relatively young. In addition, he was laboring under the burden of felt vindictiveness from his former wife, and of the children's apparently easy alliance with her. In spite of his longing for attention and however unintentionally, Alex managed to revile and collectivize Anton: Anton had displaced him, he was his mother's advocate, and he was always "one of the children" instead of a son in search. Yet it was Anton who kept pressing his father to make room in his schedule to arrange a time for therapy. And it was Anton who was present in the room. On the other hand, Anton spoke of his children's need for a grandfather rather than disclose what he wanted for himself. But in the therapy room, he was passionately present if verbally constrained. Hadn't his father abandoned them emotionally to practice medicine? Hadn't he chosen another woman over Anton's mother? Could he begin to imagine what it had cost Anton to have to act as his mother's consort and as his siblings' parent, or the disloyalty involved in having to be a substitute for his father in the family? From Anton's side, his father seemed limited and impermeable. "What would it look like to truly be with your father?" the therapist asked. "How have you been able to pursue him? What initiatives can you take? Have you guys ever tried to have fun?" "I want to go to Maine with you, to fish the way we used to do," Anton burst out. "It may have to wait a while," Alex replied. "My schedule is booked for 3 months now."

Remembering Limits

Alex's response to his son seemed to be a contradiction: Did he or did he not want to be with Anton? Could he hear the implicit rejection in his own reply? "Alex, are you aware that you can be a pretty crusty guy?" the therapist asked. "Your son is saying he wants to be with you, and you are telling him that you're booked for the next 3 months. Maybe you are not really interested in being with Anton at all." Like many people who are afraid of the intimacy of ongoing give-and-take, Alex uses his business to validate evasion as a way of life. He is unprepared for a caring response and defended against emotional touch. He is also overwhelmed by his son's hunger for him. The therapist speaks again. "There's a choice to be made here, Alex. If you feel cast aside by people around you, and your son comes forth with a passionate embrace, can you allow it?" His response was a circuitous one. "What I really want is a relationship like I have with my [second] wife's family. I like my father-in-law and brother-in-law a lot. They stop over and we have a pleasant exchange. It's friendly and easy and we never have reason to argue." "You don't have the same legacy with them," the therapist replied. "You've never had the investment in them that you've had in Anton, nor experienced the same wrench of loss. A day may come when you and Anton can just drop by each other's home with ease. And your son has just proposed a step toward that goal." "I really want to find a way to it," Alex replied, "but I'm not sure I want to travel to Maine. My whole work life is spent on a plane." Anton took heart: "It can be anywhere Dad as long as we're together. Even New Jersey will do." The rest of the session was spent in logistics. "How will you plan this trip?" the therapist asked. "When will you confirm it? How many days can you each afford to spend with each other? What happens afterward? Who will take the initiative and what will you do if your plans get stuck?" The therapist paved a way for a plan, given the tentativeness and timidity of father and son.

Real limits in dialogic partners do not preclude ethical movement. As always the therapist's storehouse of interventions includes:

- A capacity to tap into the ethical imagination of clients
- The offer of an expanded framework with which clients can think about themselves in relation to each other
- The stripping away of artificial comparisons in which people pit the merits of accidental relationships against the entrenched debits of long-term commitments whose assets remain hidden and unaddressed
- Exposure of the naivete of easy solutions while pointing toward the redemptive options of complexity

What frequently feels intransigent, limited, and impermeable between persons and their legacies may just as likely be movable, expandable, and accessible. The logical question here is, How do you tell the difference?

Therapists guided by dialogic principles and the dynamics of interhuman ethics are always operating out of the bedrock of ontic connectedness. In the case of Alex and Anton, what that means is that these people know that they are connected, and to them the connection matters. They know that *how* they have connected in the past is no longer useful to the present. At the moment, they have little knowledge of how to proceed. They have presented themselves to a therapist with whom they have a trustworthy legacy. With vague hopes and a primal longing, they wait for something new to emerge. The therapist listens to the flow of words between them—hurtful and hopeful alike—and struggles to identify the still, small voices (I Kings 19) that continue to connect them. The primary therapeutic concern here is neither their emotional state nor their failure to communicate but their ethical disengagement. Their immediate option is not to feel good but to learn that they are wanted and chosen for. They are desperate to break out of the maelstrom of prolonged intrapsychic monologue.

Faint-hearted, guarded, and afraid, Alex and Anton are nevertheless grasping for the faith of a grain of a mustard seed (Matt. 17:14–10). Anton's early declaration that he would go through hell to reconnect with Alex, for all its worth, is only a passionate description of his position. It has not yet evolved to make himself and his terms known.

The therapist has no prior knowledge of what can happen between father and son. She cannot identify possibilities between them in advance. But she can test, clarify, guide, press, reinterpret, indicate resources, brave disapproval and catalyze dialogue. As intransigence surfaces, *she can probe for movability*: To Alex: "Your schedule is overloaded? Well, what do *you* want to do?" To Anton: "You want grandfathering for your children? Can you say what you want for you?" *As limits appear, she can expand options*: To Alex: "Up until now, you've yielded your children to their mother. Can you trust Anton enough to move toward him now?" To Anton: "You've replaced your father in the family in a variety of ways. What would it look like to walk beside him?" *As impermeability asserts itself, she can challenge it and point a way to test it.* To Alex: "You use your crustiness to defend against your son. Can you imagine trusting him enough to touch him?" To Anton: "You sit in silence when you feel wounded by your dad. Can you read his crustiness as a lousy defense, and take him on without reviling him?" Intransigence and movability, limits and expandability, impermeability and accessibility are always dialectically linked. Over time they will tilt this way and that, and, in fact, may be fixed into place once and for all. In any case, what is possible in the realm of the between cannot make itself known in the abstract. *It is only in the concreteness of two people's move to connect that the sufficiency of dialogue can make itself known.*

TIME AND TENACITY

I had a wonderful conversation with my mother!

—a 45-year-old woman

After 12 years, one woman's wonder that she and her mother have actually addressed each other can be understood only from the perspective of time and tenacity. In the case of Alex and Anton, movement toward reconnecting or rejunction was directly catalyzed by interventions that took place in the therapy room. In the case of Lillian and her mother, Eunice, time and tenacity were resources that supplemented the work done in the therapy room. Therapy is preconceived by some as a well-marked road on a nicely graded hill with clearly posted signs that designate do's and don'ts for using the route to get to a specific goal within a given time. Trust-based therapy is more likely to be like Thomas Meron's seven story mountain with hidden trails and unfamiliar markers written in a strange tongue that disorient the traveler, obscure immediate goals, and defer the estimated time of arrival.

However accomplished Lillian, at age 43, had become in corporate life, she consistently felt second best to everyone, and chronically discontent. The last time she returned to therapy to review her life situation, she was depressed and having occasional seizures. She had seen a neurologist who was unable to determine any clear cause for her condition. What was clear was that Lillian was in the midst of trying to complete a graduate program, deciding whether or not she wanted to divorce, overidentifying with the trials and tribulations of her elder daughter, and generally acting like an overresponsible parent. She was constantly disappointed at her husband's lack of imagination and initiative in moving toward their children at the same time that she expected him to be a father to them *entirely on her terms.*

Lillian's legacy included a dutiful distance from her father; a contemptuous rage toward her mother; a defeated stance toward her older brother, who always seemed to be their mother's favorite child; an alliance with her younger brother, who acted as her confidant; and a cordial friendship with her youngest brother, to whom she was indebted for breaking ground in directly addressing their parents.

A Period of Incubation

Lillian had left therapy several years ago. When she returned, little seemed to have changed. She still stood in judgment of everyone and felt scathingly judged in return. Her complaints sounded as they always had. She was still bereft in her relationships both personal and professional. She had tried to change the people around her to act in a different way. But she failed with all of them. *So she concluded that something must be wrong with her. That was radically different.*

As therapist and client started again across a hiatus of several years, each brought with them the strength of their own conviction. Lillian was convinced that she was back at square one. After a session or two, the therapist was clear that Lillian had gained ground during a period of subtle incubation. She had put her familial issues on hold and had tested her wings in her professional life, but they had been unable to sustain her. In her family and work life alike, she silenced people when she thought she was pleasing them. She distanced people when she wanted to be close to them. She was didactic with people when she wanted to be dialogic with them. She had used her earlier work in therapy to inform and guide her. It had made her more self-aware, but she kept banging into walls. It was the very act of acknowledging limits that changed the ground on which Lillian stood.

Lillian was still unable to disclose her truth for, typically, she didn't know it—and if she did, she didn't know how to disclose it. So the therapist resurrected the basics of a multidirectional stance: "Everyone has merit, Lillian, and so do you. You deserve to make some claims. What is it you are really asking for?" He sensed that though Lillian was apparently surfacing the same questions and apparently facing the same limits that she had faced many years ago, her questions were now coming from a different plane. In the past Lillian was sure that she was always right. This time Lillian knew that she didn't know. She also knew that her veneer of competence and self-sufficiency betrayed her lived reality. Time and tenacity had moved her beyond monologue and psychological interpretation, beyond categories, and toward the redemptive moment of healing through meeting (Isa. 30:15).

This time around, most of Lillian's defenses were lowered, her resistances dissipated. She still made feeble attacks on the people around her, but it seemed as though a barrier had come down. This time around Lillian was prepared to *act from a multilateral perspective* rather than simply talk about it. *An integrative force was at work here*. Timidly and reluctantly, she was moving toward identifying the resources in the realm of the between. She was still caught in the categories of right and wrong. She still wanted to know the outcome of her efforts in advance. She still wanted a guarantee of reciprocity without risk. But ever so slowly, Lillian was beginning to grasp the truth that she might not be able to live life strictly in her own image. And she might be able to find a way to receive more than the disappointment she had settled for (Buhl, 1992). A willingness to test her terms in the world was the consequence of a period of prolonged incubation.

"From Metatherapy to Lived Reality" (Buhl, 1992)

Here the therapist pointed the way. The interventions that followed not only helped Lillian establish ground from which she could redemptively live her life; they also redeemed the efforts of generations past and progeny to follow. Was Lillian still caught in judgments about her parents' marriage? She learned how to extricate herself from her long-term position as mediator. Was Lillian still confused about her father's self-isolating behavior—taking refuge with his projects in the cellar when she visited? She brought him into the therapy room and found him unexpectedly articulate. Yes, he wanted to spend time with her and his grandchildren. No, he did not know that she and her brothers wanted to spend time with him. Was Lillian still critical of the ways in which her father treated the brother who was her confidant, and the ways in which her mother treated her older brother? She brought her parents and younger brothers into the therapy room to address their disappointments in each other, and to describe the weight that she carried when they complained about each other to her. She was still reticient to take on her mother and her older brother— the cost seemed much too high. But she played out some of her rage at them through railing against the insufficiencies of her husband and his parents. She wanted *them* to come into therapy, and at one point her husband brought his mother in.

In the midst of the ongoing efforts with her family of origin, she found resources through addressing her husband rather than excoriating him. Her husband responded, their marriage improved, and at her request he entered therapy with their son. It was short-lived, but Lillian regarded the attempt as a token of his good faith. In a parallel effort, Lillian brought her older daughter into therapy. Lillian was beginning to feel as unappreciated by her daughter as she felt by her mother. The therapist helped mother and daughter address each other. Lillian felt her daughter wanted more money for college than she rightfully deserved. Hadn't Lillian had to make do with so much less? Lillian resisted her daughter's suggestion that her brother was the constant object of Lillian's generosity, and that she felt shortchanged by comparison. Lillian got the point, and was somewhat aghast at the therapist's suggestion that the relationship between Lillian and her son might be uncomfortably analogous to the relation between Lillian's mother and older brother.

Lillian's unfinished business with her mother was now crashing through her residual defenses. Time and tenacity had brought her to this point. Many factors played a part in leading Lillian toward her mother. Her father suffered an acute illness, and the family members rallied around him. His treatment was at an out of state hospital, so they were forced to turn to each other as never before. The possibility of her father's imminent death awakened in her an urgency to find a straight way toward her parents. Freed from the consequences of undifferentiated rage, Lillian was less concerned about the outcome of deepening her connection with her mother than the entitlement that she might gain from it.

Her father regained his health, and Lillian regained her mother. They spoke at Lillian's initiative. Lillian raised questions that she had buried for years. The process was stumbling, halting, and circuitous. Her mother justified and Lillian lectured. Her mother explained and Lillian complained. Her most bitter lament had to do with her mother's unremitting focus on Lillian's physical appearance, most especially her hair. "Why that?" Lillian demanded. Her mother, a hairdresser by profession, was startled by Lillian's question. "But your hair has always been so beautiful," she replied. "And at age 18 I lost all of mine." Lillian had never imagined the depth of her mother's suffering from a rare if manageable disease. Her mother had never considered that Lillian's silence and scorn over time had been induced by the echo of the demand for a perfect appearance.

In this moment of epiphany, some mutual accessibility was born. Time and tenacity in their myriad forms had nudged both women beyond the binding aspects of judgment and categories, and beyond the constraining monologue of psychological interpretation—into a dialogic stance. The resources of an ethical context had been catalyzed through hard-won self-delineation and tender due consideration. Theirs was a redemptive moment of healing through meeting. Turning toward one another, they were finally able to trust their truth with one another. "In returning and rest you shall be saved. In quietness and in trust shall be your strength" (Isa. 30:15).

5

Between People and Their Parents: Key to Direct Address

How do clinicians maintain the tension that comes of imagining the
suffering of family members and still hold each one of them responsible
for the consequences of their own actions?

This chapter means to examine the nature and flow of dialogue between people
and their parents. It means to illustrate how truth and trust in the elemental
triad can serve to constrain or catalyze the healing elements of direct address—
within and outside the family context. It means to point to ways in which the
despair and desolation that often attend attempts at dialogue between people
and their parents can be diminished and recast. It means to demonstrate how
fresh resources and new options can emerge when offspring and their parents
decide to speak out of their own intrinsic authority rather than fall back on the
monologic patterns of passive pleasing and evasive protecting.

FILIAL BINDS

A 17-year-old wants to leave home. He is pressing to become an
emancipated minor, ostensibly because his father is suddenly involved
in producing another family. Convinced that his dad's life is doomed
to fall apart again, the youngster, wise beyond his years, argues that
the therapy session in process has simply come too late. The therapist agrees that father and son had put off facing one another until late
in the game. "What keeps things stuck," the therapist says, "is that
you guys are so frightened of each other." Her comment dents the
young man's despair as tears run down his father's cheeks. "Is that
really true, Dad?" the youngster asks looking straight into his father's
eyes. "I know that I'm afraid of you, but I never ever thought that you
could be scared of me."

The greatest challenge to this generation may well have to do with the ethical call to dialogue between people and their parents. The freedom won when an offspring is no longer caught *between* father and mother, but can enter into balanced relating with each of them is qualitatively different from any other kind of freedom. There seems to be no developmental and ethical task more significant, more trying and more bewildering than that of adults and their parents who choose to move toward each other, to step beyond the murky shadows and palpable constraints of factual asymmetry into the bright light and incremental gains of triadic inclusion and dialogic exchange. Picking their way through the badlands of artifice and overobligation, adult child, father, and mother find themselves on unfamiliar ground pitted with potholes and crowded with stop signs and red lights that never seem to turn green. The internal chaos, misinterpretation and failure to imagine the real that typically accompany the relationship between parents and their progeny are a particular kind of limbo, whose constituent parts usually alternate between *rueful acts of resignation* and *frantic forays designed to please*.

The inescapable questions of what I owe and to whom, and what I deserve and from whom are nowhere more sharply drawn or pungently poised than in the triadic reality that exists between father, mother, and child—linked to each other by birth and nurturance. They are linked as well to all the generations that have preceded and impacted them. The passion of a new beginning and the ability to connect oneself to what already exists belong together. The relationship between children and their parents is marked by the discrete characteristics, inclinations, motivations, and actions of each of these people—as with any other three people. Like any other three people who have chosen to be in relationship to each other, parents and their progeny are not usually involved in a straightforward attachment to each other. Instead they are part of a situation in which, initially at least, one of them stands between two competing forces and tries to meet the expectations of both of them. With parents and children, however, the binds and potential outcomes are qualitatively different in kind.

One on One

Parent and adult children can be viewed as a dyad as well as a triad. But even in a dyad, legacies and loyalties impinge. Consider Rob, age 30, a young lawyer who feels chronically silenced and dismissed in intimate relating. His reticence to address people, what he calls his ineffectiveness, has roots, he says, in his frustration with his dad.

- "At some point," he speculates, "I have to decide whether to take a leap. I have to make up my mind either to stay in the murk or accept the fact that things will get heavy."

- "I go into my exchanges with a dad-consciousness. I'm worried about the equilibrium between us before I've even begun. I come to it with that sensitivity, and then I have to shift to the sensitivity of criticizing Dad."
- "I feel like I'm not allowed to have a point of view that my father can simply take or leave."
- "The merits of any given issue are eclipsed by the familiarity of Dad being turned off when we just don't agree."
- "I need to be strengthened by someone else's presence in order to challenge Dad. Short of a crisis, I never approach him alone."
- "I don't want conflict. I am also hesitant to rush in and get a pastoral response. I don't want him to express his concern. I want him to address me."
- "I don't allow myself to get pissed off because I doubt that my anger will matter to anyone."
- "I tend to cover for him. That's what my family did for Dad for many years. We present as an all-American family."
- "I do have a position, but it's the one thing that I can't articulate very well. I want honest and direct conversation without having to risk the same thing."
- "I guess it's a standoff. I don't feel any malice. I feel a frustration that I somehow got stuck here again."
- "It feels like a missed opportunity."
- "It's not like you get nothing from the conversation. It's still something you treasure and value."
- "I've got to realize it's not Dad pulling strings anymore; it's Dad dangling."
- "Dad is physically, temperamentally, and intellectually intimidating—and I step back. But not only with him."

Direct address is a liberating choice regardless of dialogic outcome. The absence of direct address is also a choice—to remain less than free.

Timing and circumstance are always mitigating factors in efforts at dialogue. But the fundamental fact is that direct address is a loyalty issue. Speech-with-meaning tends to be confirmed in one's family of origin, or it falters and ebbs away—unnoticed and unmourned until it becomes a lethal impediment—and has to be reclaimed. Rob keeps trying to claw his way out of an impending trap: He and his father make occasional sorties. He and his mother are vitally dissociated. Rob disengages from women rather than argue his side. "Either protect me or be silent" was the message that he learned early in his life. Rob, his parents, and his sibs are committed to a dialogic process and have hurdled apparently insurmountable barriers with each other. But Rob has been silent in much of the process, and disappointed in some of the outcome. He lacks permission to proceed. First and foremost, he is a loyal son sacrificially bent on protecting his father—to the detriment of them both. Each of them knows that dialogue is an option; they simply aren't convinced that they have the permission to proceed.

Dialogue as Victim

If direct address is muffled in an adult child–parent dyad, it can literally be smothered in the elemental triad. The dilemma here has to do with the triad becoming a triangle. Three is an onerous number constantly threatened by the danger that dual loyalties, the ability to maintain balanced give-and-take within varying dyads (father–mother, adult child–father, mother–adult child), will deteriorate into split loyalties that are characterized by the preferring one, the preferred one, and the one who is not preferred. The issue here is no longer one of simply being afraid of hurting or being hurt. Now we are faced with one person who is or feels caught between two opposing forces. And more. In the case of both parents, they have known these forces as children in their own families of origin; and what is currently happening is influenced by what they won or lost there.

Consider Rita, 45, a therapist who in past therapies has "dealt" with issues around her father. She has "dealt" with issues around her mother. But she has never assessed the costs of being caught between their competing expectations and how, unable to meet them, she learned to fall silent. Rita is not free to speak for herself, she is disappointed that people don't speak for her, and she is afraid of being seen as sick if she disappoints a partner. "I don't trust that there is anyone in this world who really wants to be with me," she says. She goes on to make the following points:

- "I had the capacity to relate to each of my parents. But I couldn't be close to them at the same time."
- "There were ways I couldn't act with my father because if I did, I would be like my mother—and be subject to the same kind of ridicule from him."
- "I always carried the weight of what I thought my father was doing to my mother."
- "I've always been responsible for my father's side with my mother, and for my mother's side with my father."
- "If I were to go to my mother, even today, I would still be carrying the tendency to answer for it to my father."
- "I've always lived a war of opposites in the effort to be loyal to both of my parents. It's the thing that makes you feel crazy and makes it so hard to make a decision."
- "He would affirm me for exactly what she would punish me for."

- "At this point of my life I've chosen to spend money on therapy, on supervision, and on travel, which I love. But I can't tell my mother what I'm doing. Spending money is acceptable on Dad's side; it's irresponsible on my mother's side."
- "My mother's shadow still silences me with my father; my father's ghost still silences me with my mother, even though he's dead."
- "But it goes farther than that. I feel caught between my children and their father. I feel caught between my second husband and the children even though they aren't even his; I even feel caught between him and his parents."
- "I feel caught between my close friend and her husband. I can't bring myself to ask her if just the two of us can meet."
- "I'm never sure that I know what I want, and if I am, I'm afraid to say what it is."

Rita's dilemma is twofold: (1) How will she extricate herself from split and repetitious loyalties that make her victim and victimizer at one and the same time? (2) How can she move toward her mother and still be the master of her own being? She has already lost one sister to suicide and the other to an oscillating power alliance with their mother. She has good reason to be afraid. Can she find ways to divest herself of responsibility for her parents' marriage? Can she find a way to be married without having to give in or to give up? Can she take initiative with her mother for her own sake and that of her children? "I hate being an adult with my mother when she is acting like a child with me," she says. "If something goes wrong, she'll stop talking to me. If something goes right, she'll want a hug and a kiss, which she won't be able to give. She'll take it by implication—by waiting for me to move toward her. I'll see her standing there in anticipation, and my skin will start to crawl. There is a part of me though that wants to hug her." Rita is enraged at the seeming injustice of things. But she knows that her mother has suffered injustices from many sources, including her father, who, even after death, remains Rita's parent of choice. If her father was more fun, he was also an alcoholic. If her mother is dour and dependent, she was also left holding the bag.

PARENTAL REMORSE

Rita's mother wants to speak to her daughter but is too terrified to test her own terms against Rita's terms. She is highly defended, easily hurt, and caught in her own unfaced triad. Twice now she has agreed to therapy sessions by phone. Twice now she has backed out, always on the basis of health. "It's hard for me to talk to my children," she explains. "If I do, I have to hear things about myself that tell me I wasn't who I thought I'd been." The rest remains unsaid, but her words are sufficient to surface the degree of remorse and terror over how she may have failed her offspring and the question of whether or not, as an adult, her child will hold these failures against her. Moreover, Rita may be operating out of a hold that *her* parents may still have on her. If she is responding to her own parents' expectations and trying to please them, and if she is responding to her daughter's expectations and trying to please her, then who is she and with what is she left?

Like their offspring after them, people who are parents are typically caught between past legacies and current ledgers. Torn between unexamined asymmetrical pulls, a person who is a parent is left with no real tool for redemption other than drawing on his or her own truth and intrinsic authority. Thwarted in tentative, exploratory attempts at self-disclosure, a parent may initially retrench from direct address in order to deflect the threat of potential loss and to suppress retributive outbursts. The potential entrapment of parents is underwritten by unexamined familial, cultural and theological expectations. "Even if a nursing mother shall forget her child, Oh Israel, I shall not forget you" (Isa. 49). Left unaddressed here is the matter of what is to be done when, eventually, a nursing child forgets her parent. The operating assumption in this society seems to be that only the adult child has justification for disappointment in "toxic parents" and is therefore unilaterally entitled to disengage. Left unaddressed here is "filial toxicity" and its consequences.

Few people start off as wise parents. All children start out as an enormous demand. But neither parent nor child is toxic by design. The fact of parental limits and the misuse of parental authority are not to be confused with organic toxicity. The dilemma is that there is no way for people to raise children without injuring them. There is no way to be an adult child without wounding parents in return. The challenge of maturity comes in the recognition that alongside of parentally imposed injury and hurt typically stands a massive investment of time, money, energy, hope, good will, actual care, and parental presence as well as a parent's deep-seated anxieties over his or her felt inadequacy and capacity to bring up a healthy child. Alongside of apparent filial disengagement stand questions about parental choices and intentions, and a subterranean conviction that unbeknownst to those who should know, children have contributed to their parents' well-being in substantive ways.

Whatever its unavoidable fragilities and limits, the mother-father-child triad is the basis of interhuman justice, the starting point for ethical, spiritual, and psychological renewal. The parent-child relationship is the matrix in which hope is shaped and from which meaning flows. The volatile mix of injuries and contributions, burdens and benefits, resources and limitations, dialogue and monologue in no way negates the fact that by one means or another, adults who are parent and child are obliged to address the implications of their legacy in common or pay unnecessary consequences that rupture their common order. Paradoxically it is only when they can risk the disloyalty of surfacing their voices to parent and progeny alike in an effort to be heard that they may finally grasp the freedom that comes of direct address.

One minister father spoke proudly of how his young adult children call him once a week—but they speak only of themselves. "Sometimes," he smiled triumphantly, "I slip in something about myself." "Have you thought to tell them that you'd like things to be more reciprocal?" he was asked. "Oh no," he replied, "I could never do that." Only recently has he been able to state his terms to *his* parents. He may eventually find courage to speak his truths to beloved children—to say what he intends to them. Like this father, parents long to hear their grown children, and want their children to hear them as well. When they are partners in dialogue, a parent's voice is likely to be the voice of the children's suppressed longing, and parental questions are filial questions too:

- Who wills to make us present to them?
- Does a failure of ethical imagination make one person collude with another's untested assumptions about him or her?
- To what degree do people parentify and protect as a substitute for risking trust?
- Is it easier to stay parentified than to find the courage to say one's name?
- Parents become so instrumental in delivering their "goods" that their "it" is revered, and their "thou" eclipsed?
- Does the seeming of one's role as parent obscure the being of his or herself?
- Do personal and professional roles subvert a person's options to stand in a common situation with another and vitally expose him or herself to a share in the situation as really that person's share?
- Can a person beat the rap of being a parent? Is it an illusion for parents to persist in their quest of parity with progeny? To keep alive the primal possibility of truly being heard? To be confirmed as what they are by our adult children, and as what they can become?
- Having blindly or intentionally imposed themselves on their children from the moment of birth, are they nonetheless free to pursue a process of unfolding?
- May a parent yet step into elemental relationship with an adult son or daughter, with the hope of surprise in making an offspring present?
- May an adult son or daughter yet step into elemental relationship with the father and mother in the hope of surprise in making a parent present?

- Given the limits of parenting as well as its investments and contributions, is fair give-and-take a real option?
- If offspring, even mature offspring, continue to look to their parents for acknowledgment and approval, are parents, even mature parents, allowed to look toward their adult offspring for some of the same?

The questions before each person is *whether the search for justice in the common human order can include reciprocity between people and their parents*.

A multilateral willingness on the part of people and their parents to invite and disclose, to recognize injury and credit contributions is the movement that determines whether parental claims can ever be accepted for what they are at a given moment rather than as invariable throwbacks to days gone by. Can the blinding imbalances of asymmetrical relating ever give way to parity (ontic equivalence) between adult and adult who are connected by birth? Can parents who are painfully estranged from each other in fact, as well as those who covertly disagree while denying their divergences, ever bridge their own despair in order to liberate their young? Can adult and adults who are parent and offspring forgive each other the differences in their respective contexts rather than using them as a singular point of reference and bludgeoning each other with them? "You are free," one mother kept repeating after flying across the Atlantic Ocean to comfort her son, distraught and disappointed over marriage and divorce. "Why are you so enraged?" she asked. "You are free to live your life the way you choose. You are free even from me. Why can't you understand that?" Eventually her son would test against old images and learn to know his truth. But for the better part of his life he was bound in his elemental triad, caught in the aftermath of the circumstances of his parents' divorce, in which at 17 he became parent to both his father and his mother. And now his own sons were struggling with another brand of the same dilemma. His mother was confused by her son's volatility. "I had no father; I was illegitimate," she said. "I was handed about like a parcel when I was young. I cannot understand why you are so angry. You've always been so much better off than me."

CONTEXT VERSUS CONTEXT

Parents tend to view the future through the filter of their adult offspring's loyalty and success: (1) Will he succeed or fail in his life's work? If he succeeds, will I become insignificant to him? If he fails, is it my fault? (2) Will she eventually have a family of her own? If she does, where do I fit in? If she doesn't, who is going to be there for her when I'm dead and gone? (3) Do my children get along with each other when we are not in the picture? If they do, do they care more about each other than they care about us? If they don't, is it because of the way we've acted with our own brothers and sisters?

Offspring tend to view the past through the filter of their parents' limits, mistakes, and unspoken expectations: (1) Will my parents be okay when I leave home? How free am I to live my own life? If I do, will they have a life of their own to lead? (2) Will I please my parents with my choices of partner and career? If they like my partner, will my partner like them? If they dislike each other, will I be forced to choose one or the other? If they like each other, will I feel left out? (3) Presuming that my siblings and I outlive our parents, will we have a life in common? How will we include each other? If we don't, why?

Dialogue between Colliding Contexts

Dialogic asymmetry provides the original basis of context. Ethically, an asymmetrical structure offers survival for the young and consideration for the old. But relationally, asymmetry is a trap when its form reifies unilateral expectations—without benefit of direct address. In the last decade of the 20th century, the structural supports and institutional underpinnings of intergenerational life have all but disappeared, and given way to an emphasis on privacy and interpersonal process. But privacy can be another word for isolation. And process rooted in either a compulsion to please, or in the retributive feelings that come from not being known, constitutes a primitive double bind. Whether the topic under discussion is religion or sex or wills or funerals or holidays, the issue is the same: Can I risk saying what I mean? Can I tolerate another person's truth? Do I trust that healing may evolve out of mutual self-disclosure? Can I choose for dialogue between colliding contexts or do I flee my real context to the details and diversions of problem solving?

Problem solving suggests a practical outcome to a specific issue. *Direct address suggests a choice to engage regardless of outcome.* Problem solving suggests that something is broken and needs to be fixed. *Direct address jump starts a run-down source of energy so that regeneration can reoccur.* Problem solving is technical, instrumental, and communicational. *Direct address communicates too, but its realm is ethical and catalytic, and touches ground that people hold most dear.* Problem solving assumes a dilemma that is self-contained and produces a resolution that results from correct transactions. *Direct address assumes that the breakdown of fair give-and-take is a sign of ethical disengagement, and produces a resolution that results from assessing multilateral merit.*

Take the issue of money in the Butler family. Cliff, 28, has just finished an 8-week outpatient program for cocaine abuse. He is thoughtful, intense, and confused about why he and his father, Dwight, 61, can never resolve the issue of money.

Dwight has been in and out of contextual therapy for over 3 years. He has done marital work with his second wife, and made serious and somewhat successful efforts to renegotiate his relationship with his two sons. Dwight never knew his own father but was warmly regarded by a stepgrandfather. When his mother died 2 years ago, she left a small trust to his sons. Cliff is now asking for the proceeds of that trust to finish his college education.

Cliff's dad is black; his mother white. He has long suffered with the consequences of split loyalties. He was the only student in high school with a black parent; the only person in a black college with a white parent. He has also carried the weight of his parents' divorce and respective legacies. He is completely unaware of how empowered he is with his dad. But he knows how empowered his dad is with him: "There is no one in the whole world with whom I feel better when things are going well between us," he tells his father. "And there is no one with whom I feel worse when things go like this." Cliff is unable to reciprocate the *understanding and flexibility he is asking of his father.*

CLIFF: I just don't understand. We had a plan. I was going to take some money from the trust. You and Mom agreed that if I finished college, you would each replace the money I used for tuition. If I screwed up again, you wouldn't replace the money. Everything seemed set. And then you went on the attack the way you usually do. I never know what to expect.

THERAPIST: Do you see it that way, Dwight?

DWIGHT: Yeah, but something else was going on. After we made the plan, I learned that Cliff was driving without insurance and state registration. It felt like the same old thing. How much of this can I take? I was willing to let him have the money. I wasn't willing to pay for what went up his nose.

CLIFF: It's in my lungs, not up my nose. Anyhow, don't you think I realize you weren't responsible for that?

DWIGHT: What's more, his mother had agreed to dinner, but she had eaten before she showed up. I took that as an insult.

ANNETTE: I'm used to eating early. There's no way I could have known that that was going to offend you.

DWIGHT: Yeah, and when you offered to pay your share of the bill, you said you didn't want it to cover my drinks. That's old stuff. I've heard it a million times.

The issue of money for Cliff's tuition had technically been addressed: There was money in a trust that could be used for tuition. Dwight and Annette would replace the money if Cliff completed college. The money would not be replaced if Cliff did not succeed. The financial problem was solved, so now what was the problem?

The colliding contexts between Dwight and Cliff continue to estrange them. Cliff thinks that Dwight's outbursts are intrinsically unfair. "Even when things are settled, they're never settled between me and my dad."

THERAPIST: You're right not to want to be scolded, Cliff. But you just want your dad to do something different. What can you change in you?

Cliff falls silent. His imagination fails him.

THERAPIST: The next time your father loses his temper, can you say, "I'm taking a walk around the block. When I come back we can try to talk"?

CLIFF: That's so hard! Sure I can do it but ...

THERAPIST: Maybe your father just can't change, Cliff, but being able to take your father on, on your own terms, may be the difference between life and death. If you can ever walk away from a battle you don't want and then come back to talk again, if you can refuse to be put off and eventually join the issue that is unresolved, you may never need cocaine and alcohol again. If you can make yourself heard without allying with your mom or blaming your dad, you might be home free. If you know what you want and can fight for it instead of reacting to your father's limits, something new can happen between you.

DWIGHT: My stepgrandfather was a physician, the only grandfather I knew. When I got hurt, I came to him to fix it. He yelled at me first and took care of me then. I guess that's what I do now. He loved me so much, he couldn't stand my pain.

THERAPIST: That's what your dad is saying to you, Cliff. He loves you so much, he can't stand your pain. When you jeopardize your own well-being, it fills him with dread, breaches trust, and unleashes rage rooted in helplessness.

CLIFF: Is that what you're saying, Dad?

DWIGHT: Yes, I am. I'm willing to let you have the money, but there are no guarantees. What do I get in return?

Intellectually, Cliff recognizes that Dwight was raised without benefit of a father. Dynamically, he is destructively entitled: He blames his father for his parents' divorce. He feels he was left to take care of his mother. He feels like he lost his father's attention. He resents being the offspring of a mixed marriage. He feels he has paid an unfair cost for his parents' choices. "Why did you have me?" he asks. "Didn't you know how hard it would be?"

Dwight is self-employed and nearing retirement. He is asking if his turn to enjoy himself will ever come. How long does he have to contribute to an adult child who seems bereft of responsibility? How long does he have to settle for second place as a parent?

DWIGHT: You told me that your mother and you stand in the same corner, Cliff. Where does that leave me?

THERAPIST: Your father is telling you that he feels like shit in your eyes by comparison with how you see your mother, Cliff.

CLIFF: Is that what you're really saying, Dad?

DWIGHT: Yes. You've always been ashamed of me. I was loud, your mother was proper. I cheered you on at football games, and after the game you always walked to your mother's side.

CLIFF: I just wanted to blend in, Dad. I wanted to be the same as the other guys.

ANNETTE: I've always known how much Dwight cares for our sons. I've always known that his outbursts were a smoke screen for his pain. I just didn't know what I was supposed to do to make it better. Anyway, I think that Dwight's feelings about him and Cliff are worse than they need to be.

THERAPIST: How do you know that, Annette?

DWIGHT: Yes, how do you know that?

The tenor of this session had shifted from a discussion on how to handle money to a dialogue in which the exchange of hard truths, self-reflection, self-disclosure, inquiry, and due consideration had taken place. People may have left the session with sadness, but they also left with hope. At the mutual request of family members, the proceedings of the session had been audiotaped. For the first time in almost 3 years of intermittent meetings with his father, Cliff asked if he could take the tape with him so he could share it with his brother. The family's focus on money for tuition seemed insignificant by comparison with Cliff's ability to be in a room with his parents and see them address each other and him. His parents' financial plan to see him through college was significant. Even more significant was Cliff's realization that they could engage each other and, in the process, begin to rebalance the burdens and benefits of their lives in common—including money.

Interventions in Colliding Contexts

The therapist's interventions among the members of the Butler family were based on the following premises:

- In their anticipation of going unheard, people and their parents get caught on the horns of dialogic asymmetry.
- *Dialogic asymmetry is an inevitable consequence of loyalty*: Children want to please their parents and tend to conform to what they are told. "She has a mind of her own" is a phrase that is often used to express a parent's helplessness in the face of a child's oppositional stance.

- As children become adults, *dialogic asymmetry has to be reworked.* Young adults tend to assume that their parents have a powerful hold on them and tend to overlook real and felt parental helplessness. Parents tend to see their adult children as distancing and evasive, and often overlook the compelling power of filial attachment.
- Relational maturation requires the young to eventually embrace the tension of the realm of the between. To embrace the realm of the between requires the discipline of expanding interhuman knowledge to include the dynamic realities of give-and-take in families and beyond.
- Context is the organic connectedness that provides impetus, motivation, and the will to engage in the realm of the between. The potential collision between the contexts of people and their parents is the *sine qua non* of intergenerational life.
- Confidence in the flexibility and pliability of contexts as they converge and meet frees people to relinquish stagnant asymmetrical patterns of relating and to attain dialogic parity. Disengagement from inevitable collisions, on the other hand, reifies dialogic asymmetry and can freeze people into modes of dependent child and caretaking parent for the duration of their lifetimes.
- Parity is the corrective to dialogic asymmetry. To create parity out of dialogic asymmetry, ethical imagination has to be employed.
- Ethical imagination requires a capacity to grasp the paradoxical nature of trust-based relationship: That self-delineation requires due consideration, and due consideration requires self-delineation.
- The freedom to act on one's own behalf while acknowledging the merit of other people's sides *without having to endorse their stance or conform to the pressure to agree* is the developmental apogee of interhuman ethics.

It is a common and tragic flaw in intergenerational life that allows people and their parents to fantasize that it is easier for one of them to initiate, engage, and speak directly than it is for the other.

WORDS THAT WORK

What will we do if we let go of our rage, and then have to figure out who we are in relation to what we don't have to be or do anymore?

—A 48-year-old mother of two young adult sons

In contextual therapy, interventions are guided by the imperative of speech-with-meaning. The words that count are neither cosmetic nor created *ex nihil.*

They are words that are teased out of the pulsating ground of people's respective existences. No therapeutic manipulation or cajoling or linguistic gimmickry can suffice to elicit these words that alone clothe each person's nakedness. Speech-with-meaning has no abode in statements like "I feel shut down," "You never support me," "Why do I always have to initiate?" and "We never communicate." *Who can imagine that the full measure of human life in common can yet emerge from the darkness lighted by the truth and trust of two basic words—I and You?* Neither the rampant silence nor the torrent of empty words that constitute masks in this society can produce meaning born of presence. *Only living intercourse offers a third alternative.*

Human beings usually live in a world of language whose primary manifestations are instrumental, defensive, reactive, withholding, evasive, submissive, and deferential. In family life where ethical disengagement is typically a norm, language also assumes a *dutiful* characteristic: "Hello Mom, I don't have time to talk but I thought I would call." These manifestations of language collectively result in a life of monologue whose unilateral movement estranges rather than connects. They also convey a message that is mixed rather than straightforward, exclusive rather than inclusive: "My world cannot tolerate your scrutiny." "I'm too busy to let you in." "Why don't you know what's precious to me without my having to tell you?" And, "Why don't you mind your own business?" Nowhere is the life of monologue more apparent or potentially more destructive to present and future generations than in the relationships between people and their parents. Nowhere is living intercourse more unlikely or more remote for fewer legitimate reasons than between the generations.

The subject matter of living intercourse in ordinary events is always secondary to the humanity of people who share a connection in common. Consider the simple if sad example of Mark, 69, and Betty, 66, who asked Bea and Don, their daughter and son-in-law, to be with them in the aftermath of a brutal and bitter argument. Mark was very ill, and Betty aggrieved at the weight of her responsibility and her impending loss. The tension in the air was palpable. As Bea and Don got ready to leave, Mark asked them to go out to dinner. The invitation seemed outrageous given the intensity of the moment. Burdened and dismayed at the hopeless repetition of her parents' quarrels, Bea declined. The memory of her father's invitation has lingered with her for years. Might it have been different, she has since wondered, if Mark had disclosed his limits and terror in the situation and simply said, "I desperately need you to stay." Might it have been different if Bea had been able to disclose the degree to which she was burdened by her parents' conflict, saddened by their desperation, and then offered them terms on which she might have been able to be with them at that particularly poignant moment?

The cry for living intercourse is everywhere and nowhere: *everywhere* because this is a time in which people speak and are not heard (Ps. 115), and hear and do not speak; *nowhere* because in the main, people are profoundly unaware that living intercourse is an option, that there is a level of self-delineation that offers a communion of mind and heart. *There are words that work* because they embody truth and elicit trust. It is not the mechanics of the spoken word but the mutual self-disclosure of the human spirit that time and again creates meaning and catalyzes healing in the realm of the between. Ordinary moments comprise the bulk of any relationship. *Speech-with-meaning is the self-corrective intervention that challenges the routinization of ordinary moments.* People may come to therapy in crises, but almost without exception it is the routinization of meaning that provides the backdrop of crises.

The Potency of Unspoken Words

Life requires routine to structure reliability. On the one hand, even a cursory awareness of life's potential for chaos creates an absolute demand for habit and ritual. On the other hand, the longing for predictability tends to flatten passion and eclipse awe. The paradox of close relationships is that the very loyalty dynamics that are meant to convey reliability and continuity are also the repository of stagnant ritual and routine. Gravitation toward the familiar can be an expression of loyalty; it can also be an expression of ethical disengagement. Repetitive stories, unvarying holiday "celebrations," and unstated expectations and untested premises based on the past may provide the stuff of family lore; but they are also the cracked and dried glue of boredom and resentment. "I could never say that to my daughter" and "My parents would never understand" are formulaic expressions whose intention it is to predict the essentially unpredictable, and whose outcome is to sterilize and neutralize interhuman vitality.

Collisions over religious disloyalty often demonstrate the chasm that lies between parental disappointment and filial reactivity, and filial disappointments and parental reactivity. Chronic mismeetings over religious education, money, and sexual preferences, to name a few issues reveal the absence of words that work. Consider Joan, 31, a therapist who has just returned from her nephew's First Communion. The event was both a source of pleasure for her and a reminder of how her religious stance and practice are an ongoing source of disappointment to her father and brother. Her initial response toward them was defensive and reactive. *At no point did she take recourse in the merit of her own conviction, or even recognize the potency of her own unspoken words. Her refuge in silence* not only denies the significance of her presence to people who love her, it also *blinds her to her family's longing to know her rather than conform her.*

JOAN: I get a lot of pleasure from my nephews and niece. They are very important to me, and I get affirmation about how important I am to them. I'm Jack's godmother and I went to pick him up at school Monday before I left. The parochial school teacher was very brusque when she asked, "Jack where are you going? I don't know who this person is." "This is my godmother," Jack replied. "How could you even ask?" he seemed to suggest. "Why don't you know?" It was lovely. Mike and Donna make a big deal out of godparents. The reserved pew for First Communion was for parents, grandparents and godparents. That was very special. Still, there is always tension about religion— between me and my dad, most specifically, and me and my brother. It is ironic because in our younger years Mike was the one who broke every rule in the book and rebelled against our parents. Now he is very loyal to Catholicism. I know that he wishes that I were more of a practicing Catholic, especially as Jack's godmother. He wants me to be part of his son's Catholic education. It would have been good to say something to him rather than just handle it through humor.

THERAPIST: What would you have said?

JOAN: Part of it is my regret—I'm sorry to disappoint my dad mostly, but also Mike.

THERAPIST: That doesn't say much about you. What is your ground?

JOAN: I struggle around religion and finding my way. I think what I can offer Jack at some point, maybe even now, is talking about developing some kind of relationship with God.

THERAPIST: I didn't ask you what you could give Jack. I asked what your ground is.

JOAN: At this point I can't afford to be a practicing Catholic, according to strict definitions.

THERAPIST: Can you talk about it from a resource side? Your side, as you describe it, is in reaction to—it's not ground of your own.

JOAN: Ground of my own is I'm not reacting or rebelling against Catholicism.

THERAPIST: If you could put words on it, your family might rejoice in what you have to say. You're defending yourself in ways that you rarely do. Religion in your family seems to remain an unaddressed reality for you. If you could say, "This is what I stand for…"

JOAN: What I stand for is my word, and how I live it has to do with relationships—connecting with people. I don't know what is more sacred than that.

THERAPIST: You seem not to have developed it enough. Just in your work with bitterly broken families you talk about love, justice, compassion and forgiveness and reconciliation and death and resurrection every day. You could go on indefinitely about how your tradition informs you. You just haven't put words to your truth. You seem to be defending against the fact that you are less ritually observant than other family members. What you have taken for granted and are letting them take for granted too is how hard you try to embody your religious conviction.

JOAN: Some of it might even be lack of education. I'm not really grounded in what the tradition stands for.

THERAPIST: Have you read Matthew Fox? His is a resource orientation. It is dynamic and nonjudgmental. If that appealed to you, you could write letters to your nephew. Everything that you do every day is closely linked to a living faith in Catholicism. Why do you let your father and brother make judgments without knowing what gifts you have to offer? Have you failed to tell them because you haven't put words around it yourself?

JOAN: Somehow I worry that in saying that it sounds judgmental of Mike or my dad.

THERAPIST: What are you calling judgmental?

JOAN: If I say I have found my own way, it's different than...

THERAPIST: The minute you say "I've found my own way" it may be heard as defensive. But you have a gift that embodies much of the tradition. Maybe it is you who is taking you for granted by not putting your conviction into words. Maybe creation theology can help you see how your investment in youngsters in court is an expression of living Catholicism. Then you might write to your nephew and tell him about the youngsters you treat. You could talk to Jack about love and fairness and forgiveness. You could tell him stories of social justice. You have it at your fingertips. You don't have to jump into someone else's skin. You don't have to justify not going to Mass. That's your judgment call. What you might do is say that you stand for something; and convey what you stand for to Jack. It's an entitlement issue. You are looking at it as disappointing someone. That may be the hardest piece of work in all of relationship—for adult children to turn their blind loyalties into a claim for dialogue, and then reroute the dialogue: Then you are not conformed to someone else's terms. You do have ground. I'm not sure that you know that.

You may feel insecure about what living Catholicism is for a mature person. At another level you may feel shut down by your father. Is your world in your head? Do you presume that people know where you're coming from? Are you defended out of loyalty to your family? Do you believe that anything that your father dislikes is not worth saying so you fall silent and then get enraged because he doesn't know your faith? Is there a difference between *feeling* shut down and *being* shut down? Do you have to attack, or can you reroute the direction of dialogue? Can you say, "I know you have certain expectations, but let me tell you how the tradition is significant to me?" "Are you aware of how my work [in family court] brings me face to face with issues of death and resurrection and choice?" Most people emphasize religious form. Joan, you operate out of religious substance. You may or may not choose to act on ritual yet.

JOAN: I moved to my present apartment for a lot of reasons. It is across the street from a Roman Catholic college. I used to go to daily Mass in college. It meant a lot to me. Being so close to the college gives me a chance to find a way to reembrace what is mine. It is so convenient that I do pop over there for Mass. Not every Sunday—but on occasion.

THERAPIST: Does anyone know that?

JOAN: I have said that to Mike and my dad, but probably more defensively than I needed to. I use humor, but I know that there are some underlying issues that need to be addressed directly. I knew that I need to say something, but I haven't found a way. At one point I said something to my dad that probably sounded defensive and made him feel judged. He said, "Maybe you are more advanced than I am." He was not sarcastic at all.

THERAPIST: You might say something like "There are a couple of ways to look at it, Dad. One is an emphasis on substance and the other is an emphasis on form. I know I'm short on form, but I chose an apartment, across the street from a Catholic College. I'd like you to understand my religious ground, Dad, and I want Mike to know too." I suspect that two or three letters a year to your godchild could also make a difference. They would help you crystallize your own thinking and disclose your own integrity. It's a lovely way to gain adult ground vis-à-vis your tradition without having to be self-justifying.

JOAN: There is a fine line between saying my side and having to defend it.

THERAPIST: It is hard.

JOAN: Are you saying the line's really not a fine one?

THERAPIST: The difference between defending yourself and delineating yourself is more like a massive border than a fine line. It's like sitting back and saying, "Dad, I know what you would like, but this is what I have to offer." The issue with your nephew is a little different and requires direction from you.

JOAN: If something were to ever happen to my brother and sister-in-law, my brother is very clear that he wants the children to be together, and he would prefer that they be with me. He would want them to be raised Catholic. It's very important to him.

THERAPIST: Since you are his children's godmother, your faith stance becomes your brother's business. That's why dialogue counts. It would be heartening to your brother to have you guide his son. There are some wonderful children's books in Catholic bookstores. You might want to look at them to see if they hold something you can embrace. It is not because Mike or your father wants you to do it but because it is your choice. You could begin sending Jack some books with a little note inside. You could write him letters at Easter or Christmas.

JOAN: I *would* like to acknowledge the religious piece. I really don't know how. Not a Bible, not a rosary...

THERAPIST: Your best bet might be to share your heart with him. You can do it in terms of the parables about the kids that you see. You have so much at your fingertips. You seem scared to take yourself seriously. Your choice of an apartment near a Catholic chapel may be a gift to your parents. It seems like a real return—maybe an accident, maybe not.

JOAN: Not much of an accident! On some level it *is* coming back home.

Rerouting Monologue

> *Only in partnership can my being be perceived as an existing whole.*
>
> —Buber, *The Knowledge of Man*

Coming back home for Joan means exchanging filial reactivity and monologic entrenchment for living intercourse. The shock of recognition here requires her to take her rightful place as *partner to her parents*; to grasp the fact that *her* longing to be addressed as an existing whole is matched by her parents' selfsame longing; to assume full responsibility to speak her still unspoken word rather than collapse and disappear under the weight of stale or despised parental utterances.

Consider also the situation of the 33-year-old daughter who has chosen a woman lover. She is hurt and perplexed by her parents' hurt and perplexity. Her notion of healing has to do with a demand for parental affirmation of her choice. Still constrained by childhood images of parental vulnerability and power, she is withholding of her word and reluctant to hear theirs. Her father pleads for a different kind of balance: "We cannot affect your choice," he says, "nor can you alter our felt loss. But can we breathe life back into our ruptured connection? You ask us how we are; we tell you. We ask you how you are; you are silent. It feels like you cannibalize our words. We give; you take. Nothing comes back in return." Implicit in her father's frustration is an invitation to partnership.

If adult offspring are often double bound by their parents, parents are as frequently double bound by their offspring. Can this daughter move her longings for carte blanche parental affirmation to the bedrock of a personal stance that can afford to be inclusive? Is her reflexive insistence on privacy a mask that conceals her fear that what life she has will be ripped from her by parental ground that diverges from hers? Can she find words that delineate her own reality as well as credit her parents' reality? Being partner to a parent requires ownership of one's own words. It requires a conscious resistance to pleasing as a primary relational mode. Most significantly, *it requires a filial choice to be as responsible for the specific direction of dialogue as parents seem to be. To the degree that adults address their parents out of dialogic asymmetry, there is no dialogue.* To the degree that they address their parents out of parity and the passion of their conviction, genuine dialogue can evolve. It takes courage to stand over against parents at almost any stage of life. It takes mature imagination, however to embrace the fact that parents want filial approval as much as progeny want parental approval—and that parity eludes parents as well as offspring.

What's a Father to Do?

Consider the situation of Emily, 40, an only child, and her 80-year-old father, Mr. B. The request of Emily and her husband, Aaron, to borrow money from Mr. B. to buy a house has precipitated a family crisis. By any measure, Emily and her father actively care about each other. Moreover, he has embraced his son-in-law as a son and is deeply invested and involved in his grandchildren's well-being. However, Mr. B., a successful lawyer and businessman, speaks with a certainty and a sense of authority that, unbeknownst to him, silences his daughter and enrages his son-in-law. This is particularly so when it comes to finances, a realm in which Mr. B. seems to presume his own competence and Emily's ineptitude. Her father's attitude triggers helplessness in Emily: She does feel inept in financial matters. She is also convinced that her father's decisions always overrode her mother's—a view with which Mr. B. vehemently disagrees. She feels caught between her father and her husband, a position in which she colludes by never identifying her own side.

Mr. B. is a man who speaks with a certainty that belies his accessibility and vulnerability, and overshadows expressions of gratitude for how much he is resourced by Emily and her family. Since his wife's sudden death 18 months ago, Emily and Aaron have literally been a lifeline to Mr. B. They have incorporated him into their lives and household, and he has willingly let himself be received. He continues to live on his own and is currently resuming his own life—but he leans heavily on his children and grandchildren for emotional security and mutual consideration. After his wife's death, Mr. B.'s increased involvement in Emily and Aaron's context introduced tensions that were as understandable as they were inevitable. For example, Mr. B.'s take-charge attitude with his grandchildren placed him in competition with the children's father, however unintentionally.

Emily's request for financial help from her father has exacerbated these tensions—not because Mr. B. is unwilling to help but because of the shutdown of dialogue between them. *Theirs was a nondialogic kind of caring that, however well-intended, resulted in ethical disengagement.* Their fear of direct address left them bereft of direction when they differed or disagreed. Short of dialogue, they proceeded along parallel lines without a bridge on which to join their colliding concerns. Emily and Aaron's need for financial help was therefore one more expression of the chaos that ensued when they thought they were speaking and being heard. At one point in the negotiation for a house, Emily used her father to deliver a statement of financial disclosure to the bank. Though she had offered no instructions to the contrary, Emily was outraged when her father read it. Though he had asked no permission to read the financial statement, he presumed the prerogative by virtue of his anticipated contribution. He thought he had a right to know the degree of his children's indebtedness. Aaron and Emily felt so intruded upon that they ended negotiations for the new house. Other factors also entered in.

Discouraged, upset, and insistent that she be heard, Emily asked her father to come into therapy—no small request given the knowledge that her father felt they could talk about anything. So why the need for a therapy room? When Mr. B. came into the therapy room, he reiterated that he felt entitled to know about Emily and Aaron's financial situation. He was confused, not so much by the fact that Emily disagreed with him but by her characterization of their relationship, that is, that he had all the power. He could credit the fact that Emily felt caught between him and Aaron. *He was stunned that she felt unable to stand shoulder to shoulder with him.* During this session, his aggressive and articulate way of speaking silenced Emily once again. The therapist encouraged Emily not to fall silent and withdraw into herself; and to help Mr. B. understand that while he may see his daughter as a peer, his daughter did not see herself as his peer. The therapist challenged Mr. B.'s assumption that Emily could make her views known. "Your daughter may speak well on behalf of her husband and children," the therapist said, "but she is not a good advocate for herself." "I'm sorry to hear that," Mr. B. replied, "I never knew that was so." "She has no precedent for knowing her ground and articulating it," the therapist went on. At this point, Emily decided to address her father in the midst of her dread and anxiety. After a half-hearted attempt at parrying her statements, Mr. B. stopped and listened. *Once his daughter began to draw on her own authority instead of anticipating his, he no longer needed to assume the responsibility to provide answers or to take the situation into his own hands.* Emily had tentatively found her voice and her father was able to hear it. At this juncture, father and daughter became present to each other. The patterns of accommodation between them had been shattered, for however brief a time. For the moment, Mr. B. was able to assert his right to have a say in a transaction that drew on his generosity. With the therapist's help, Emily was able to lay out her contributions to her father, especially over the past 18 months. Her father readily acknowledged Emily's significance to him and the joy he drew from her family. "What's a father to do," he asked, "if he can't take care of his child?" Mr. B. remained unattuned to the upheavals between him and Emily, and other members of her family, or even that these upheavals had taken place. He was perplexed by his capacity to intimidate his daughter—a perplexity that Emily was unable to comprehend. Even so, the tone of the session had been palpably transformed as Emily began to grasp the significance of her own spoken word.

In a follow-up session, the therapist led Emily in an examination of her reactive behavior toward her father, her overexpectations of him, her static answerability to Aaron, her husband, and her underexpectations of herself.

EMILY: All the way home, I was just so ... that was such an emotional thing.

THERAPIST: I was glad when you came forward because for a bit it didn't look like you were going to.

EMILY: I just felt like saying, "What difference does it make if I say anything?" I felt so overwhelmed that ...

THERAPIST: What you were overwhelmed about?

EMILY: Dad started talking about me with you. It was like I didn't exist. My mother and father used to do that a lot.

THERAPIST: That's what he fell into.

EMILY: They would have this discussion about me while I was in the room. I know that is a really common thing for parents to do to kids. But for me I just immediately fall back into being 6 or 7 years old and not having any kind of power in the situation at all.

The therapist hears Emily presuming intentionality and premeditation on her father's part to exclude her from dialogic parity. The reality is that her parent does not know how to include his offspring or how to ask to be included by her. As often as not offspring fail to face their part in reciprocal objectification or what they want to do about it. From childhood on, Emily had been excluded from her parents' *discussion about her* rather than *included by direct address*. In adulthood, she replicated her childhood pattern of silence, which, in effect, resulted in self-objectification as well as in objectification of her parent. Here intervention evolves from the therapeutic conviction that the leverage afforded by residual trust and merit between the generations counterbalances and outweighs the leverages attached to untested perceptions of power.

The therapist acknowledges Mr. B.'s relational limits and their impact on how he approaches the issue of money. He also points to the fact that Emily's father would have given her the money regardless of their disagreement over how he had handled their discussion until then.

THERAPIST: What you don't see is that he did that out of helplessness. In terms of what you're saying, he needed to address you but he wasn't addressing you any more than you were addressing him. If you could see that as a failing or a limit rather than as arrogance or presumption, you could gain a lot. I think he'd give his life for you.

EMILY: I knew I was going to face this again. I had to do it with you here because I didn't want to have it become an issue down the road. I wanted to be up front with him. But I didn't want him to be involved in this decision, whether I chose to buy the house or not.

THERAPIST: Right.

EMILY: The point was that I needed his help, and last night he gave me a check for the full amount that I requested.

THERAPIST: Emily, help me with this. I know it's hard for adult children, astute adult children, to see their parents' limits. But when you asked him for help this time, I wondered what you meant to offer in return. Do you think you owe him anything for that kind of consideration even though power in terms of money lies in his domain?

EMILY: What do you mean?

THERAPIST: When you ask him for money, do you owe anything back?

EMILY: What happens is that I fall into feeling like I owe something back; but I wind up divulging everything and I give myself away.

THERAPIST: Is that the dilemma ... ?

EMILY: Then Aaron challenges what he sees as my capitulating. "You don't have to tell him all of this," he says. And I say, "But I just did." Then he says, "Why did you give him the power of knowing all of this information when you don't have to?"

THERAPIST: In the best of all possible worlds, you might sit down with Aaron if he were willing. Given his issues with his own parents, he may or may not agree to it. Then you might say, "Look Aaron, this is what I, Emily, am willing to do. I'm willing to ask my

	father for money, but in return I think he deserves to know some stuff about us. And this, A, B, C, and D, is what I'm willing to tell him. If that's workable for you, fine; if it isn't, I'm not going to ask him." If we were friends outside of this room, Emily, and you wanted to borrow a substantial amount of money from me, I suspect that you might ask me what I want in return. The assumption might be that I was owed for consideration given. Contractually, because you trust you father, I think your wish is to share with him. But then you lose your side in both directions because Aaron is displeased. Is that a fair assessment?
EMILY:	Yes, real fair. I think I've never been able to negotiate right, or to negotiate with my father as a peer. It's always been as a child asking a father. I fall into that trap. I don't want to work myself into a situation like that again. I know that I've given my father a lot as far as relationship is concerned. That is something I can freely give, that I have to give and I want to give. Money becomes so significant probably because we've never had much.
THERAPIST:	Do you make money more important than other aspects of relating, Emily? Can you see finances as your father's veneer? He was kind of cute at the end of the session. He stood at the door shaking his head after you left and said, "I just came from a meeting with 18 other guys, all of them lawyers, and I was doing the same thing that you were doing here. I think I can join your practice." Let me press it this way, Emily. I hope you heard his misconceptions about you. He sees you in his mind's eye as an aggressive, competent advocate for yourself. Now if he sees you as an aggressive, competent self-advocate, then he sees you as a peer. Just because you don't see you as a peer doesn't mean he doesn't. Once again, there has been a significant mismeeting. He thinks he has someone standing shoulder to shoulder with him. He has no way to know that you are still sitting at his knee.
EMILY:	But only on some levels. When you get into the financial end ... NO.
THERAPIST:	What you did here was to reroute the dialogue. I frankly did not have anymore rabbits to pull out of the hat until you finally spoke. I did think you were so wounded you were going to back off. Then you came back in. What you did was teach him the relational part of money. He said something like, "I was the delegate so I had a right to read that data." I remember saying, "No, I don't think so." You failed to instruct him initially, Emily. When we spoke briefly 4 weeks ago there were a couple of

places in which your silence empowered him. One, you might not have to read him the stuff, or you might not have given him the stuff to begin with; two, not laying out the terms under which you would borrow from him. If your father plays God with money, it may be because it is the way he relates to money in his business life. When he said, "What's a father to do?," he adds money to his mandate as a father to take care of you. He is fairly blind to how to care for an adult child.

I was very touched when he said he took Aaron as a son but he is naive to the point of ignorance about the consequences of his own behavior. He doesn't know a hell of a lot about intimacy. He is absolutely devoted, but that doesn't mean he knows about fair give-and-take. You have something to teach him about how money impacts relationship. Or even his statement about taking your daughter to Florida. He saw that as his decision. He didn't recognize the nuances of what it means for an adolescent and how she is entitled to be consulted. But that is his ignorance and limit. He comes on like a panzer division, which is potentially intimidating. He does not realize the implications of his behavior, but he can stand still when you spell them out.

Here the therapist lays out the difference between a punishing parent and a confused person. He realizes the courage required for Emily to bring her father into the therapy room against his deepest wishes. He also takes a multidirectional position that says, "There is a side to your dad that you seem reluctant to acknowledge."

The therapist's freedom to advocate for her father's terms against Emily's comes from trust earned by crediting Emily's merit. Now the therapist can risk holding Emily more strictly to account. Now Emily is more willing to recognize her father's limits, credit his merit, and acknowledge her own intrinsic authority. Now she can begin the process of recasting her childhood stance. She is beginning to get a visceral hold of *the fallacy of parental infallibility*. She no longer has to ask why she should have to instruct her parent. She no longer has to demand that he *a priori* know what she needs or wants. She is beginning to identify the benefits of moving beyond the feelings of a 7-year-old into the freedom of an adult in relation to a parent.

Emily has chosen to embrace this most formidable task of maturation: standing shoulder to shoulder with her parent in full knowledge that she is as empowered as he by virtue of the fact that her word holds full parity with his. She is beginning to identify how she has trapped her father, how her ambivalence has confused the question of whether or not she wants to be seen as a peer, how her silence and withholding have falsely empowered her father whether or not he wants it, how she has avoided adult-to-adult status through maintaining a childlike role, and how she has blamed her father for obliterating her side when in fact her obliteration was self-imposed.

EMILY: My father made these statements about my daughter's behavior. I was able to ask him to address her. "Then you will always know exactly where you stand with her. Isn't that better than being afraid of what's really going on under the surface?"

THERAPIST: So you can do it for your children but not for yourself.

Emily describes the exhaustion that set in after the therapy session with her father. She takes note of her ability to overcome the emotional cost of dialogue between her father and her; and regrets how she gets in the way of dialogue between her father and her husband by taking a go-between stance.

EMILY: Right. It's very hard for me. When I got home, Aaron and the kids made dinner and were walking on eggs. They didn't know how Mommy was going to be when she got home. I was exhausted from the whole thing, just blown away. I literally ate dinner and got a blanket and watched television and went to bed. I left everybody and pulled the covers over my head. The next day I called my dad in the middle of the day, not a frequent occurrence. I asked if he was okay, and he said yes. Then I thanked him for going with me yesterday. He said, "Okay," and then in his typical way, asked if it had helped me. That's Dad. I realize that I interpret Aaron for Dad and Dad for Aaron. I try to make Dad understand where Aaron is coming from, and get all of Aaron's stuff together and present it for Aaron to Dad. Then I take all of Dad's stuff and wrap it up and try to present it to Aaron in an acceptable package.

THERAPIST: That way you eclipse yourself ...

EMILY: Right! I told Aaron that I'm not doing that anymore. If you have an issue with my father, you talk to him about it.

THERAPIST: Good.

EMILY: I told him that I have a hard enough time working out my relationship with my father, "I cannot work your relationship out with him too. You do it," I said. "If you have a beef with him, you take it to him." Now I haven't said that to Dad yet, but I think I will say, "Dad, if you have something you need to talk to Aaron about, please do."

THERAPIST: There is even more to say. For example, "Dad, let me tell you *my view* on this. If there is residue left over and you need to talk to Aaron, go ahead." By not stating your own position, you might still get caught between them.

EMILY: That's true. In other areas of my life, this skill works fine. I am able to work with a kid's parents and explain each person's side. But I can't do it with these guys.

THERAPIST: You do well with explaining other people's sides, Emily. It is your own terms that tend to disappear. In a sense your husband and your dad are each claiming you as their own. Now *you* can assess what you are willing to do as well as to consider the merit in their claims. The important thing is to learn to slow down long enough to figure out what it is you want. Then you can lay it out. It is a matter of entitlement. Getting out of the middle is simply not enough. You have to know what you want.

EMILY: This is just typical of women in my generation. We are caught in that framework. The difference between my mother, myself, and my daughter is so incredible.

THERAPIST: It's still untested. Your daughter is not up to this yet.

EMILY: But her verbalizations are so...she is so on target.

THERAPIST: But your father thinks your verbalizations are on target too. Entitlement is an issue that men and women struggle with in different ways. Your father and Aaron feel entitled to speak professionally. But when it comes to intimacy, to whom do they go? You. You may not have a mandate from your mother to speak up, but don't underestimate how timid the men in your family are. If you do, you make it into a gender issue. But entitlement is not a gender issue. Once your father realized that you were not a good advocate for yourself, everything shifted. He backed off and listened. Everything changed once he knew he had misread what was happening to you. He was more combative when it came to Aaron, fearing that Aaron was a source of your pain. But when he was made aware that he had injured you, he shut up.

EMILY: That was the farthest thing from his mind. He never believed he had done anything like that. Part of that is my inability to tell him, but I don't know how.

THERAPIST: *You do know how and you did.* It is not your inability to tell him, it is your lack of permission to proceed.

In this exchange, the therapist is challenging Emily's slippage into an ideological position. He is demythologizing a political interpretation of her family context. He is questioning Emily's parentification of her daughter. He is exposing her hiding places: In effect, he is saying that people cannot take refuge in an ideological position, in professional credentials, or in a stagnant role in the family and still expect to be heard.

THERAPIST: What would your mother have said in this circumstance if she were here with the two of you?

EMILY: The way my father described my mother was far removed from my memory of her. I think she was an entirely different person when he met her. The view I have is so different from his. The mother I knew was a woman who kept herself very quiet and medicated. She also drank. We never attached a label to it because she was not a falling-down-drunk, crazy woman. Every night she had a glass of sherry. It was only before Lauren was born that it became a social problem. We addressed it as a family, and then she stopped a lot of it. But the sherry at night continued. She had my grandmother to put up with.

THERAPIST: She may have been silenced in her own family of origin.

EMILY: She didn't know how to deal with Grandma, who was absolutely miserable. Grandma was alert but not physically well. When Dad gave us this check, Aaron said that he did not want Dad to know anything about the financial circumstances around this house.

THERAPIST: Emily, I want to go back a step. I would like to know if you recognize how dependent your father was on your mother. That is what he was trying to say. However the decisions actually got made, he was as dependent on her as she was on him. The same situation exists between Aaron and you ...

EMILY: I know.

THERAPIST: Well, yes and no.

EMILY: I am beginning to realize that more and more. I am beginning to be able to say that this is where I am and this is what I will do. I was never trained that way. It's a whole new way for me to think of things in that regard. When Dad started to talk about his legal background, I should have said, "So what?" I might have said, "Look, that is great and I am an educator and I am pretty damn good at it." I don't mean to speak out of anger but to say, "I respect you for that, but don't hang that over my head as if you know better than I." Does that make sense?

THERAPIST: It does make sense as long as you keep understanding that his aggressive statements are defensive statements ...You may also need to say, "What we are talking about does not belong to the law but to the way we wound each other unnecessarily. Let me tell you how that happens to me." He can hear you at this level. The important piece is not to join him in his defensiveness, which comes across as aggressiveness. He talks fast and he talks hard and he makes sense. But there is a limited context there. He does not know that, but you do. So take yourself as seriously as

	you take him. You give yourself away in general. You give too much away to him. He is educable. What has happened to Aaron in this whole process? Does he feel inadequate or competitive with your dad?
EMILY:	He does. I often misread him because I do not see Aaron as inadequate.
THERAPIST:	You do not see your dad as inadequate either. That is the single missing piece in your education. Once you get that piece in your viscera, I think you will be on much stronger ground.
EMILY:	I don't read either one of them that way. When he referred to his mother humiliating him, I was surprised. I never heard that before.
Therapist:	That's why I try to resist your sociological definitions of women of your age. The issue here is not gender oriented. It has different gender manifestations. But everyone feels inadequate. Everyone has a limit. God did something screwy with people in not teaching men about women or women about men.
EMILY:	There are only two women I can think of who don't do what I do.
THERAPIST:	But you are of an age when that shifts one way or another. When you assign power to men, are you saying that women don't know how to use power?
EMILY:	I am really just saying that this is the first generation that women have not just stayed home and watched kids. Now we do a lot of things, but still don't know to speak for ourselves. I see such a difference in my daughter. She is saying things and calls things the way they are. I can't do that at my age. On the whole she is standing on firmer footing that I am. I look at the women in my office, and every one of them defers to men.
THERAPIST:	I want to repeat that she is untested. When she comes into her own and is clearly aware of her vested interests and is afraid of losing in a way that she is not afraid of losing with her mother and father, then she will struggle too. It is the stuff of every generation. No one skips it.

ESTABLISHING ADULT-TO-ADULT CONTRACTS

You have got to know, Mom, we will always work it out.

—Ben, age 20

The freedom for direct address is both a consequence and catalyst of merited trust. Every relationship between people, whether between family members, between friends, or in the marketplace, is predicated on some degree of truth and trust built on mutual self-disclosure. Truth in lending, for example, presumes that a full disclosure of facts is necessary to establish a viable contract. *For what is apparent is not necessarily real.* A mortgage for $75,000 on a house is more likely to cost $200,000 over 20 years. Do potential purchasers know what they are really about to spend if they are not told? Is the banker obliged to tell the purchaser even though that might endanger the anticipated transaction? Fairness and trust require a mutual exchange of truth. But truth in relationship, unlike truth in lending, can never count on full disclosure. It counts, instead, on the human capacity to exercise fairness in the realm of the interhuman. Ben's conviction that he and his mother will always work it out is a fact, a hope, and a promise rooted in their primal connection, shared legacy and present reality. To wit, this is what we have to work with. Are we going to work with it or not?

Establishing an adult-to-adult contract between people and their parents always requires a dialogic process that transcends emotional and transactional expediency. *Interpreting feelings as the basis of reality rather than as signals for unaddressed injustice is an example of emotional expediency.* It is a choice for isolation. *Seeking a solution without surfacing unfaced injuries and crediting mutual contributions is an example of transactional expediency.* It is a choice for evasion. Establishing an adult-to-adult contract between people and their parents includes emotions and transactions but is essentially ethical. It too is a choice. Feeling close, understanding, pleasing, and disengaging are all components of an implied contract but are ethically deficient. The deficiency of an implied contract is that it fails to surface and to join each person's terms. It precludes an ethical process for the sake of psychological safety. And it perpetuates an illusion of intimacy without the risk of mutual disclosure. *Ethical engagement depends on the existence of an explicit contract or covenant whose terms are rooted, dialectical, and always in transition.*

Implicit Contracts

In a milieu that underwrites children's impulses to divorce their parents and parents' inclination to abandon their children—to wit, disadoption—only active testing can provide a corrective to unilateral processes that are essentially unethical. Ethical reengagement is possible not because people are supposed to forgive each other but because people are covenanted to each other—whether they know it or not. It is ontology rather than morality that provides the glue of relationship. What was, what is, what still may be are contractual questions begging to be asked. A therapist is able to identify fresh resources and new options between people and their parents not because the therapist creates them ex nihil but because resources are seeded in hidden and unexplored crevices between the generations. The tendency to renounce the contractual nature of relationship when we hit stone walls does not nullify the ethical consequences of interhuman connection. "Raised with a positivistic and pragmatic overevaluation of science, we are inclined to doubt whether there are any valid ethical issues left between hypocrisy on the one hand and neurotic guilt feelings on the other" (Boszormenyi-Nagy, 1973, p. 44).

Examine the implicit contract in the Z. family.

At the age of 38, Ms. Z. and her five children left Venezuela to come to the United States. Driven by her husband's reckless business dealings and gambling debts, she abandoned an upper-class existence replete with servants and privilege as well as cultural roots and the security and convenience of an extended family. Ms. Z.'s shame over her loss of status converged with her husband's shame at bankrupting his family; and though he joined them only a year later, the emotional and economic ruptures that each of them sustained had ethical consequences for their relationship.

Everyone suffered in the upheaval. The eldest, dutiful daughter became a stereotypical yes-man whose loyalties allowed no room for her to live a life of her own. The second-born and eldest son was his father's favorite child by everyone's consensus. His increasing involvement with the drug culture in the United States eventually led to his indictment by the DEA (Drug Enforcement Agency) and, shortly after his father's death, he fled to Venezuela, where, ironically, he lives in permanent exile from his family. The third child, a daughter, was divorced twice and struggles to sustain ongoing relationships with men. She is also the truth sayer in the family, whose adolescence and young adulthood has been a relentless demand for physical affection and emotional confirmation from her mother. Mr. Z. died when his fourth child and second son, currently a successful professional, was 10. His teenage struggle with drugs and sexual identity forced another geographic relocation for the family when his mother moved from New York to Arizona to protect him. The youngest child and third daughter, who has spent most of her adult life wrestling with a weight problem, is caught in chronic passivity and, like her mother, is massively infantalized.

The implicit contract among siblings in this family is that Ms. Z. has suffered enough and deserves a reward for having rescued her family. They have decided to protect her from further suffering. But none of them could have foreseen the long-term consequences of their implicit if collusive contract. None of them could have understood at that point that in acting for their mother they failed to act on their own behalf.

Making the Implicit Explicit

THERAPIST: You are desperately trying to have your mother confirm you by getting her to understand what it has cost you to get to where you are. I wonder what it cost her to get where she is.

JUANITA: I knew I wanted to ask her these questions, but I was too afraid. So I told her my therapist wondered what it cost her to leave her homeland. What did it mean to leave her family and friends and husband behind? Was she trying to shield me from her losses? My mother smiled and began to respond. She said things I had never heard before. When she was done, the pain that I had carried all these years seemed to lift and disappear. I suddenly decided that my mother is not cold and removed; she is just afraid of losing more. She was willing to tolerate my rage as long as I did not leave her. I suspect that her lack of overt affection was never a rejection of me. She still cannot hug me easily. But now I can hug her.

In one fell swoop, the connection between Juanita and her mother had been transformed from an implicit contract into an explicit contract, from a unilateral position to a multilateral stance, from an individual to a relational focus, from monologue to dialogue, from a context of psychology to ethical reengagement. The silent suffering between caring people was broken; a process of repair had begun.

Juanita had been in individual therapy for 3 years when her brother invited her into a therapy session with him. Family legacy had cast Juanita as the problem child; Miguel was the family's good boy. Recently, Juanita had taken to calling Miguel in the middle of the night after a drunken brawl with her male friend. After two divorces and the loss of a pregnancy, she turned to her brother to make things better. He offered solutions, she refused them, and he withdrew—always failing to disclose how her phone calls assaulted him. In the session, discussion shifted from the phone calls to their respective and collective losses. Then the therapist asked them what they now want of each other. Miguel could say what he did not want. Juanita could talk about her disappointments in Miguel. But neither of them could articulate what they specifically wanted from each other—other than "to get along." *The therapist credited Juanita's feelings but challenged her ethics.* To be sure, her emotionality was her attempt to hold her family accountable. But she was never present to her own challenge. In this meeting, she took pains to validate how hard she had worked in her 3 years of therapy. But she had come out of individual therapy with the absolute conviction that she was justified in feeling what she was feeling, and expressing what she was expressing. She seemed to take little account of the consequences of her part in the injustices that lay beneath her feelings. But she knew that she needed something more than insight. She had been comforted by her experience in individual therapy. Her therapist had helped her to feel good about herself in the face of a lost pregnancy and a broken marriage. Juanita had needed solace. But, beyond her therapist, she needed the solace from members of her context. Eventually Juanita used contextual work to reassess her premises. Borrowing on the trust that she drew from the therapeutic relationship, she began to make choices that reflected newfound freedom. She initiated a process characterized by some of the following steps:

- A *conscious decision to recontract with her mother*—born of the fact that none of her other efforts seemed to work.
- A *willingness to test*, which brought her face to face with her mother's story and prepared a way for her mother to speak.
- A *choice to fight for dialogic parity* as an alternative to a childlike demand for asymmetrical confirmation.
- A recognition that her *volatile expression of feelings often served to obscure her truth and drove her further away from reconnecting with* people she loved.
- A *fresh understanding that her desire for responsible relationship was not solely dependent on external referents*, for example, on her mother's ability to confirm her, her brother's ability to embrace her, or her lover's ability to respond to her.
- A choice to take initiative in the face of her mother's limits.
- *Her mother's choice to receive her daughter's initiative and attempts to respond in kind.*
- *A ripple effect that extended to other members of her context* and continued to impact everyone in unanticipated ways.

Within a time frame of 3 months, Juanita was able to move from an unmitigated need for personal comfort to a claim to ethically reengage. She had begun to use her truth to elicit truth, to build trust through earning it, and to receive consideration by offering it. In facing her parents living and dead, she had gone beyond automatically being determined by them. She was now able to reroute some of her life energy and goals. She was increasingly able to channel them from the bitter wasteland created by people and their parents who overreach reality, and finally move to the fertile soil of due consideration. And in the testing, implicit contracts became explicit, the invisible became visible, as each person's word was increasingly set free.

6

Truth and Trust
in Peer Relating

How do clinicians catalyze the justice dynamics that alone provide the promise of reliability and continuity between peers, that is, mates, lovers, friends and siblings?

The rampant absence of self-knowledge and the destructively elevated expectations that people bring to members of their contexts tend to obscure the fact that peer relationships require fair give-and-take in order to survive. Whether or not people say what they mean or trust that they will be heard, the struggle toward meaning between relating partners in a seeming society still depends on a dialogic stance. Our intention in this chapter then is to demonstrate clinical *interventions that maintain a vision of relational justice between mates, lovers, siblings, and friends*. We also mean to explore the dilemmas of peer parentification, and the promise implicit in the recognition of gender-neutral realities and interventions. This chapter means to challenge the dual illusions that between peers anything goes, or conversely, that there is a sacrosanct way to ensure sin-free relating. It means to argue that neither hedonism nor moralism can adequately address the relational complexity presented by a society steeped in cynicism, in cultlike proscriptions, and in the chaos perpetuated by group and family disintegration. The term "peer" is used to describe relationships between siblings, between mates, between lovers, and between friends.

FRIENDSHIP BETWEEN SIBLINGS

The term "peer" technically applies to relationships between brothers and sisters in their adulthood. What differentiates siblings from other peer relationships is that they are held together by an irreducible ontic reality: Siblings are usually connected by blood and parentage. Genetic and long-term connectedness provides a level of life in common whether siblings want it or not. Beyond childhood, brothers and sisters are faced with all of the pressures and promises of any peer relationship—and then some. For they share family legacies that they may interpret from diametrically opposing stances. Like marriage partners and friends, siblings have choices to make about how deeply they want to engage. But, unlike marriage partners and friends, siblings are bound together by an irreversible connection that weights, predetermines, and predisposes them to how they make a choice. *The primary obstacle to friendship between sibling and sibling is their respective unfaced relationships to their parents.* Almost as important are their untested assumptions about who siblings are to each other.

When a therapist draws up a genogram and asks family members to characterize how they relate to their siblings, "close" and "distant" are the most frequent replies. *When brothers and sisters say they are distant, what they are typically describing is relationship by default*: They are ethically disengaged; they are estranged by unfaced injuries; they are polarized by alliances with opposing parents; they are defined for each other by parental labels like good or bad; they are caught in split loyalties with their parents and use those splits against each other; and they substitute pseudomutuality for direct address. *When brothers and sisters say they are close, what they are typically describing is making do with the unaddressed consequences of their legacies in common*: They are usually vitally associated but verbally withholding; they are joined by shared injustices; they may be allied with each other against a parent(s) and other siblings but maintain a loyal silence with others to ensure peace at any price; they justify each other's actions and paper over resentment and real and imagined guilt; they are reliable in a crisis but avoid intimate disclosure; and they tend to talk *about* other family members in lieu of direct address.

Whether close or distant or a mixture of both, the connection between adult brothers and sisters is almost anomalous. Structurally, they are peers. Dynamically, they are more impacted by the third-party reality of their parents than by each other.

In other peer relationships, people are drawn to each other and then explore what is possible between them. But siblings are imposed on each other and are then left to assess resources exist between them. In any case, they remain critical factors and potential resources in each other's context. Whether or not brothers and sisters choose to be friends, in adulthood they are faced with the developmental task of demystifying how consequences of their filial legacies predisposed them to each other and who they are vis-à-vis each other.

Embracing Complexity: A Trust-Based Intervention

Therapists who treat brothers and sisters are immediately thrust into multidimensional complexity. Their primary intervention is to draw siblings into a recognition of that complexity through helping them grasp the justice dynamics in their context in the following familial relationships:

- Sibling and sibling
- Siblings and sibling in relationship to other siblings
- Siblings and each parent
- Siblings and both parents
- Siblings and their parents' parents
- Siblings, their parents, and their parents' siblings

The following vignettes demonstrate the span of this complexity.

- The 40-year-old woman whose eldest brother committed suicide at 22 feels panicky about the chronic arguments between her 6-year-old daughter and 11-year-old son. She inevitably blames her son.
- The well-to-do father of a 45-year-old single parent constantly rejects her frequent requests for financial help for her son. His new wife objects. He disinherits his eldest child, a son who has been indifferent to his wife. He is more generous to his younger daughter, who accommodates his wife. As he lies dying, his new wife asks him to change his will. He assigns his remaining assets to her. His three children are at odds over the use of extraordinary medical measures. After he dies, his son draws satisfaction from "pissing on his grave." The distribution of material goods, medical decisions about an aging parent, and a lifetime of dutiful distance from each other now stand between these siblings and their children.
- A 60-year-old man feels crushed by his parents' decision to leave their estate to his siblings, each of them of modest means. Nor were his hard-won achievements recognized by any other means. Even worse, his professional and financial status seemed to estrange him from other family members. His parents felt unneeded, his siblings felt competitive. Everyone chose to interpret each other by the disparities between them. In my family, he said, you get rewarded for failure.
- An eldest brother, 40, and an only sister, 35, of four siblings, both highly accomplished professionals, meet once a year at Christmas time. The brother's material success underscores the sister's felt insignificance in the family. His recent career change has been cloaked in "strict secrecy," a fact that his sister resents. She desperately wants to connect with her brother but doesn't have the vaguest idea how. Nor does he. Asked if she had called him, she replied, "He doesn't call me." She is embittered at her brother's apparent lack of reciprocity. She uses her brother's success to judge her parents for not guiding her to his financial heights. Her brother's

suffering may parallel hers but is probably obscured by his early material success.

Psychologically, sibling relationships are characterized by feelings that range from impassioned to estranged. *Ethically, sibling relationships are character-ized by the consequences of invisible ledgers and legacies*, that is, by the com-pilations of recorded entries of burdens and benefits, injuries and kindnesses, competitiveness and complementarity, real or imagined betrayals and caring—even sacrificial—acts between them, and between and over the generations.

Colliding Triads

> *I have the very strong feeling that brothers and sisters should sit down and talk to each other.*
>
> —an embattled parent

Direct address between siblings is always an option whether people know it or not. It can be catalyzed by a parent's sense of entrapment between his or her offspring, by one sibling's evolving determination not to be held captive by another, through two or more siblings' determination to inquire of each other rather than continue to judge each other, or through the sheer weight of stag-nation by intention or default that polarizes and silences family members from generation to generation. The effort to talk often comes about in the wake of a crisis or by frustration about what one person has confided to another.

Consider the case of the Johns family, whose lives together have been pro-foundly shaped by two major factors: their father, Joseph's, struggle with al-cohol, and their sister Eileen's congenital medical problems, which required lengthy hospitalizations and repeated surgeries. In their adult lives, Martin, 45, Eileen, 44, Joe, Jr., 42, Ann, 39, and Marie, 32, unwittingly perpetuated the consequences of their parents' marital struggles as well as the consequences of their own breakdowns with each other. After a holiday incident in which Eileen accused her brother of ignoring "her" mother, Joe realized how fed up he was with the injuries he had suffered from years of silence in his family. *All his efforts to better himself through education, marriage, and professional attainment were insufficient to overcome his discouragement over the "fact" that in his family things never change*: That his mother would never say what she wanted no matter how deep her need; that his father, now dead a year, would always be characterized as a drunk rather than credited for his gentle-ness, intelligence, and humor; that his elder brother, Martin, would always remain invisible; that people would always yield to Eileen as the family's *enfante terrible*; that Joe himself would continue to surrender pleasure in life to duty and obligation; that in her attempts to make peace at any price Ann would forever be "caught in the middle"; and that Marie, the baby, protected from her family's grief by four older brothers and sisters, would never imagine their pain.

Put in terms of colliding triads:

- Both Martin and Eileen defined their father only in terms of biology and saw their mother as his victim. Joseph Sr. adored his firstborn son and thrilled in his firstborn daughter. But the impact of his war experiences left him poorly prepared to endure any further human suffering, especially that of his own suffering infant; and so little by little he distanced himself from her. Marge relied on Martin as surrogate mate and buffer. But the connection between her and her daughter deteriorated around the escalating demands of Eileen's medical problems. Her illness became the visible sign of the family's deprivation—relational, psychological, spiritual, material, and physical. Eileen's behavior became the outward sign of an invisible reality, that is, a signal of each family member's despair and an inability to speak from his or her own suffering ground.

  Unable to help his daughter get well, unable to better his mother's life with his distancing, authoritarian father, and in competition with Eileen for the attention of his wife, Joseph saw no options for himself. Unable to imagine that he had a right to more than what might flow from facing the sources of his grief and loss, he pulled back into the place he knew best. With his war experiences and the legacy of his immigrant parents, who themselves struggled to survive, Joseph retreated into the intimacy of alcohol, his only identifiable resource. Well liked by many people, he was nevertheless bereft of a capacity to trust the adult world. Joseph clung to his 16-ounce bottle of beer as one might cling to a best friend. Marge, faced with the increasing demands of the care of an ill daughter, of raising four children, and of preventing Joseph's steady retreat from the intimacy of marriage and fatherhood, trapped Eileen in a double bind: "Look at how I sacrifice for you."

- Joe sensed that each of his parents loved him, though he wouldn't have necessarily used that word. "If they loved each other," he reasoned, "and loved their children too, why the chaos? Clearly love can't vanquish chaos, so why love?" Joe's father, one of nine, was at a loss to express his love to Joe, though Marge described Joe as her husband's namesake and favorite. All his mother asked of Joe was that he be good and not add to her trouble. Her own neediness always preempted Joe's entitlement to receive from his mother.

- Ann's unspoken message to her parents from childhood was, "Why can't you be happy so I don't have to be so afraid?" Easy to parent, Ann was an invisible daughter as Martin was an invisible son. Marge and Joseph were overwhelmed by the time Ann came along and saw her as their last child. Their relief that she was healthy, unlike Eileen, freed them to enjoy her as long as she didn't make demands.

- Marie was born 10 years after Ann. The "golden child," she was everybody's pet. Marge and Joseph were far more available to her than they had been to their older four children. By that time, Joseph was depleted and didn't want a job outside his home. Marge reluctantly went to work 6 weeks after Marie was born. Joseph became the stay-at-home parent. Marie alone found a way to be loyal to each of her parents while her siblings were all caught in split loyalties, choosing their mother over their dad.

Colliding triads are the *sine qua non* of sibling relationships. It is virtually impossible for siblings to claim each other as friends without sacrificing someone in the process if they are blindsided to the uniqueness of their loyalties to their parents, jointly and respectively.

Resentful and confused, Joe set out to clarify what he owed and what he deserved in his family and from whom. Eileen had vowed that she would never do therapy with Joe, himself a therapist, but his mother agreed to reenter therapy with him. Eileen became the immediate object of exchange. It was only later that the therapist was able to help Joe and his mom transform their mutual resentment of Eileen into a self-delineating stance with each other and by extension with Joe's dad. And it was one year later when Joe and Eileen attempted to address each other through delineating themselves and inviting each other to make a claim.

Reengaging Siblings: A Birthday "Surprise"

Part I

Joe, Eileen, and their mother, Marge, faced each other in the therapy room with fear and trembling. They had met time and again at ritualized family gatherings. But this time they knew some things would be different.

THERAPIST: Joe, I promised to begin this session by asking why you wanted your sister and mother here.

JOE: I asked them to come in because of an incident around my birthday. It raised issues that we have had to face over the years, or not face, as the case may be. I think I've suffered for a long time over my relationship with you, Eileen—suffering for you and as well as for myself. I was disappointed and relieved that my 40th birthday party didn't come off as a surprise. I have so much difficulty in receiving, much less being honored. I'd like a clearer delineation or separation of my relationship with my mom and my relationship with Eileen. If my mom wants to get caught between Eileen and me, or Eileen gets in the middle between my mom and me, I can't prevent that. But I want them to know that I don't want to get caught in the middle.

THERAPIST: So you would like to push for a dyadic relationship with each of them and break the triangle that you've experienced.

MARGE: What I want is a better understanding between Eileen and Joey.

THERAPIST: What do you want for yourself?

MARGE: That would be everything for me. I don't like family infighting. This isn't even infighting. It's a silent war. When that burden is taken off you, it's a feeling of great relief. Now you can have one or another of your children over without the worry of who's mad at whom. I don't like being the filling in the sandwich. I really don't but I have been placed in that position by a couple of my children ...

THERAPIST: And allowed yourself to be placed in that position.

MARGE: I admit that willingly. I do not speak up for myself.

EILEEN: What precipitated this meeting is that there was going to be a surprise party for Joe. His wife, Grace, and I spoke about it. There was a complete breakdown of communication at that point. When I finally got back to Joe to tell him what was going on, and explained what was happening to Grace, Joe asked me if I would be willing to go into therapy. To be very honest with you, I don't feel like therapy is my first line of defense. I feel like you try to talk things out and if it doesn't work, you bring in a third party. I did not feel we had ever talked. Of course a few years ago there was a problem, but that was another whole issue. I do not feel like there is a silent war, as my mother put it.

THERAPIST: How would you define the relationship between you then? What has broken down?

EILEEN: As I said to Joe over the phone the other day, if I live to be 100 and you live to be 98, you are my baby brother and you always will be. And I'm really proud of where you are and I respect you and I admire you. I know I don't say that often enough. My feeling is that therapy is the way that Joe deals with problems. I'm more than willing to do that if that's going to help us in the end.

JOE: Historically, Eileen, working with you one-on-one has been very difficult. It is not that I haven't made attempts. Last Labor Day was like a sucker punch. You came up to me and told me all these things *I* did to Mom. I was mindful that two things were happening in that moment: (1) You were advocating for Mom and not for yourself and (2) we had different views about what was or was not going on. In either case it left me no context through which to address you because you walked away. And then in subsequent phone calls, you refused to address the issues.

THERAPIST: What do you mean that Eileen refused to address you?

JOE: She wouldn't return my calls. All I am saying is that if you hold that view of me, Eileen, then we are in very different camps in terms of how we do relate.

THERAPIST: Why don't you spell out your own view of how you see therapy and why?

JOE: From my standpoint, a therapeutic session is a way of catalyzing a process that has already begun. Sometimes it hasn't begun, and then people come in because they are desperate. What I am aware of too is how I've tried to protect you, Eileen, and Mom and probably others as well from what was going on with me over the years. Part of my thinking unilaterally was that this would be a safer place for you since you did not seem able to handle the one-on-one piece—particularly since all of us came into therapy 6 months after Dad died. Everyone had a good sense of where we were at the time.

EILEEN: That's funny. I thought it was safer for you. We are still protecting each other.

THERAPIST: That's an important statement, Eileen. Obviously, when people protect each other, no matter how much they love each other, they can never really be intimate. If you are protecting each other, you will never be able to say to Joe, "Sit down and hear me out." Nor will he have permission to say, "Sit down and hear me out." Protectiveness functions like a block to keep you from ever connecting. I do not know where the invitation comes from when people protect each other.

EILEEN: We were on the phone for an hour when this issue about the birthday came up. I told him my feelings, my perceptions, and my thoughts.

JOE: It is true that the connection was there. What I did not trust was that the connection wouldn't die down again and simply disappear. I did not want it to be a one-shot deal. That is what we've done as a family—go from crisis to crisis.

THERAPIST: And only a crisis might elicit the kind of connection that you and Eileen finally made. Were you able to ask Eileen, "Can I count on our continuing"?

JOE: I don't think a claim was made—directly. It may have been implied.

EILEEN: I don't think it was necessary.

JOE: That's another place that we differ. My perception of our history is that all the injuries get registered but are not usually talked about. Rarely were anybody's accomplishments acknowledged in the household.

THERAPIST: Joe, let me stop you. You keep speaking in the passive voice, and it's covering over your "I."

JOE: I could not tolerate the risk of being cut off after such an intimate connection, Eileen. And when you cut off, there is never any softness in it.

EILEEN: I know I can be that way. I am either hot or cold.

THERAPIST: Is that your defense, Eileen?

EILEEN: No. I really believe it's my personality. I don't know if it is age or attitude. It is probably selfish, but I have a lot of physical problems. It takes a lot of energy to deal with them on a daily basis. Then there is a lot of mental strain associated with part of the physical problem. Things like, Why me? How come I can not do this or that? Why can't I have a baby? I allow myself to feel sorry for me for brief periods of time.

THERAPIST: But there is a real deprivation.

EILEEN: I deal with that 24 hours a day. I have constant harassment from a government agency who employed me to prove that I do have a disability. On the other hand, I spend the rest of my life trying to deny it. So I get real self-contained. And I eliminate the stress from other areas of my life.

THERAPIST: Why would calling Joe up be a source of stress rather than a request for help? I am weary, I am discouraged, I just need a pat on the back—what gets in the way of that? Why isn't that the first option?

EILEEN: I'd be the first one to offer help if anybody needs it. But it takes a lot for me to ask for help. To ask for help in some way is to say, "I am weak," and I don't want to admit that I am weak.

JOE: I have that kind of fierce self-reliance too. We used to band together in a crisis. It was actually group survival. There wasn't really ever any room for self.

THERAPIST: Was it self-reliance or isolation and insularity?

JOE: I was suicidal when I was 25. Last year Mom asked me why I never said something. That just wasn't what we did in our family. The ethic was that you handled everything yourself. It was an implied ethic.

EILEEN: We were trying to survive.

JOE:	Survivors. That's what I realized we were. I could not keep going on that way. What I now know is that I have to consciously fight the inclination to say, "Fuck it, if they don't call me, I won't call them."
EILEEN:	The essential issue last time we fought was between you and Mom. I remember telling you not to hurt my mother. Then when you two got into therapy I felt like it was not up to me to interfere. When Mom and I argue, I argue. She says you're entitled to your opinion. There is no argument.
THERAPIST:	There is no connection either.

Part II

EILEEN:	That is what happened around the birthday party. When Grace called up and changed all my plans, Mom said, "Let's have it anyway." So just because I said Grace called, she jumped up, and is going to do this and that. I tried to make her react. I was so enraged. I said, "Two years ago you didn't even buy me a birthday present or birthday card. But oh, we're going to have a surprise party for Joe aren't we?" She looked at me. I said, "You do what you want to do."
MARGE:	(arms crossed) And then what happened after that? I called Grace, and I told her it had been called to my attention that I did nothing at birthday time for any of my children for their birthdays. I could not do it.
THERAPIST:	That was a courageous step for you to take, Marge—to try to balance the scales from your perspective once Eileen brought it to your attention. It may have seemed like favoritism. But that was to disengage. What did that do in terms of you and Eileen, for example, "I don't know how to figure this out. Why didn't I give you a birthday gift?" Or say, "In a sense we are estranged and we can't seem to connect with one another."
EILEEN:	Well, we are in a sense.
THERAPIST:	You might have said, "Can we find a way to celebrate together?" Because as old as we get what you say applies to every one of us: *How come you are giving a party to him and you forgot me?* So you get triangled in talking about Joe when there are issues that haven't been addressed between you and your mom.
EILEEN:	That is why my anger came out. It wasn't that I begrudged Joe in any way, shape, or form. I just told Grace that when she first called.
THERAPIST:	You and Grace were supposed to give the party. Was that it?

EILEEN: It was a little more involved than that. She wanted to have a party, but she couldn't make up her mind whether to have it at her house or my house. Just because I love a party, I said we'd have it at my house. We went into the details of it, it just kept mushrooming, it got to be 60 or 70 people, and then I realized I could not handle it. In the meantime, I had spoken to my two sisters and my sister-in-law to say we were having a party here. What can we all do to make this work? And especially trying to surprise Joey. That was an old challenge anyhow. His general attitude in life anyway is that he doesn't deserve a party. Birthdays suck, Christmas sucks, why bother with these things? In fact, when I did talk to him about the party and said we were going to go ahead with it, he said (and I think I'm quoting), "There are going to be a lot of people there who I've suffered with over time." I thought, fuck, is there going to be anybody there to have a good time? To me party and good time go together. Suffering and sadness go together.

THERAPIST: Eileen, Joe may not have caught up to parties and a good time.

EILEEN: Yeah, he did good at the party. I am proud of him. We went back and forth, and there was a total breakdown in communication between Grace and me. I wasn't getting my point across to her. Either she was not hearing me or I was not hearing her. Finally I said, "If you want to have a party, you have it at your house." Mom was talking to her one night and let her know that we were going to have the party at their house. I asked Mom what Grace said about it and she said, "She seems a little upset about it." I thought, why does this have to be a problem? It's supposed to be a party. Then she called me up about 10 times. With our schedules being different, I did not take the time to call her. I was getting frustrated with the whole thing. When I finally did get to her, there were going to be two parties, one at her house and one at my house. It was going to be Joey's friends and family at my house, and Joey's colleagues up at his house. Then I interpreted that as separation of church and state—the specials up there and the slummers down here. I would rather not party with these people if that was how it's going to be. This is the dumbest ass party I've ever been at. As it turned out, they were going away that particular weekend. The more I'm thinking, I think it's a good deal if you can get away with it: You're going away for a weekend, I'm watching your kids, and you're going to come waltzing in and we'll yell "Surprise!," and Grace will say to Joey, "Isn't this wonderful? Look what I did!" It came off like, "Eileen, I want to have this wonderful party, but you're going to do all the work, all the preparation, I'm going away. You are going to watch my kids, and I am going to come to a wonderful party."

It was not that I was giving a party for credit, that has never been the case. It's like, "Just hire somebody who will do the work for you." When I finally did talk to Grace about it, they had decided to have one party at their house. Again, it was a matter of taking the time to straighten it out. I do admit that when I am ready I call.

THERAPIST: There is a parallel here to Joey saying, "You can call me on my terms." There is a mirror image here if you can see it. Joe, I hear Eileen saying you rarely talk in resource terms, you talk in terms of suffering. It creates a disjuncture for her. Is it possible for you to say, "This is what's happening to me and why it is hard for me to get the phone. I'll call you in the morning or right before I go to sleep"? I know that you have to draw boundaries, but *I don't know where your invitation is.*

JOE: I guess it is a part of my family legacy: Why bother asking? You're not going to get it anyway.

MARGE: Joey, do you remember getting a birthday gift from me?

JOE: No.

MARGE: Eileen, do you ever remember getting a birthday gift from me?

EILEEN: Yeah, except for one time. You were pissed off at me. You always get me birthday gifts.

JOE: I remember two birthdays. One when I was 13. In this case Dad was drunk.

EILEEN: Ahh, I find that hard to believe.

JOE: We were in the kitchen, there was a birthday cake, a neighbor said, "This must be a big deal." I said, "Yeah," but I thought, let me get the hell out of the house.

EILEEN: It's your choice if you don't want to celebrate your birthday. But don't knock people who care about you and want to celebrate.

JOE: *That is precisely what happens.* I have a position. The whole family draws a conclusion about my position, and never comes to me to say, "It seems as if this is what you are saying." I never get tested against. On the other side of that, I'm learning to do this more. I am learning to pursue them in the present tense. I'll say, "What do you think is going on here?" I am learning to say, "I just got a cold shoulder. What are you doing here?" I'm not going to let those issues go unaddressed. I also am not going to get a migraine headache about what you think or what you feel. I'm going to ask.

Justice Dynamics and Sibling Friendships

The probability of friendship developing between sibling and sibling hinges on a variety of factors, chief among them their respective willingness to recognize and address the justice dynamics that lie between them and between each of them and their larger family context. Topics may differ, but a balance between what each sibling owes and deserves is always one issue at hand. To wit:

- Eileen can acknowledge her desperate longing to be credited rather than resorting to overgiving, to command attention, or punitive with-holding, to protect herself against further disappointment.
- Joe can emerge from an embattled defense of his father to reen-gage the siblings who cannot exonerate their father.
- Marge can exonerate her own mother whose past demands elicit Marge's current rage at her daughter Eileen. And she can find courage to disclose herself to her daughter as she could not do with her mother.
- Joe can take on his other siblings to disclose his hurt and isolation and risk the claim of asking them to pursue him.
- Grace can identify elements of her own context in Eileen's com-petitive reaction to plans for Joe's birthday party. Does she recog-nize her own unfinished family business in the virulence of her reaction to Eileen?

Whether or not they recognize them as choices, these family members can continue to collude in their disengagement from each other or they can choose to tap into the residual resources that exist among them, as well as between each of them and their parents. The therapist who can help siblings face into the complexity that characterizes brother-sister relationships, identify the triadic basis of the justice dynamics between them, and point to self-delineation as the intervention by which old injuries can be transformed into due consideration has already begun the process of catalyzing friendship between siblings.

BETWEEN FRIEND AND FRIEND IN THE THERAPY ROOM

Sex with my friend kept me from a premature divorce. But when my husband and I reconnected, my friend and I began to lose touch.

The grace of friendship may lie in the fact that it has no immediate identifiable contract, no ritualized social sanction, and no predetermined function. Unen-cumbered by past legacies and untouched by preexisting injuries, in the first instance, friendship can be a resource, a refuge, and a consolation.

On the other hand, fair give-and-take with its primary questions of what is owed and what is deserved applies to friendship as well as to family. When can I say no? When can I do things my way? Why do I always have to take the initiative? These questions reflect justice dynamics between friends as well as between family members. The justice dynamics that present themselves when friendship is long-term are more subtle and complex, and eventually develop a legacy akin to a family. "I thought we had something going here" is a clear if disappointed expression of prior investments, earned merit, and entitlement. Friends sometimes, though not often, present themselves as a unit for direct intervention in the therapy room. In any case, friends can have a profound impact on each other's lives and on each other's families in ways that influence the course of therapy.

People often feel safer with friends than with family members. "I am an entirely different person when I'm with my family" is a common lament. "I am at ease with my friends; I am guarded with my parents." "I can say anything to my friends; I expect sarcasm from my husband no matter what I do." "Other people my [adult] children's age enjoy me; but my children make duty calls." "My friends call and it is fun; my father calls and it is deadly." "My friend's parents take care of me; my own parents expect me to take care of them." The tendency to compare the merits of friends and the insufficiencies of family members constitutes a negative loyalty to family that begs consideration if fairness is to be served.

"Roommates" with an Option for Sex

People find ways to be comforted. Failing to find mutual consideration in one relationship, they seek it in another. People often turn to friendship unaware that they bring the full force of their family context with them. We usually flee frustrating family relationships without facing them, unaware of the residual trust and potential comfort that still may await them there. Hunger for connection characterizes the 1990s. So do relational chaos and the lingering illusion of the 1960s that in relationship anything goes—without consequences. Joe, 41, and Celeste, 39, are cases in point.

- Celeste presents herself as a boundaryless person. She describes herself as spacey, gullible, and an air head who is also spontaneous, creative, and artistic.
- Her life was marred by the death of her 16-year-old brother when she was 18, an event that is yet to be addressed by her and her family. She married a "real jerk" the first time around but stays in touch with him on behalf of their 11-year-old daughter. The second time she married she was intent on having fun.

- Joseph is the only son in a family of four children. In the face of an often harsh and distancing father, he learned to live within himself and came to present himself as insular and indifferent. He married late and quickly discovered that it was safer to develop a relationship with his stepdaughter than with his wife. He continued to pursue all of the activities of a single man.
- Celeste felt excluded by Joe's single-minded pursuit of his earlier interests. She never tried to address the issue of her loneliness with Joe. Instead she sought refuge in her artistic community. By definition, she put a lid on the marriage, and Joe's absence clamped it into place.
- Joe's friends were surprised that his marriage didn't constrain him and pleased that he was still available to them. Learning of Celeste's dismay, her friends advised her to cling to the status of marriage and find a lover as well.
- At one point, Joe and Celeste were examining his calendar to try to establish more time together. She noticed a woman's name written into Joe's calendar on Valentine's Day—in Joe's handwriting. Joe was unable or unwilling to explain who the woman was or how the name got there. Celeste cited the incident as another example of Joe's apparent indifference. Joe was confused about why Celeste was so upset.

Celeste was finally catapulted into therapy by an article on male invisibility. She set up a session and initially went alone. Joseph, befuddled by his wife's expectations, was relieved at her initiative and eventually came with her. In the therapy room Celeste poured out her disappointment: "He keeps everything separate. He has his money; I have mine. He has his friends; I have mine. I cook my meals; he cooks his." Joseph was reluctant to let her do anything for him, on the one hand. On the other, he earned $30,000 more than she did each year but expected her to carry an equal load. Their sex life was nonexistent: Joseph had trouble sustaining an erection, and, in any case, he was disinterested.

The therapist's early efforts included acknowledgment of past and present losses; an inquiry into how their 3-year-long arrangement before marriage worked, what initially sparked them about each other, and how Joseph imagined life would be with his ready-made family. Celeste's confusion was rooted in Joseph's double message. He wanted to maintain a single life, *and* he wanted the apparent security of a committed relationship. Joseph's confusion was rooted in the fact that whether as friend, lover, or mate, he knew nothing of what a partnership implied. Celeste and Joseph took refuge in friendship outside the marriage. The therapist's effort at this juncture was to help these partners *distinguish between what kind of friendship they wanted between them and what it was they wanted of friends.*

Flight into Friendship

> *I intended to tell him that we couldn't get married. Instead I cried. And then we got married.*

Celeste and Joseph were both clear that they didn't want to be alone. But they had few touchstones that allowed them to connect. Neither of them knew what they meant by friendship or understood what they wanted of friends. Nor had either of them defined terms or specific criteria for how to stay together. Instead they had an amorphous *sense of friendship* that allowed them to proceed. Moreover, their idealized views of friendship were paralleled by romantic views of marriage and sex. The tough work of hammering out linkages that can bridge two separate lives, and facing legacies was as far removed from their hearts and minds as it was from their parents'.

They handled their failure to know their own terms and to offer each other due consideration by fleeing into the arms of "understanding" friends. The therapist's efforts here were to do the following:

- To surface a comparison between the two married people's initial expectations of each other and their present disillusionment
- To demythologize the assumption that the structure of marriage is sufficient to maintain the forward motion of its respective partners
- To encourage them to consider their parents' marriage, what they learned from them, what they drew from how their parents lived with each other—for good and bad; and, if possible to explore with their parents directly
- To identify the invisible resources that were latent between these two partners
- To recognize that each of them was operating out of a marital contract whose terms had never been recognized, much less articulated
- To help them indicate the terms by which they were willing to live together in a common effort to renew their relationship and establish trust
- To help them balance their loyalties and investments in themselves, in each other, and in their respective friends

A segment of dialogue touches on a number of these points:

THERAPIST: Celeste, why did you marry Joseph in the first place?

CELESTE: I was looking for reliability for myself and a father for my 5-year-old.

THERAPIST: Have you ever said that to Joseph?

CELESTE: No.

THERAPIST: Has your expectation of reliability been fulfilled?

CELESTE: No, I did not get what I wanted.

THERAPIST: What have you done with your disappointment?

CELESTE: I've turned to friends, to Linda in particular. But don't get me wrong. Linda has her own baggage. I would never want to be married to her.

THERAPIST: What do you get from Linda that you're missing in your marriage?

CELESTE: She is emotionally accessible, reliable, you can talk to her.

In her continuous comparison between her partner and her friends, Celeste found marriage wanting and friendships comforting. She had entered the structure of marriage without anticipating the process of marriage. She had contracted for security as a static entity rather than as an evolving convergence of two sets of identified and negotiated terms. She had entered into a dyad with little attention given to the weight and consequences of the intergenerational legacies that each carried. She had expected fatherly involvement in her child to the exclusion of husbandly demands on her time that left her chronically split between her daughter and her mate. She had entered the early phases of marriage with an "assumed we," that is, an expectation of common agreement that would override the requirement for direct address. It comes as no surprise then that direct address was as absent from Celeste's and Joseph's friendships as it was from their marriage.

Friendships had filled a void in Celeste's and Joseph's lives. Friends provided company, direction, comfort, enjoyment, and consolation. Each of them had called friends on the spur of the moment, got together if they could, called on another friend if one of them was unavailable. To some degree their friends were interchangeable. Boundaries of time and energy gave form to their friendships and implicitly limited the scope of expectations and demands. Because they were free of the consequences of bed, bills, children, and family legacies, friendship offered them a respite from the mundane. *But with their marriage friendships became less of an oasis. Now they became a source of competitive demands.* How to choose, whom to choose, and under what circumstances to choose became pressing questions. Time, money, energy, and passion were now subject to division.

The therapist's operating premise was that friendships can be a resource to marriage and a married couple can be a resource to friends. He affirmed Joseph's and Celeste's investments in their friendships at the same time that he challenged them to identify their loyalties and priorities. He asked Joseph how long he expected to play squash and rehearse with the band without considering what he and Celeste might pursue together. He faced Celeste with her tendency to unjustly compare the satisfactions of long-term friendships with the discontent over short-term relationship with her spouse. He encouraged them to address friends with their new realities rather than triangulating friends into their marital shortcomings. He helped them face into the terror of losing their friends by limiting them. And he urged them to discover reasons why they might move toward each other at times when they preferred to be in the safety zone of their friends. All of this took place in the therapy room concurrently with their respective self-exploration, surfacing their unfaced terms for their own lives, and for marriage and parenting, sharpening their investment in the development of a viable partnership, and addressing significant events and people in their respective family contexts. The paradox here is that in the long run, much of what can be said about marriage can be said about close friendships.

- Whatever the context, people who consistently take each other for granted become ethically disengaged.
- Accumulations of unspoken injuries are inevitable in long-term relationship. So is the promise of healing when people can risk direct address.
- Over time friendship can assume a familylike quality for good and for bad, and will acquire complexity, nuances, and burdens as well as reliable presence, directness, and immediacy.
- Marriage and friendship can complement and provide balance to each other when all members of this complicated context can address rather than discuss each other.

The reality is that the marriage context can be massively overloaded and brutally lonely without the component of genuine friendship. And the context of friendship can be ephemeral, empty, and overpromising when friends compete with each other's primary loyalties rather than try to complement them.

BETWEEN MATES AND LOVERS

Mirrors of Marriage: Woody, Mia, and Us

Images of mates, lovers, and friends usually anticipate love, hope, safety, and care. The dilemma with these kinds of associations is that too often fantasy overrides reality, and leaves little room for hate, despair, danger, and indifference, which also characterize peer relating. The fact is that everyone in relationship is instructed by explicit and implicit expectations and impacted by positive and negative consequences that in the long run dictate the viability and continuity of peer relating.

Whether peer relating is shaped by tight structure and clear expectations—British royal couples, for example—or by free-floating chaos bereft of any apparent landmarks or structures—Woody Allen and Mia Farrow, for example—is secondary to each partner's part in establishing terms of commitment that can evolve through their respective courage for direct address.

Mia Farrow's in-gathering of needy children and self-vindication by overgiving, on the one hand, and Woody Allen's insistence that the platonic nature of their relationship for the past 4 years absolves him from being accountable to her and their collective brood, on the other, represent a mutual terror of intimacy and a failure of fairness based on insufficiently designated terms. The essence of the Allen–Farrow matter has little to do with the sensational aspects of incest and adoption. At base it has to do with an idealization of emotions, and a shortfall in the evolution of commitment born of a lack of will to completion. It has to do with two people's inability to decide the degree to which they want to become mates, lovers, and friends. Theirs was a willful collusion, which in some ways characterizes every relationship until each party to a relationship decides what he or she is actually choosing for.

We have met the enemy and they are Woody, Mia, and us. In a culture obsessed with the products of intimacy, we are bound together by the absence of intimacy. We are linked by a common thrust away from facing the terms of peer relating. We are joined in a voyeuristic intimacy that is titillated by the thrill and fantasy of what can never be. Marriage as an institution, for example, is a shaky proposition in a fluid society. Without children, it is a friendship at best, a temporary way stop at worst. Attempts at marriage for two people who work and have children is often a footrace for resources in which every family member may be competing with each other for time, energy, and money.

The massive if momentary reaction created by the media typifies the mythology surrounding relationships. The irony of the public outcry is that it was characterized by judgment, provoked by profound disappointment that not only had we been failed, but our personal causes had been failed as well:

- Groupies cried foul. Creative geniuses are not bound by the same rules as others.
- Feminists cried foul. One more overgiving woman who's been screwed.
- Adoption advocates cried foul. Would Woody have been more justified if the children were theirs by birth?
- Mental health advocates cried foul. "Incest" and "abuse" were the buzzwords of the day.
- Family and social theorists cried foul. Parenting figures ought to act like parents—as if there were a working definition of what a

man and woman owe their own children—much less each other's children in or out of marriage.
- Hero worshippers cried foul. When the fantasies of the rich and famous crumble, the rest of us are forced to fabricate our own.

Whether or not Allen's movie *Husbands and Wives* was partially autobiographical, it is useful as a commentary on relationship as a legal fiction, action unmindful of consequences, stagnation bereft of engagement, reactivity as a substitute for meaning, and the therapeutic setting as a person's only safe place to examine truth and trust. There wasn't a grounded person in the lot. There wasn't a word of genuine dialogue in the plot. The goals of their individual searches were never stated. Their loyalties were never refined through the ordeal of direct address. They moved between the poles of order and chaos in a desperate attempt to find meaning in relationship without benefit of anyone's intrinsic authority. Listen to the words placed in the mouths of the script's characters:

The Situation

- "Sometimes you can be a lot more alone when you're with somebody."
- "You use sex to express every emotion but love."
- "Why did you have an orgasm with Michael and not your husband?" "I didn't."
- "Somewhere along the line it slipped away. We had two separate nice experiences."
- "I never said it was all your fault."
- "I'm beginning to see why your husband got a bit crazy. You have an answer to everything."
- "I wasn't completely honest with Gabe. I didn't want to hurt him."
- "Everything about it was wrong, but that didn't deter me. My heart doesn't know from logic."
- "In that quiet way of yours, you're always there for me. You call it supportive. I have no room to breathe."
- "I didn't mean those things. I don't deserve you."
- "Do you ever hide things from me?"
- "You really trust no one, do you?"
- "They don't want to know men."
- "It's hard to keep a marriage going smoothly."
- "I have a penchant for kamikaze women."
- "I fall in love with the situation."
- "Your I.Q. is suddenly in remission."
- "I'm tired of being corrected or criticized."

- "Judy is passive–aggressive. Poor me! But she always gets what she wants."
- "You can stay together out of fear. Then you know what you become? My mother and father."
- "I'm begging to have a baby I don't even want."
- "It's been a while since she's been courted or romanced. She just ended a long marriage."
- "Sooner or later everything turns to shit."
- "We put up bigger and bigger fronts."
- "What the hell am I doing with the midlife crisis set?"
- "I didn't know what I wanted."
- "What about all the years we had together?"
- "So I did a couple of things wrong. Does it have to be irreversible?"
- "Show me a couple who doesn't have problems."
- "Sperm cry out, 'Let us out; let us out now.'"
- "He wanted himself—but as a pretty woman."
- "The only time Richard and his wife experienced simultaneous orgasm is when the judge handed them their divorce."
- "You're weeping, I'm counseling you, and suddenly you turn on me."
- "She wasn't just a passive little worshipful student."
- "I love it when someone thinks highly of Judy."
- "I was so full of hurt and rage."

The Resources

- "I went back to psychotherapy today."
- "I've discussed this with a therapist."
- "I couldn't get my feelings straight so I went to an analyst. Then he fell in love with me."
- "It's like $50,000 worth of psychotherapy dialing 911."
- "Change is what life is made of."
- "Love is like a buffer against loneliness."
- "Whatever works is the deal."
- "We're doing fine. We've learned to tolerate each other's idiosyncrasies."
- "The true test of relationship is how you weather a crisis."
- "Here's to a good marriage. Finally the best that two people can hope for."
- "Maybe the real secret in life is not to expect too much."
- "I'm out of the race at the moment. I don't want to hurt anybody. Or be hurt."
- "Can I go? Is this over?"

The real Woody and Mia may reflect everyone's ambivalence and overreach. We are never told of their joys, only of their travail. The clamor and passionate polarization around their public statements may well have to do with our illusions of intimacy as well as theirs; and with our reduction of marriage to a legal fiction as well as theirs.

One client put it this way: "I stay married because he cares for the kids; we function as a couple in a world that doesn't know what to do with singles; I don't have to have a physical relationship; I've been sick and I'm still hooked on the notion that the family will take care of you; and there's no way in which I want to be a single parent. He still kisses me good-bye. I don't kiss him good night; I don't even want his arm on me." Stunned by the unanticipated marriage of a former lover, she says, "The passion was so incredible with John. He provided the spark." Another client puts it this way: "Five years ago she wrote that she was married to a very wonderful man—me. Her house of cards fell apart when her mother died. A hole ripped open in the fabric of her existence. My humanity wasn't enough to fill it. Then all the demons rushed in."

In the beginning of the movie *Husbands and Wives*, a television commentator cites Albert Einstein's comment that God doesn't play tricks with the universe ... to which Woody mutters, "No, he just plays hide and seek." Abraham Heschel put it another way, "How embarrassing for a man to have been created in the likeness of God and to be unable to recognize him." There are still other ways of putting it:

- How awkward it is for people to claim to be in relationship and not know what they deserve, what they owe, or how to disclose themselves
- How demeaning it is to give our selves away in the lust for a secure, nonexistent world.
- How diminishing it is to blame someone else for failing us, while we stand bereft of a vision of what constitutes relational success.
- How disillusioning it is to thirst for speech-with-meaning without ever taking the risk of saying what one means.
- How useless it is to flee into illusions of intimacy as an alternative for being and doing and speaking out of the sanctity of one's own ground.

People can be friends and not lovers, lovers and not mates, mates and not friends. Some people can be all three, some people none. The determining factors have to do with the justice dynamics between partners who know the merit of their own ground and can imagine the merit of the other's. Fantasies of peer relating can never be made to do the work of fair give-and-take.

GENDER-NEUTRAL REALITIES

I call heaven and earth to be my witnesses that the Holy Spirit may indeed dwell upon heathens and Jews, upon man and woman, upon man-servant and maid-servant, depending solely upon the human deed.

—Seder Eliyahu Rabbah IX

There is neither Jew nor Greek, there is neither slave nor free, there is neither male nor female: for you are all one in Christ Jesus.

—Galatians 3:28

Dialogic psychotherapy as manifested in contextual theory draws from premises that are rooted in the very order of interhuman existence, and are embodied in the mystical layers of Judeo-Christian tradition. *Loyalty and justice dynamics are the essential ingredients of committed relationship inside and outside of biblical literature.* Conviction and merit are the stuff of loyalty and justice. In dialectic relation to each other, they are products of the human spirit ethically engaged in "the strict sacrament of dialogue" (Buber, 1965a, p. 17). From the book of Genesis to the book of Revelation, and from Jeremiah to Jesus the biblical imperative has been to do justice, to love mercy, and to proceed with a humble spirit.

What the Bible calls faith and works, contextual therapists call conviction and merit. Conviction and merit are the distillation of people's capacity to turn and address the balances of give-and-take between them—and are in no way delimited by gender, race or class, or any other manifestation of a person's particular identity. Conviction and trust are the outcome of the struggle to rework loyalty and to rebalance justice. When mates walk into therapy, a contextual therapist presumes that each person carries conviction and merit shaped by the past, skewed in the present and laden with consequences for the future. Whether conviction and merit are informed by gender differences that are biologically rooted in each partner, or by gender differences shaped by deeply held family loyalties, for example, specific gender-determined roles, is under constant scrutiny by women and men alike. What is absolutely clear, however, when a man and a woman, or a woman and a woman, or a man and a man, walk into the therapy room, is that there is no way in which to predetermine—or perhaps ever determine—a couple's capacity for fair give-and-take by nature of gender alone. Even their proclivities toward stereotypical gender expectations may say more about their contexts than about the constituent parts of what it means to be a man or a woman.

Gender differences, the subject of massive research in this era, exist and influence perceptions and interpretations in relationship. Overt aggression, isolation, territoriality, boundary setting, and protectiveness among men, on the one hand, and covert aggression, physical vulnerability, initiatives in relationship, social cohesiveness, and nest building among women, on the other, are frequently cited gender differences. But in a technological society these differences are often subterranean and blurred. A woman in a jet fighter may be able to kill as efficiently and aggressively as her male counterpart. A house husband who stays home to free his wife to pursue her career may also be protecting himself from the hellish demands of corporate life. The issue here is rooted in the reality of the particular, which tolerates no sweeping conclusions about gender, either in its most parochial interpretation or in some fictitious, androgenous norm.

It is increasingly difficult to discern which gender differences are inherent and which are a consequence of gender loyalties learned in the family context. A man looks at his daughter and son and wonders: Are they loyal to me differently from how they are loyal to my wife? Is there any part of their loyalty that has to do with the fact that she is a woman and I am a man? Or that one is a girl and the other a boy? Or do their expressions of loyalty have to do with their living experience of me as a person who is a man? Or of their mother as a person who is a woman? What about their unique integration of their mother's and father's expression of gender? In any case, from an ethical perspective gender differences may be redundant or even obsolete. While that may be true, stereotypes remain entrenched. For years women have held the stereotypical view that men cannot understand them, are evasive, distancing, and emotionally withholding. In the face of that charge, men have further mystified women sexually, objectified them and defined them as emotionally volatile. How else to contend with stagnant charges? Conversely, men have reinforced the stereotype that women are strong ... by which they typically mean loud and verbally aggressive. In the face of that charge, women tend to throw up their hands in despair and feel that one more time men have confused female vulnerability with its frustrated expression.

Descent into Hell

He worked so hard for so long for so little and had such bad luck.

—suicide victim's wife

Consider the case of Ellen, a 55-year-old woman who entered therapy weeks after Glenn, her husband, committed suicide by shotgun. She burst hungrily into the first session, frantically and speedily speaking of Glenn's goodness and her massive confusion over how he could have left her and their two adult children so utterly bereft—without a note, without a clue. Shortly before his death, Glenn and Ellen had been faced with the fact of their son's divorce, a disclosure of their minister's sexual misuse of their son when he was a child, and preparing their daughter's wedding. They were also mired in a deteriorating marriage. To the outside world, Glenn was the consummate lawyer, father, husband, and churchman. He undercharged fellow congregants for his services if he even charged at all. He was protective, compliant, and invisible to his family. He had undergone extensive surgery on his hips, which were destroyed by a crushing car accident. After suffering much pain over a long period of time, he had to have more surgery. "He began to die that day," his wife recalled. He had encouraged Ellen to have a life of her own and then was threatened by her professional success. People who defined him as laid-back overlooked the melancholy that enveloped his life. He was passive about work and seemed indifferent to money. He lived in his father's shadow, in his sister's shadow, and eventually in the shadow of his wife. He seemed kind, caring, gentle, giving, compliant, strong, reliable—always there for everyone—"except for himself and us."

On the other hand, Ellen seemed hard driving, purposeful, strict, organized, self-assured, opinionated, and frenetic in her activity. Her parents were separated when she was very young. She was sent to a convent at the age of 2, saw nothing of her father, and little of her mother. She married the fantasy of a man she thought would counteract her roots, and basically lived with a phantom for 25 years.

From the perspective of their individual characteristics, Glenn may be viewed as feminine and Ellen as masculine. But in point of fact, from the perspective of relational ethics, the primary determinants of their lives together may be more usefully grasped as gender neutral.

Mates, lovers, and friends typically operate as a dyad. In peer relationships each partner walks between constantly shifting dynamic polarities. Life happens between these poles. A choice to live on either side of them results not only in imbalance but in *situationlessness*, an imaginary context that admits of no one's reality, including one's own. These polarities exist in dialectic relationship and—held in tension—shape and define the actual terms of the contract that exists between any two people in ongoing relationship. These poles include the following:

Ideal	Reality
Seeming	Being
Promise	Action
Isolation	Inclusion
Longing	Cynicism
Passion	Duty
Love	Fairness
Hope	Despair
Pleasure	Denial
Self-service	Consideration of others

Chaos	Order
Communication	Direct Address
Presence	Problem Solving
Individual Ground	Common Ground
Convergences	Divergences
Undisclosed Ground	Self-Disclosure
Parallel Choices	Joint Decision Making
Self-Advocacy	Redemptive Sacrifice

The dual aspects of each of these polarities are gender neutral.

A Morality Play

In flight from stagnation and disappointment in their families of origin, Glenn and Ellen fell in love with their respective ideal of who a mate should be. Each of them was essentially deaf, dumb, and blind, as most young marriage partners are, to the justice dynamics that alone are the sustaining reality of long-term peer relationships (*reality and ideal*). Pleased to please, they seemed like the answer to each other's dreams. But when they began to awaken from their dreamlike state, they were no longer satisfied simply to please. Now they wanted to be. They subtly began to blame each other for getting in their respective ways. The problem before them, however, was that they didn't have a clue what it meant to be (*seeming and being*). Ellen did what she thought Glenn wanted. Glenn did what he thought Ellen wanted. Neither of them disclosed what he or she wanted, or imagined the efficacy of saying what he or she meant. Eventually family, home, church, and job were all in place but failed to stave off the disengagement between them. Their early longings turned into cynicism. Sarcasm, volatility, and punitive withdrawal became signposts of their crumbling spirits. Their longings seemed stillborn, their cynicism abortive (*longings and cynicism*).

The by-product of their cynicism was a resignation to loss. Their passion receded into duty. The religious fundamentalism that ordered their lives distorted daily existence into absolute rights and wrongs. So exclusively informed by what they thought they owed, so dismally deadened to what they might deserve, they in their every act deformed the command to love as you would be loved (Lev. 19:1). In a few short years they had distorted the injunction to do unto others as you would have them do unto you into a maxim to please others no matter how it binds you or deepens your despair. The implicit promise of *the marriage vow that joined them for better or for worse nowhere taught them that two people can best act on behalf of the other when both can act on behalf of themselves (promise and action).* When partners choose to face the deprivation, injury, and exploitation that inevitably accompany relationship and finally conclude that the capacity to redress these imbalances belongs to them and to no one else, not even to their mate, then they are truly free (John 8:32). Two people who are free to act on their own behalf are the ones who can best afford to respond to the world's demands, and even to their mate.

Self-consideration and due consideration exist in dialectic relationship to each other. To assess relational balances—and now choose for self and now choose for another—is the stuff of relational justice. The reduction of this dialectic to an answer-oriented paradigm is a kind of fundamentalism that is as stultifying as religious parochialism. Ritualized pleasing at the expense of self-knowledge inexorably leads to insufferable silence that burdens the soul and paralyzes the imagination. Isaiah's suffering servant knew his own terms and acted on them. His leverage was neither automated pleasing, blind service, nor spiritless duty but an unshakable conviction that *the redemptive sacrifice of the servant lay in direct address.*

GENDER-NEUTRAL INTERVENTIONS

Ask and it shall be given, search and you shall find, knock and the door will be opened to you.

—Matt. 7:7

The failure to attain personal freedom results in stagnant marriages. *Stagnant marriages can best be characterized by a failure of self-disclosure and a chronic propensity to assign blame.* Consider the situation of George and Kate. In Kate's context, men are always right. In George's context, men simply don't count. Both are unaware of how their childhood patterns continued to shape their adult interpretations. George presumes that Kate has never needed him. Kate presumes that George has never wanted her. The therapist presumes that the dilemma facing this couple has little to do with their goodwill and intentions. Their confusion over how to consider each other and still choose for themselves is something they had never witnessed in their families of origin.

Kate was encouraged by George's willingness to attend therapy, but fearful that he would get highly critical once it was again confirmed how bad she really is. Kate and George have been married for 24 years. With all three children away at college, more focus has been placed on their marriage. They entered therapy a year and a half before the last child left for college. Their initial desire was to have a "better relationship." Kate felt that George never really wanted her from the beginning of their marriage. She felt driven to try to please him but never seemed able to do enough. George, on the other hand, consistently rejected Kate's overgiving. A quiet, emotionally unexpressive man, George dealt with Kate and life by distancing himself emotionally. "I've been extremely passive most of my life," he reported. "I'm comfortable being in the middle." Intellectually sharp, George confided that he was "emotionally retarded."

George describes his father as a "distant" man whose own father committed suicide when George was 2 months old. He describes his mother as a woman for whom nothing was ever good enough. "She made all the decisions for me up and through the college I attended." Kate came out of a traditional family where women stayed at home to raise the children and manage the household. Her dad worked for a major company for 15 years only to leave to begin his own business. Kate remembers the shift as difficult for her. She was in ninth grade, and suddenly her father went from being a top-level executive to selling hamburgers. Twenty years later he would retire a multimillionaire. The cost to Kate, her mother, and her sister was that their husband and father, respectively, was rarely available to them.

Where George and Kate were concerned, the therapist operated from the premise that their vision of commitment and their way of relating in marriage were no different from their way of relating in all of their other relationships. The sole difference lay in the fact that they had children together. *A couple who have produced children can technically end their relationship at a specific time but are forever sealed in their partnership in the imagination and expectations of their offspring.* Kate lives through the children at everyone's expense. She extends herself to community functions and organizations. George lives through Kate, whom he expects to protect him from his social limitations. For the past 10 years, he has earned a living as an engineering executive. Before that, he worked for his father-in-law over Kate's objections. Originally, Kate's father saw George as the son he didn't have. George saw his father-in-law as a warm and accessible father. In George's family men didn't count. In Kate's family women waited on men. Kate felt directionless. "I know I beat up emotionally on George, but I don't seem to be able to stop myself," Kate confesses. A compulsive buyer of things by her own definition, Kate has resisted any suggestion from George to "get rid of this stuff." "There is no more room in the house for anything," George complains. Kate stubbornly refuses to clean out the house because "No one is going to take what is mine."

George has attended two or three sessions with Kate during her 6 years of therapy. Kate has characterized the marriage as "me trying to please George, his putting me down, my attacking him, and me blaming myself for what a rotten person I am. The more I bought, the more he complained, the more I attacked." The marriage stands on the brink of divorce. George and Kate are angry, frightened, and driving themselves into increasing isolation, all the while silently begging for deeper intimacy.

Neither George nor Kate had a life of their own, and could not imagine how to act on their own behalves. The stagnant interpretations and images from their respective childhoods; their untested assumptions throughout their marriage; and profound confusion about how to work through it all threatened to end their early attempts at therapy. George was "extremely doubtful that it would do any good." "She has been in therapy her whole life [6 years]," he argued, "and nothing has changed." Stunned to find out that unaddressed issues with his parents might have something to do with his marital disappointments, George was unsure about what he wanted for himself. His psyche's pulsating message that told him that men didn't count was now being challenged by the thought that he actually had a side of his own that deserved to be heard. He felt like a dormant volcano suddenly threatening to erupt.

Therapists, Gender and an Ethical Stance

Whether or not a therapist can take a gender-neutral stance has consequences for the quality of fairness in therapeutic interventions. Here we mean to differentiate between a therapist's limits and therapeutic focus. A therapist's particular skew born of unfinished family business may be imposed upon clients and perpetuate a distorted view of gender. On occasion, a woman will report that her male psychiatrist or psychologist has called her a bitch. In another situation, a male family therapist was physically restrained by family members from attacking a client's father who adamantly denied any part in his wife's chronic depression and his daughter's acute anorexia. Having lost his mother in a tragic accident at an early age, the therapist saw women as helpless, and men in need of protection. One woman was still grieving over what she considered the precipitous encouragement of her divorced female therapist to file for divorce. When therapists are constrained by invisible gender bias, clients suffer. When therapists are free to focus on the gender-neutral realm of the between, gender impacts but does not define.

Whatever form relationships take, therapists are obliged to help people integrate the tension that exists between the *poles of individual and common ground*, between *presence and problem solving*, between *legitimate convergences and inevitable divergences*, and between *communication and direct address*—among other polarities. *A person's eventual ability to hear each parent's distinctive voice and to address them accordingly frees the client from the two-pronged demon of idealization and vilification.* For example, in distress over how his mother is idealized by his father and stepfather alike, one 23-year-old described how chronically disappointed he is in women who are his peers. He recognized that his elders' insistence on maintaining an unrealistic view of his mother was *their* problem. But it violated him.

Male and Female Created He Them (Gen. 1:26)

The question of whether a therapist is a man or a woman is secondary to his or her capacity to embrace, affirm, and acknowledge men and woman in con-

text—and only in context. In the case of Ellen and Glenn, for example, the therapist is a woman. In the case of Kate and George, the therapist is a man. What difference does it make?

How does a woman who is a therapist address a suffering client whose husband has abandoned her by suicide and who is now deeply mistrustful of men? In the initial session Ellen is in deep mourning. She both misses her husband and stands in judgment of him. How can her life go on without him? What has he done to her, she wonders, and why? Glenn's death leaves Ellen not only bereft of a partner but once again having to pick up the pieces that lie between them—this time without being able to physically reconstruct the marriage. What are her options? And what are her goals? If Ellen comes out of the therapeutic process convinced that she was responsible for her husband's death, or embittered over the fact that her husband chose against her, what hope does she have for facing herself, or for establishing a trust-based relationship with another man? If Ellen uses the event of her husband's suicide to justify long-standing disappointments in her son, can mother and son ever speak of Glenn without withholding their truths? If Ellen can never talk to her son, how will her silence impact the grandson on whom she now dotes but who will soon grow into a man among men? And what about her brothers who have often been there for her? Do they fall into the category of untrustworthy men?

If personal and interpersonal balances of freedom and responsibility are the legitimate goals of contextual intervention, then clients are entitled to help in learning how to differentiate between what belongs to them and what belongs to others. Ellen and Glenn, by Ellen's report, had absorbed their respective families' loyalties and blindly embraced them. Ellen's family disengaged by flight; Glenn's family by denial. The notion that marriage partners could have individual ground as well as common ground was foreign to them. Problem solving was used as a surrogate for intimacy and presence. Converging preferences were seen as "Christian" and acceptable. Divergences of any kind were seen as selfish and threatening. They felt they weren't communicating. In fact, they *were* communicating their discontent born of a failure to assess themselves and address each other.

As Ellen grieved her situation, the therapist credited past and present suffering but pressed her to review the past in order to create a future.

Q.   What would happen if you were to marry again?

A.   I simply refuse to risk that chaos and pain again. It's hard to be alone. People are afraid to ask me how I am. But I work a lot. I'll make it.

Q.   But what about your part in what happened? What would you do differently if you had a chance at it again?

A.   I'd tell him that I couldn't be who he wanted me to be. Our pastor told me that I frightened Glenn by my success. I don't understand that. Glenn is the one who wanted me to go to work.

Q.   If it took place today, how would you address Glenn's part in what was happening?

A.   I would not automatically think he was right. I would ask him how come he could do for others and not for us. I would tell him that I couldn't make him better no matter how hard I tried. That really was on him.

In point of fact, Ellen was using past breakdowns and injuries to guide herself into an awareness that she was entitled to individual ground.

This process might have been skewed by a female therapist who was disengaged from her mate at the same points that Ellen and Glenn were when Glenn died. To wit, Glenn used his despair to bind Ellen to him. He wanted more of her; she was his whole life. All she had to do was be happy and he would be content. When their children were little, Ellen remembered that he was the one who was busy but made time for church and even to be with them at home. But had he and Ellen ever found *time for each other*? Before his death, Glenn presumed that his wife was too busy for him. He hadn't been able to tell her how his business had fallen off, how little money was coming in, how clients in general and church members in particular rarely paid their fees, how responsible he felt for their pastor's deleterious involvement with their son. He had never been able to spell out what was happening to him in any case. He certainly had little to say that was good about his life now. His mother seemed needy, his children distant, his profession slumping; his wife had taken refuge in her own world. He was in physical pain from repeated surgeries. What more was there to do?

How does a contextual therapist help a client take a multilateral stance in the midst of the torrential flow of guilt and resentment attached to the suicide of a mate? Ellen's volatility and grief were shaping factors in the early months of therapy. So was her fear that her daughter might commit suicide too. Was Ellen even allowed to face into the immediacy of her own suffering? To what degree was she entitled to resist the neediness of her daughter, who was in a downward spiral into her own brand of despair? Her son's desperate struggle over whether to remain in his marriage was still another factor in the therapist's decision about how to proceed in this situation. The suicide had its impact. The unimagined consequences of such a sudden and severe loss in a family's life were expressed in everyone's competing needs—to such a degree that all of them moved centrifugally rather than toward each other to try to make room for their own pain. Navigating her way through the turbulence of the family's collective chaos, and bombarded by the unremitting pressure of their longings for premature answers, the therapist offered solace as she could. More significantly, she looked for handholds in the sheer rock face of the family members' entrenched ethical disengagement. Her immediate task was *to point to the residual trust that she knew continued to undergird their connectedness*, and to catalyze the resources that lay dormant in their panic and remorse. Her subsequent task was to help Ellen and the other members of her context—inside or outside the therapy room—reassess the current balance of burdens and benefits among them:

- To hold Glenn accountable for his contributions and culpabilities even though he was dead
- To reconstruct Glenn's unfaced justice issues with his family of origin and their impact on him, Ellen, and their children
- To gauge the degree of Glenn's ethical disengagement from his mother, father, and sister as a limit on what was possible in their marriage
- To assess their choice of religious fundamentalism as a means of nurturing at a time when there seemed to be no other source of nurturing; or if there were, no one knew how to claim it
- To help Ellen address her own contributions and culpabilities as she tentatively surfaced confusion and shame over ways in which she was absent to Glenn, rebuffed him, and was enraged at him
- To help Ellen travel the distance over mountainous levels of unfaced injuries that she imposed as well as suffered
- To make Ellen aware of the stagnant quality of the marriage that she and Glenn had settled for, given their failed imagination
- To attune Ellen to her limits, to help demystify her self-image of being everything to everyone, and to entitle her to withhold when she could no longer give—by way of helping her face and reconnect with her own family of origin
- To guide Ellen toward ethical reengagement with her daughter and son, given finite resources on everybody's part

A female therapist might have entered into a power alliance with Ellen. She might have caricatured Glenn as one more emotionally inexpressive male. She might have identified Ellen as the victim of one more man used to controlling his wife. She might have played on the irony that Glenn found acclaim in his profession and community; but where had he been for his wife and his kids? Or she might have allied with Glenn over Ellen.

A male therapist may have viewed Ellen as an overly demanding wife and mother allied with her children against their father. Or seen her as playing a power game now that she had her own money and didn't need his. What was

Ellen doing with all her time anyhow? he might ask. Was her job really that demanding or was there someone else?

How does any person who is a therapist address clients, men and women alike, who are critical of their common ground and blind to their respective individual ground? Who immerse themselves in problem solving, through which they move from crisis to crisis without ever taking the time and effort to be present to each other beyond the "problem" in gentle and tender ways? Who see converging ground as "good" and potentially healing, and diverging ground as "bad" and inevitably threatening? Who communicate blame and bitterness to each other and then wonder why they are not communicating? Who time and again stop short of the risk of direct address, but feel bereft and abandoned because nobody else has the motive or courage to risk addressing them?

Clients may choose therapists by gender for a variety of reasons, including gender-based identification; compensating themselves for the losses of ethical disengagement from a mother and father; or attempting to find a "good" surrogate for a "bad" parent. A client may choose an opposite-sex therapist in a frank longing for romantic confirmation, or a same-sex therapist for anticipated safety or comfort. Conversely, therapists may be more at ease with same-sex or opposite-sex clients for all of the same reasons. What is significant here is not that the therapy room is unaffected by gender, but that gender-neutral interventions provide the means to deliver the promise of reliability and continuity between mates, lovers, and friends.

Any therapist, male or female, who proceeds along the lines of unilateral conjecture instead of multilateral testing in the matter of gender or any bias of that nature is party to distorting the reality that may exist between person and person. On the other hand, any therapist, male or female, who can be faithful to the merit side of men and women alike is establishing unshakable ethical ground for trust-based interventions.

PARENTIFICATION BETWEEN PEERS: DILEMMAS AND INTERVENTIONS

Mates and lovers inevitably enter a commitment to each other with an eye to long-term relationship. Security, continuity, and reliability are all values that are factored into mutual involvement and investment. But rarely, if ever, are two consenting adults in the early stages of relationship aware of what they are consenting to. The intensity of the early phases of relationship tend to be seductive at their core for they lead people to expect more of each other than any two people can ever hope to deliver or sustain. *The illusion that sexual passion, emotional intensity, and idealized compatibility are the basic build-*

ing blocks of long-term relationships typically results in parentification between peers. The retrogressive longing to sustain a stage of relationship that at best is only a prologue to commitment creates a mythology. This mythology may be initially viewed as romantic but turns destructive when it results in a subtle mandate to one partner to become the responsible extension of the other partner's wishes, limits, and fears. This stance produces relational stagnation but also represents ethical disengagement. This unrealistic set of expectations is further burdened by both partners' unfaced loyalties to their family of origin.

Mates and lovers usually start out with impenetrable fantasies about their future. They eventually drop into the crevices of a chaotic purgatory where the creeping tentacles of stark disappointment constrict, dispirit, and demotivate. A realistic if painful individual and mutual assessment of where they have been, where they are, and where they want to go is typically enough to forge a pathway out of situationlessness onto the high ground of relational ethics.

Relational ethics are always impeded by parentification, a term that was originally used to describe a person's maneuvering to turn a child or adult into a functional elder (see Boszormenyi-Nagy & Krasner, 1986, p. 419). *To be sure, parentification between peers has its ordinary and benign usages.* For example, two adults recognize their respective constrictions: One is embarrassed to return new purchases to a store. The other is loathe to inform creditors that payments will be late. They agree to swap tasks to lighten the burden of each other's vulnerabilities. Benign parentification allows room for each person's inhibitions and vulnerabilities, which are noted, addressed, and negotiated. On the other hand, destructive parentification between peers is characterized by chronically unspoken expectations, unacknowledged limits, and unilateral imposition, which, unfaced over time, destroy the fabric of just relating.

Purposeless Efforts

ARTHUR: She is asking to vicariously share in my life. She never describes her own.

SHARON: Initially he was like a god to me. He was everything I ever wanted in a person. I felt like a stammering idiot in his company. He seemed intimidating. I always stood back and waited on Arthur. I never forged anything for myself. Now he doesn't want to talk. It kills me. His withdrawal kills me.

ARTHUR: She has no imagination for me. She counts on our vows instead. "Till death do us part" is fine, but there are other ways of dying. There is a certain sickness about living with a dead institution. I fall silent to avoid unfulfilling discourse. I exist in her mind, but she never sees my person.

Parentification and ethical disengagement usually exist in dialectical relationship to each other. One amounts to the exploitative use of others, the other amounts to a defeated retreat from the will to face and meet. The parentifier and parentified each pay a heavy toll—the one through overdependency; the other through undue isolation; and both through unsought disengagement.

Whatever the actual issue, life of monologue invariably leads to a life of parentification: I define you as more than you are; therefore, I blame you for making me less than I am. Parentification creates double binds, and double binds lead to parentification.

- (Time) "I don't have any time for myself, but you never pursue me." *Translation:* "I can't make up my mind what I want from you, much less what I want for me."
- (Feelings) "You never tell me what you feel, but when you do it upsets me." *Translation:* "After all this time, you still don't feel like I do."
- (Friends) "We don't have any friends because of you." *Translation:* "It's hard for me to make friends, and you are not helping at all."
- (Function) "You know I want the house painted. How many times have I asked you to call the painter?" *Translation:* "I don't know how to negotiate with him, you do it better than I do."
- (Finances) "You're always spending our money." *Translation:* "I provide a handsome living for us, and never even get a pat on the back."
- (Sex) "When she wanted kids, she couldn't get enough sex." *Translation:* "I want to love her, but she may not want me."
- (Travel) "When we go on a trip, I have to make all of the plans." *Translation:* "I take the responsibility, and you take the liberty to criticize."
- (Taxes) "We always have to pay more taxes than you planned on." *Translation:* "Tax time upsets me. I wanted to put that money into savings."

In each of these instances, the speaker conveys a demand quality, personal disappointment, feelings of helplessness, and an inability to act without his or her partner's permission. Double binds preclude the possibility of reasonable solutions. Reasonable solutions between two or more people depend on the interplay of self-delineation and due consideration. Chronic failure of self-delineation and due consideration always results in parentification or its counterpart, infantilization.

Therapeutic interventions in destructive parentification emerge from a multidirectional interpretation of justice dynamics. Therapeutic methodology includes the following elements:

- The operating contract that led to parentification is surfaced and its premises examined.
- Questions are focused on the underlying sources of a client's lack of entitlement.
- Residual trust in long-term relationships is identified in an effort to help clients test options instead of presuming rejection.
- Attempts are made to help clients differentiate between current peer parentification and entrenched patterns of past parentification stemming from families of origin (revolving slate).
- The existential relief that comes of knowing and disclosing one's terms to a parentified other is underscored.
- The burdens and benefits of relationship are examined and the balances of give-and-take reconsidered.
- Dialogic alternatives are explored.

Destructive parentification has innumerable forms and manifestations, which can yield to innumerable interventions.

The Corporate Wife

Her job excites her the way I never can.

Most people enter a long-term relationship with the immediate goal of pleasuring and being pleasured. Michelle and Marilyn are a case in point. Together for 11 years now, they each came out of a marriage that ended in divorce. Michelle has two young-adult children who live away from home. Six years ago she agreed to raise an adopted child with Marilyn. They sought an alternative life-style for complex reasons of their own. Foremost among them was the wish to simplify life, reduce stress, and optimize personal freedom. What each of them bumped into were parentifying inclinations and structures, which they then spent years in therapy trying to undo.

At first these two women seemed essentially compatible. They held many things in common—among them age, interests, friends, sexual attraction, religious affiliation, and a concern for social justice. They were affectionate, fun loving, and invested in each other's family of origin. Over time their initial attraction began to wane under the strain of disappointments. The intensity of their arguments seemed disproportionate to the apparent causes. Like any couple, they tended to buckle under the weight of everyday traumas. They were also buckling under the weight of stagnant relating. Earlier therapeutic work had ended prematurely. Their therapist had been confounded by the ongoing intensity of their arguments. Her therapeutic orientation stopped short of the complexities of legacy issues and colliding entitlements rooted in family loyalty systems. Their new focus altered their therapeutic course by challenging the illusion that better communication and a dyadic analysis of their transactions would be sufficient to undo their adversarial stance. The degree to which Michelle and Marilyn were parentified in their family of origin provided a direct parallel to the degree to which they parentified each other.

Their hunger to make things right obscured overt resistance to the therapeutic process. On the other hand, they were stuck and they knew it. They were also fed up with what they knew: Their arguments led them nowhere, their 4-year-old successfully managed to split them, Marilyn usually wanted more intimacy than she got, and Michelle was desperate for more space in the relationship. She had already raised two children. She was invested in Kerry, their adopted daughter, but she was not enthralled as was Marilyn by the joys of being a parent for the first time. In fact, Michelle liked her work but parentified its demands. She also drew from the structural predictability of the workplace. Their terror of direct address had led these partners to a bifurcated stance. On the one hand, they were clear about what they no longer wanted. On the other hand, they lived in monologic misery. The injured trust brought into the relationship by each of them and the breaches of trust that continued to occur between them had dulled their capacity to imagine the merit of their own terms, let alone each other's.

Logically then, peer parentification became the drug of choice. If Marilyn prefers to operate close to home, why isn't Michelle free to spend more time at work? If Michelle is put off when Marilyn wants to hold her, why would Marilyn want to continue to try to make love? If Michelle is turned on by challenges and excitement in the workplace, is there room or desire for homelife or a mate? If Marilyn's emotional world relies on getting more than Michelle will give her, are her hopes illusory and has the relationship ground to a permanent halt? If, if fact, Michelle does make her share of investments in the family, can Marilyn rework the demand quality of her requests and give Michelle room to pursue her? If Michelle has learned that it is dangerous to take initiatives because what she offers is never enough, can she hold the tension of still risking and being able to say no? Or is Marilyn the proverbial corporate wife—always to be defined by the overloaded, never-ending tasks of a mate who is the proverbial corporate executive?

The relationship between Michelle and Marilyn was a study in ethical disengagement. The equal and opposite patterns through which these people chose to live out their lives presented the therapist with the immediate task of pressing beyond individual and transactional interpretations.

Cross Parentification

Couple work in contextual theory is insufficiently explored for some justifiable reasons: Words like "couple" and "marriage" are self-limiting; they are structural terms that indicate the form but never the substance of an identifiable contract that two people enter by commission or omission. A couple per se can try to fill the gap in each person's ledgers and unfaced legacy issues. They can cling to each other to protect themselves against unfair treatment from a hostilely perceived larger world. They can turn to each other for compensation for felt losses from earlier days.

But couple as context is no substitute for a three-generational context, which alone allows for a thorough assessment of justice dynamics with their potential for healing through meeting—in marriage as well as in other long-term relationships. A therapist's capacity to elicit multiindividual truths can lead to a trust base that may catalyze people's ability to face each other and in the process develop the capacity to do the following:

- Reengage apparently estranged family members
- Shift the burdens and benefits among them—even if only one family member recognizes a skew
- Establish and identify the existence of residual resources among them
- Indicate entitlements already earned as well as indebtedness that remains outstanding

If healing through meeting cannot be attempted between the generations through sustained efforts at direct address, prospects for healing through meeting between peers of significance are likely to remain elusive and dim.

Peer parentification is often overlooked in the therapeutic process. If two partners are very verbal and speak with apparent authority to and of each other, a therapist may easily confuse peer parentification with direct address. The complex elements of the parentifying process can always be traced through following the protocol of a multiindividual paradigm. This protocol includes the following elements:

- Crediting each person's suffering
- Eliciting each person's grounds and terms
- Identifying points of breakdown and mutual overexpectations
- Exploring points of ethical disengagement in other relationships
- Acknowledging parallel points of ethical disengagement in the current relationship
- Identifying long-term patterns of sustained parentification between self and parents, siblings, friends, colleagues, and supervisors

Making functional elders of the world can be the result of chronic indebtedness and depletion. It is also the cause of chronic disappointment, resentment, and stagnant relating.

A therapist's interventions in the deparentifying process begin with addressing fundamental causes of relational disruption.

Marilyn feels abandoned by Michelle's constant inaccessibility and apparent intransigence on the issue.

Q.   To what degree is Michelle's inaccessibility justifiable?

Q.   Can Marilyn legitimately insist that Michelle modify her inaccessibility without prior consideration of the aggressive style of her own demands?

Q.   Can Marilyn assess the overburdened nature of her relationship with Michelle and find her way out into a broader world of relationships?

Q.   To what degree is Marilyn's longing for another child a reasonable and valid desire? To what degree is it a defeated resolution linked to unrequited love from her mate?

Q.   To what degree does Marilyn's disappointment in Michelle's lack of accessibility fly in the face of her experience with an available father who was also a corporate executive?

Q.   Is Marilyn's unfaced loyalty to an image of the former availability of her now deceased mother a factor in shaping her current overexpectations or undue demand that Michelle be more readily available?

Marilyn has clearly parentified Michelle by assuming (1) that Michelle can alter the course of her time demands outside the home; (2) that Michelle could comply more readily with Marilyn's ideal of how a family should interact; and (3) that she is a victim of gross negligence on Michelle's part without any realistic view of how she is "victimizing" Michelle.

The deparentifying process itself involves intense dialogue between Marilyn and Michelle in an effort to have each of them take responsibility for her part in this particular breakdown. When, for example, the therapist asks where Marilyn got the idea that what she says needs to be fully complied with, Michelle pointed to Marilyn's older sister, born with congenital defects. Marilyn agreed but took the question one step further. She noted with some surprise that her mother, typically passive, acted in a similar way. "My mother was always surrounded by her five little chicks. She was caring and gentle but she expected us to do what she wanted."

Michelle feels crowded by the demanding character of Marilyn's continually expressed needs. She wants more time to herself and more room to pursue Marilyn on her own terms.

Q.   To what degree is Marilyn's sense of being abandoned justifiable?

Q.   Can Michelle legitimately insist that Marilyn ask less of her without considering the withholding and self-protective style that she uses to defend herself?

Q.   Can Michelle assess the unreasonable burdens of her workplace, and find her way into the more intimate world of family relationships?

Q.   To what degree is Michelle's resistance to raising another child a reasonable and valid position? Or is the issue of another child surfacing Michelle's unfaced disappointment in the overburdened quality of life that her commitments have imposed?

Q.   To what degree is Michelle's chronic withholding a defense learned at the knee of parents who early on expected her to be an uncomplaining but responsive daughter?

Q.   Does Marilyn's failure to sufficiently credit Michelle's real contributions to their family context trigger Michelle's resentment at the imbalance between what her parents required of her by comparison with how little seemed required of her brother?

The subtle and not-so-subtle patterns of peer parentification obscure the justice dynamics between partners and their respective legacies. They serve to defer the possibility of direct address and in the process short-circuit trust building between mates and lovers and their families of generation. They intrude, impose, and limit the vital association born of mutuality among peers. Spontaneity, enthusiasm, and excitement in long-term relationships slip away under the hammer blows of chronic parentification.

The Resource Side of Infidelity

The excitement comes not so much from the physical act but from a feeling of intimacy, of being received.

—55-year-old corporate executive

At base the term "infidelity" may best be understood as an act or series of acts that abrogate a contract previously established by two consenting parties. It may also be understood as the logical conclusion of one person's impulse to find comfort and consolation outside of the boundaries of what is expected and approved of by mate, family members, friends, church, and society. This search for consolation is usually accompanied by one marriage partner's muted awareness of or earned indifference to its consequences or impact on the other partner's life. Rubbed raw long enough, people stop caring and can justify their disengagement. Marriage partners rarely know the person whom they have chosen to marry, much less grasp the terms of the contract into which they are entering. Most marriages find premature closure—either dynamically or legally—because of the absence of self-delineation and the presence of overexpectations on each partner's part. By the time sexual infidelity becomes a reality, marital infidelity has become an accomplished fact, and personal infidelity (knowing and acting according to one's own terms) has become a stagnant way.

Sexual infidelity has a variety of functions:

- It can be an expression of a revolving slate: punishing one's partner for unfinished business between members of one's family of origin.
- It can be a demand that someone else, anyone else, take charge of one's own helplessness or happiness.
- It can be a flight into fantasy or an effort to sustain the fantasy of marriage by compensating for its shortfalls without undoing its intrinsic structural or dynamic fabric.
- It can be a vehicle for testing new parameters of safety, security, excitement, and intimacy.

In any case, whether or not sexual infidelity is a human and interhuman resource is fully dependent on whether or not a person can turn and face his or her own context, and consider the weightiness of his or her decision *regardless of legal outcome.*

The promise of partnership represents two people's choice and willingness to try to build a life in common over a prolonged period of time. Structurally, they throw their lot in with each other, allegedly for better and for worse. Dynamically, they bring their respective expectations, which, untested, they presume to be mutual. Sooner or later they face inevitable disappointments and setbacks, and, more significantly, *they set aside no time to invest in themselves or in each other.* Paradoxically, people balk at the notion of scheduling time for intimacy. Jobs, duties, children, parents, siblings, and friends can all be unwitting divergences or accomplices to ethical disengagements between partners.

It may be that no other social institution is so heavily assaulted, carries such massive expectations, and receives so little day-to-day attention as marriage. It comes as no surprise then that so many people under so many circumstances seek comfort and hope in the illusory shelter of infidelity. In one person's words, "I just wanted a buddy. Instead I had a whole series of affairs."

- "They served a need in me. False intimacy was better than none at all. I misled my lovers into thinking that they were individually significant to me. In the end I discovered I was violating the real me."
- "In these relations I found pleasure in being sought after; I found hope in being received; I found consolation in physical closeness; I found relief in not being blamed. In the end I found little substance. What is more, whatever solace I was offered was offset by an equal if opposite sense of chaos and despair. I did not want to live a life of deceit."

Too often "infidelity" is a static word used to describe a dynamic reality. It implies disloyalty and is often used to label the fallenness of one person whose sexual transgressions have resulted in a "deliberate" betrayal of another. From a justice perspective, however, the term is meaningless outside of context. For left to itself, the use of the word not only imposes one person's truth upon another but results in a further deterioration of trust.

Rarely if ever do people have an affair for the sole purpose of sex. Overt motives—for example, unexpected flattery, fear of aging, or use of sexual exploits to bolster self-assurance— are typically secondary to other more powerful agents. Among them are existential vulnerability; the dulling quality of ordinary life; and confused and conflicting cultural, social, and religious prescriptions that cultivate male and female imagery. Even more powerful agents include the failure to grasp one's own terms, let alone another's; unexamined intergenerational mandates; and a longing to reclaim what might never have been. In point of fact, people may be less threatened by the occurrence of sexual infidelity by a mate than by more subtle factors, such as the following:

- An immediate sense of insufficiency
- An impending loss of companionship
- Impending bereavement
- The loss of context
- Betrayal of an initial contract
- Unsolicited exposure of the fantasies that undergird a prior contract
  —That the original contract was once and for all
  —That one person can be all sufficient in another person's world
  —That the rate of growth in partners is parallel in time and degree
  —That a structured commitment confers protection from each other and the world

A partner's announcement or discovery of a sexual liaison typically has the force of a lightening bolt and paradoxically serves to obscure long-standing issues of injustice, which are not only motivational but often more significant and profound. For example:

Tony, 26, close to hysteria, calls the therapist. He has been sexually involved with a woman outside his marriage. The woman's husband has just telephoned Tracy, Tony's wife of 8 years. Years earlier Tony had been a part of his parents' efforts at therapy. At that time, he had left home to join the Navy. "Eleven years ago, when I was 15, your last words to me," he reminded the therapist, "were that one of these days I would have to face my parents in order to find my way and to sustain a relationship with a woman. Well, here I am and everything is in shatters. On the surface of things I have a wonderful wife, two fine little kids, a good job. I'm finishing college and we live in a nice house. Now this," he cried. "Tracy wants to know why I did it. I don't know why; I don't know why!"

The couple comes into a therapy session. Tony is crying; Tracy is distraught. "I could understand it," she said, "if it happened early in our marriage. But why now? When we first got married I got involved with another guy, and I could understand his getting back at me for that. But this started 3 months ago. I was pregnant with the baby. Everything seemed to be fine. Why now? What did I do wrong?"

"It is hard to know where this stuff belongs," the therapist replied. "What else is happening in your life?"

"My mother and I are still at war," Tony replied. "But Tracy and she are best friends." "I can say almost anything to his mother," Tracy added, "and she will listen. My own mother either doesn't want to hear or she will repeat anything I say to everyone in sight." Tony and Tracy have little contact outside of Tony's family. Tony works at home. Tracy has just quit her job to attend to their two little kids. A depleted, parentified child, Tracy has cut herself off from her entire family. On the other hand, Tony's parents babysit. They want Tony and Tracy to join their church. They pay for Tony's education. And they offered to pay for the young couple's housing if Tony and Tracy were willing to move in from out of state where Tracy's parents lived.

The night before the couple came to therapy, Tony told his parents what was going on without consulting Tracy. His father offered to come to therapy if that would help. His mother turned on Tracy: "You have no right to leave Tony now," she admonished, "after all we've done for you."

"Tony's always so mean to me," Tracy cried. "He's never hit me but he's always mad. He verbally abuses our 5-year-old daughter, and now he's started on our 3-month-old son. He is even mean to his two little nieces." "Yes," Tony wept. "That is how I am and I don't know how to stop." He pointed to his parents' file, which the therapist held in his hands. "What is written in that folder probably holds the answer to my life."

From the outset, the therapist was faced with two distinct if unequal dilemmas: Tony's affair, with its short-term havoc, and the massive, minimally three-generational injustices that were now converging in this young couple's lives. *Paradoxically, Tony's affair was functioning as a resource.*

- It represented a cry for help.
- It surfaced the extreme degree of his ethical disengagement from the people who mattered to him most, especially his two children.
- It alerted him to what he already sensed—that he was again sucked into the chaotic vortex that he had tried to escape when he was young.
- It revealed the negative consequences of crossed loyalties:
  —Tracy used Tony's parents as a substitute for her own. But they were Tony's parents.
  —Tony used Tracy as a buffer from his mother but then suffered from his mother's apparent preference for his wife.
  —An element of intimacy appears to exist between Tracy and Tony's mother that eludes and bypasses Tony with either his mother or wife.
  —The material contributions made by Tony's father toward the young couple's upkeep induced shame and rage in Tony, and underscored the already apparent insufficiencies that Tracy ascribed to her parents.
  —Tracy's parents became ancillary to their daughter by virtue of (a) their preoccupation with their younger children, who had earlier been in Tracy's constant care and (b) their inability to compete for Tracy's love with Tony's family, who outstripped them in money, status, and class.
- It disclosed the adequacy of the couple's sexual function and the affairs irrelevancy to the justice issues of truth and trust that, unaddressed, left Tony hostile and Tracy confused in the bright light of day.
- Sex was purely a physical release for Tony but in no way confirmed his uniqueness or merit.
- Sex temporarily accessed Tony for Tracy but failed to sustain intimacy.
- Tony moved to protect his vulnerability after sex in anticipation of the inevitable loss of his partner to her preoccupation with his parents and their kids.
- Tracy moved to extend the momentary intimacy of sex with Tony by sheer dint of longing. She was befuddled when lovemaking drove him away rather than drew him to her.

What seems evident here is that like any other significant act sexual infidelity can be as much a resource as a liability. Sexual infidelity can be a resource when it is an effort at responsibility, however irresponsible the act may initially seem. Sexual infidelity can become a resource when it surfaces unfair and stagnant balances of give-and-take—real or perceived—that rob relationships of *any vestige* of promise or hope. Sexual infidelity can become a resource when it offers an oasis of temporary nurture and relief in an unremittingly barren and destructive landscape that seeks resolution through violence and despair. Sexual infidelity can be an expression of invisible loyalties in which it is safer to "act out" than to force people to face each other with the hard truths of their respective stances. As such, it may be a resource that invites loved ones to face the injustices that estrange them. In the long run, sexual infidelity may function to forestall a premature termination of a committed relationship.

It is striking to note the degree to which sex outside of marriage can force partners to reassess their reality, reconsider what they owe and deserve, who they are, and what images they want to convey to the next generation. There are as many variations of "sexual" infidelity are there are variations of marriage.

- Same-sex relationships that can be construed as protecting the dignity of one's marital partner
- Long-term liaisons that sometimes span the gap between partners who are widely disparate in age
- Affairs that dynamically become marriages in terms of long-term give-and-take and marriages that become affairs in which each person is prostituting himself or herself in order to maintain the semblance of a marital relationship.

Whatever its purpose, sexual infidelity can be a trap as well as a resource. It can distort, defer, and evade the basic issues of commitment. People can use infidelity for purposes of comparison, humiliation, and self-exoneration. Whether infidelity is eventually seen as a resource or a trap heavily depends on the willingness of each partner to harness rage and disappointments long enough to explore what at base the occurrence really means.

7

Truth and Trust After Divorce: Dialogic Interventions

with Janet I. Filing, Ph.D.[*]

What are the clinical leverages to help family members tap resources after divorce—if estrangement, polarization, and mistrust were facts of life before divorce?

Divorce is a journey ended and a journey begun. It has a legal end point. But in its aftermath there are dynamic consequences that impact people for good and for bad. These consequences are multilateral, inter-generational, and transgenerational. The connections between father, mother, and child are elemental and irreducible and are no less so after the event of divorce. This chapter is based on the therapeutic conviction that each member of an elemental triad stands to gain from a willingness to face each other member in the wake of divorce. It means to demonstrate clinical strategies, leverages, and interventions that underscore the binding and compelling nature of ontic attachments.

EX–HUSBAND AND WIFE

I feel a sense of relief and groundedness when I can say to our children, "Your father and I have talked."

—parent 16 years after divorce

Divorce is a product of failed expectations and tragic stagnation. When people who have no children divorce, they may or may not remain emotionally connected to members of each other's families. *When people who have children, divorce they may or may not be emotionally connected, but they are always ethically bound.* It can be argued that in the justice of the human order, people

---

[*]Janet I. Filing, Ph.D. is a contextual psychotherapist and teacher at the Center of Contextual Therapy and Allied Studies. She is co-primary investigator and clinical supervisor of the Women's Study for cocaine addicted women at the Medical Center of the University of Pennsylvania Treatment Research Center.

who are parents are informed by a law of nature and by a law of human beings: Parent and child are bound by biology and care, if not by intent. Given this reality, all clinicians who face the fallout of divorce in the therapy room are forced to grapple with the implications of ontic connections. Do they move toward unilateral alliances or toward multilateral siding? Do they join their clients in condemning the former partner or help clients test the difference between common grief and conflicting claims? Do they move prematurely to solve logistical problems or can they link problem solving to the greater healing force of vital reengagement?

Clinicians are tempted to side with children against their parents. Clinicians are tempted to label one parent good and one parent bad and to try to be an even better parent. Clinicians are predisposed to identify problems and look for solutions rather than to stretch their client's imagination for how to honor connections that still exist.

In any case, contextual clinicians are obliged to identify resources that make it possible for people to face each other even when they prefer to flee and blame. After divorce, when separate lives, separate housing, warring factions, and new relationships assert themselves, clinicians are bound to point to resources when everyone else concerned is pointing to futility. The aftermath of divorce is as varied as the aftermath of marriage. Clinicians can choose to underscore pathology or prod people toward healing through meeting.

Take the case of the Kent family. Sixteen years ago Jean left Rob and sued for divorce. They were 34-years-old, and their children, Carl and Jim, were 8 and 5 at the time. Their marriage was stagnant, their imagination for change limited, and each had a legacy of parents for whom distancing was expected to do the work of relating. During the divorce passions ran high, for Jean was in love with a longtime friend. The couple sought out a therapist with mixed intent. In retrospect, Jean may have bolted too quickly, and Rob may have fled into resignation. Over the years the couple was emotionally estranged. Jean remarried and was overwhelmed by the disruption in her new husband's unfaced context. Rob married later, divorced, and married again. The children were forced to make sense of their loyalties and family ties, which had now catapulted them into at least three different directions: their family of origin and two new families engaged by virtue of each parent's new relationships. There were new stepparents, new stepgrandparents, new stepsiblings, and new stepaunts and stepuncles. They were suddenly engulfed by the sheer sweep of numbers. Rob and Jean set up households only two blocks apart. They worked hard to shield their sons from the trauma of divorce. But Jimmy had recurrent dreams about living in one house with two separate doors. That way he could have immediate access to both of his parents.

Over time Rob and Jean brought their children into therapy. They worked hard and long with genuine success in the following areas:

- Jean and Rob became friends.
- Their sons were relieved of the burden of being caught between their parents.
- Rob and Jean were able to become a parenting team that made room for colliding claims between them and between their sons and them.
- The children maintained contact with their maternal and paternal families.
- The children were able to sustain their ontic connections and were freed to develop new ones.
- Rob and Jean helped their sons find ways to relate to their respective grandparents.
- The boys were able to develop discrete relationships with each of their parents.
- The parents helped their sons address the added burden of divorce on their sibling relationship.
- Carl became a resource to Jim, almost a surrogate father.
- Jim eventually became a resource for Carl by virtue of his willingness to test new options in life.

How did they get there? How was this different from what would have been if Jean and Rob had stayed married? How was this different from what might have been if Rob and Jean had refused to address each other? What were the therapeutic interventions that not only helped these people stay afloat in the maelstrom of emotions that surrounded them, but also impelled them to strike out toward the safety and freedom of the nearest ethical shore? Nowhere are the questions of what is owed and what is deserved more sorely tested than in the aftermath of marriage and divorce.

It can be argued that divorce is like marriage, only more so; that in the long run all of the same basic circumstances of a given context exist after divorce as existed before it—and more. If people enter into marriage blind to their own ground and confident in the illusion that someone will provide it for them, they usually leave marriage in the same way.

Whatever else divorce portends, it always represents a ruptured contract, whose invisible terms were probably never understood in the first place. The mandate of a contextual therapist faced with the consequences of divorce then is to help people sift through the wreckage of each former partner's entire context: the divorce process itself, failed attempts to make the previous marriage work, grieving children, threatened family members, pulled and indecisive friends, and the groundlessness of two individuals impaled on blame and propelled by reactivity. In the case of the Kent family, the therapeutic mandate was driven in five differing but connected directions, which in every respect informed the truths and deepened the trust base of the Kent children and their children yet unborn. These directions involved (1) former partners, (2) former partners and their children, (3) former partners and their elderly parents, (4) former partners and their siblings, and (5) current partners and their stepchildren.

Initial Efforts at Trust Building after Divorce

After 5 years of upheaval in and out of the therapy, Jean decided that she no longer wanted to continue her relationship with Rob. It seemed to be her decision, but Rob later was to say that he too wanted to end the marriage. He wanted to try new career options without having to answer to Jean about the extended travel his job required. He wanted to expand his contacts with other women and no longer needed the cover of marriage to do so. He wanted the freedom to visit his family of origin without feeling caught between his father and wife. For her part, Jean wanted to be alone because to be with a partner meant either to be parentified or to be blamed for doing things her own way. In the divorce process, Rob and Jean chose to see the same lawyer at the suggestion of their therapist. By choosing for a lawyer in common instead of two competing lawyers who might overstate their differences, the couple hoped to save money, energy, and the unnecessary adversariness that often characterizes legal interventions. At no time, however, did they turn to their family connections. Their therapist's stance was to use *himself* as a resource to the exclusion of family resources. Only when Rob and Jean had clearly decided for divorce did the therapist suggest that Jean bring her mother and sister into the therapy room to help break the blow of the decision. In fact, Jean's mother, Susan, used the meeting to blame the therapist and Jean's best friend for leading her in the wrong direction.

Among decisions facing them now was *how to tell their children*, who in fact already knew. Jean had moved into little Jim's room, Jim had moved back in with his older brother, Carl, and Rob had stayed alone in the bedroom that had once belonged to Jean and him. Jean, who had never had her own room before, put a lock on the door to assure herself that she finally had a place all her own. The children noticed and wanted to know why. Other decisions that had to be made were, which of them was to move out? Where? When? And at whose expense? Which school district would the children attend? All the way along Jean and Rob carried second thoughts, resistance to the path they had chosen, and excitement about what they had decided to do. They also carried the weight of their friends' insecurities and judgments. In point of fact, they were largely cut off from their context and were very much alone. Nevertheless, Jean saw the option of divorce as a new lease on life. Rob saw divorce as more of the same—Jean doing things her own way.

Jean, Rob, and the boys remained in constant contact. Initially, the children rotated parents every week and after 3 years stayed with each parent bimonthly. Rob moved close by and Jean found herself objecting. Her new partner, Tim, felt pressured by Rob's proximity; and Jean herself felt burdened every time she walked by the house of Rob and his new wife. She also felt safe. He represented continuity—but this time on Jean's terms.

Jean continued in therapy and involved Tim in the therapeutic process— and life went on. She had massive struggles around whether to remarry, stood by Tim as he ended his marriage, and eventually decided to make a life with Tim, fully knowing how much she still didn't grasp about what she was deciding. Ten years later Jean found herself stuck, in pain, and repeating old patterns, and decided that this time something different had to be. More self assured than she had been 10 years earlier, Jean began to reassess her life—this time from the perspective of her relationship to her family of origin rather than from the perspective of what she owed or could expect from her mate. From the time that her father died 2 years before her divorce, she had been without a radical advocate. The suddenness of his death at 62 had not only encompassed her in grief but ended the illusion of security that had rotated around her father's axis. Now Jean was faced with Jim, now 15, who still cried when he left his mother's home to visit his father. Carl, now 18, and ending his senior year of high school, was puzzled, if not enraged, about why his brother's pain was being heard when he had been expected to make do with his. "Everybody is in pain, Carl," his mother used to say. After 6 years of marriage, Tim seemed giving and generous to Jean and had now replaced Jean's father as a surrogate source of meaning. After 6 years of divorce, Jean was acting as mediator between her former husband and their sons. Rob was unsuccessfully trying to incorporate Carl and Jim into a relationship with his wife of 6 years. Jean's younger sister, Bea, continued to mourn the loss of Rob as her brother-in-law; she seemed loyal to him and distant from Jean, who in any case had kept Bea at arm's length. Jean's mother had maintained a staunch if blind loyalty to her daughter, a one-sided advocacy that seemed to have more to do with propriety than the realities of her daughter's life. Jean used silence to cut off any relationship with her former in-laws, who were also passing acquaintances of her parents. They responded in kind.

It was under these circumstances that Jean returned to therapy, this time with a contextual therapist who was more focused on ethical reengagement than on individual feelings. From the start, the therapist recognized Jean's isolation from almost everyone she held dear as well as the family legacy that mandated Jean to make it on her own. Initially Jean was disoriented by the fact that the therapist was saying what Jean already knew: that she needed to address the sources of her isolation rather than collude with them. Jean's life and context were more accessible to the therapist through Jean's work than through her self-awareness. Her job was to encourage disenfranchised teenage women to get their GEDs (general equivalency diploma) in order to find a job and remove themselves from the welfare rolls. Although Jean was bound by loyalties that constrained her from ever asking anyone for help for herself, her success on her job was to a great extent dependent on these youngsters seeking help from their family members. She was doing something right in her job, but she didn't know what right meant. In danger of being grounded in her personal life for everyone but herself, she knew she was doing something wrong but she didn't know what wrong meant. Her analysis of what was happening to youngsters in her charge confused her. Overburdened, she knew she could not provide for others what she had no way of getting for herself. So she directed her charges to test the available resources in their lives no matter how estranged they might feel, and in the main they were received. Why then, she wondered, was she without a place to be received?

Jean's therapeutic journey was divided into four parts. In essence and without conscious intent, Jean had removed herself from each and every member of her context in the name of self-protection. Her contact with Rob was essentially functional rather than ethical. Her contact with her mother was not even functional. It was pseudomutual. Her contact with her sister was functional at best, and completely disengaged at worst. And her contact with her in-laws ended well before her divorce began. She was tired of overfunctioning, though she had never done anything else. She knew that she wanted help but was cynical over claiming help from anyone in her family. On the other hand, what she wanted for her boys was a trustworthy relationship with her, with each other, with their father, with their respective grandparents, and with their cousins, uncles, and aunts. What is the bridge between cynical, overfunctioning self-isolation and the ethical imagination that finally frees a person to get a grip on his or her own stance—without having to wipe out those who have an opposing stance?

The therapist knew that Jean's therapeutic journey had at least six self-evident directions:

- Jean's ongoing judgment and rage were consuming her energies and searing the children. *She deserved to become a priority in her own life.*
- Rob had not yet yielded the illusion that Jean could do it all, even after divorce. *He deserved to be heard; but in order to be heard he had to decide what his terms were and say them.*
- Carl and Jim had to keep proving that they were okay to everyone in order to justify their parents' divorce. *They deserved relief from that burden; they were entitled to act more like the adolescents they were than like the mature adults that everyone expected them to be.*
- Jean's and Rob's respective parents were in various forms of relational disarray: guilt for having failed their children, anger at their children's having failed them, and panicky overinvestment in their grandchildren's well-being. *They deserved to be credited for*

> *their own pain and travail, to be engaged with their adult children as peers in a struggle in common, and to be precious resources to their grandchildren.*
> - Jean's and Rob's siblings were taking sides along loyalty lines. *They deserved to be credited for their loyalties and addressed as potential peers and resources.*
> - Tim encouraged Jean to pursue her goals vis-à-vis her former mate and their context. He was also confounded by her intensity and persistence. *He deserved to make his own terms known to Jean, however oppositional. He also deserved the option to engage members of his own context rather than overinvesting in his new marriage to Jean.*

The paradox here is that Jean's decision to ethically reengage with members of her context put her into an overfunctioning position yet one more time. The difference here lay in the intent of her interventions: (1) They were made on her own behalf and (2) they made a claim for other people's full participation.

Distributing the Therapeutic Burden

The therapist too was threatened with overfunctioning. Over a long period of time, she was engaged with people, their biases, and their passions. She recognized the merit in each of their sides, their high degree of motivation, and their will to make sense of their estrangement and injuries. Her temptation was to advocate for vulnerable children against struggling parents. The reality was that the merit of each member of this three-generational context deserved to be credited. Even more, merit that existed in every family member and between them was to guide the course and outcome of the therapy. The residual trust that typically lies dormant between grandparent, parent, and child remains the bedrock of therapeutic interventions and strategies—whether the context belongs to disenfranchised teenage girls struggling to find resources to earn their GEDs or to highly educated, materially comfortable, and strongly motivated divorced middle-class parents struggling to find toeholds on the future for themselves and their posterity.

The following dialogue from four therapy sessions is meant to demonstrate the therapist's address of the justice dynamics that are always and everywhere linked to the primal fact of ontic connectedness. The dialogic material represents summary exchanges among family members that span 10 years of life, testing, and various forms of therapy. In preparation for a summary review of their years' long attempt at relational justice, these former spouses met to test the level of trust between them. In their preliminary session, Rob, Jean, and the therapist probed areas that remained raw and unaddressed. Questions rather than answers evolved out of their effort:

- How did I translate my experience of my parents into my marriage?
- Who was I to my father and mother?
  —What did they expect of me?
  —What did I expect of them?
- How do I translate my experience of my parents into my parenting?
- How did my parents use me as a compensatory source of consolation when one or both of them were disappointed in each other?
- How did or do I use my children as a compensatory source of consolation when I am or was disappointed in my ex-mate?
- How was/am I caught between my parents?
- How was/am I caught between my children?
- How was/am I caught between my ex-mate and my child or children?
- How was/am I caught between my ex-mate and another partner in my life?
- How were my parents or grandparents caught in like fashion?
- How do I address the pertinent members of my family to extricate myself from being caught between them?
- How do I rework the gap between fantasy and reality in family life and convey a greater sense of reality to the next generation?
- How do ex-spouses deepen their friendship without unduly threatening their current mates or confusing their respective families of origin?

These questions were formulated and distributed to family members before they met for dialogue.

FATHER, MOTHER, AND CHILD

Jean began the session with Rob and their two sons by responding to the question of what forces were at play to bring the family together now.

JEAN:	I think a precipitating event was Carl's graduating from college. The problem for me was having to talk to Rob's parents after all these years. What was I supposed to do?
THERAPIST:	Are you saying that you and your former in-laws had not been in each other's presence since your divorce?
JEAN:	I had not been in their presence, and I knew I was going to be for that weekend. A second precipitating event was Jim's going

to college. There was a misunderstanding about when Jim and I were to meet, and I was enormously angry at Jim. I was frightened when I couldn't find him and wondered who I should call. I felt strongly that Rob, rather than Tim, needed to know. I called him from the hotel. I can remember Rob saying, "I don't know how I can help." It was a watershed experience. It was clear to me that you were the only person that could understand what I was feeling about Jim.

THERAPIST: Rob, how did you respond to Jean's phone call?

ROB: I was flabbergasted! First of all I tended to be judgmental, and then I realized that you were in an emotionally difficult situation. I was scared to death. The next couple of hours were very traumatic. But it made me feel good that she did that, that she came to me and really affirmed what had been going on for years. I don't know that I ever really saw it as focused as that. We are in this thing together. I know I always thought like that and acted that way, but I felt privileged. When you finally called and said you found the son of a gun, I rejoiced a great deal.

THERAPIST: Were you aware of your entitlement? That you were where her call really should have been placed? If your son was lost, that it was you who was owed that information rather than anyone else?

ROB: I didn't think entitlement, but you're right, that is exactly how I felt at that point.

THERAPIST: What did you make of the fact that your mother called your father?

JIM: I thought it was a little strange at first, and then when I heard Dad's side, I thought it was right. It provided great assurance to her to call him, I guess.

THERAPIST: Carl, do you want to say something?

CARL: I always thought that whenever Mom called Dad it was going to be a rather serious issue, but I think I was in the mode of not seeing it in the light that these two are my parents and she should call. I think that gets lost all the time in the shuffle about the divorce, of dealing with Tim and dealing with my father's second wife. Even being here now, I have a feeling for Tim about his feelings about what is going on here.

Therapeutic Interventions

- In addressing previously unmentioned divorce issues, the therapist tenaciously emphasized resources over pathology.
- She consistently challenged the idealized notions of marriage that cast a shadow on everyone's way of addressing each other.

- The therapist repeatedly invited these parents and children to face each other, convinced that there is simply no other way to catalyze the latent resources that exist between people burdened by estrangement but bound by an ontic covenant.
- The therapist made room for Carl to surface the loss of not seeing his parents on a day-to-day basis, and extended the exchange to help the boys assess the burdens and benefits of having a mother and father live apart.
- The therapeutic acknowledgment of parental investment elicited relief and gratitude on everybody's part.
- Each therapeutic effort to remove barriers of blame encouraged claims and counterclaims that diminished fear and freed each family member for an ethical stance.
- Jean's therapeutic process had freed her to transform stagnant despair into dialogic claims. She could now address her former husband rather than blame him. Her recognition of Rob's significance in their children's well-being directly paralleled her grasp of how generations of her family of origin had invested in her.

On the other hand, Rob remained loyalty bound to his parents. His freedom to choose *for* his children, *for* his current wife, and *for* his ex-wife, to say nothing about *for* himself, was constrained by the despair that he was *caught between people* rather than believing that he had a side of his own that counts.

ROB: The image I have of marriage is that two people are one. My mother gave up early on who she was to become Mrs. Rob Lyon, and that is where she is today. Jean would then raise issues, and I didn't know how to respond, and I can recall being scared. *I never saw my parents work anything out so I didn't know how to do that.* I think I was married once to two different people. I often felt that we were to speak as one, and to act as one. I was caught between the children [Carl and Jim] and Sally [ex-second spouse] in some way and caught between Sally and Jean.

THERAPIST: Did you ever have a clear notion of not only what you owed but what you were owed?

ROB: I feel after the last 3 or 4 years of hard looking at myself and working on myself that I am owed certain things.

THERAPIST: Carl and Jim, how do each of you register that your mother was somehow clear that it was she and each of you who had the primary connection and that your dad maybe was less entitled to lay claim on you?

JIM: I always felt like I needed to take care of you, Dad, more than Mom. Over the past 5 years, I've tried not to take care of you. I

| | could never understand why you wanted to make your second wife part of the family. |

CARL: One of the reasons I get angry about this, Dad, is that I didn't feel you had a side. *You were choosing Sally's way over your own way.* Jim and I would have preferred you to have your own terms. We perceived men as giving women a lot of power in a lot of ways. Tim [stepfather] gives up his power too. I feel that loss. That's why I commented to you, Mom, about the triad, about bringing the father back into the family. It is really important. It is hard to learn how to make claims.

THERAPIST: *I have never felt that the terms "weak" and "strong" were relationally useful.* Your mother struggled to address her own parents in an effort to break free from what she considered was holding her back. What your father is saying, as I hear you, Rob, is that like the rest of us you carried and copied very strong loyalty ties. What our parents do is typically what we do until we figure out it doesn't work for us. My guess is, Rob, that those loyalty ties inhibited you from even knowing that you had the freedom to have a side of your own.

ROB: Absolutely.

CARL: Then I would feel that everything I would talk to you about would be interpreted by you as what Mom would say and the same when I went to talk to you, Mom.

THERAPIST: You weren't heard.

CHRIS: I felt like I wasn't right. Then I got into the mode of playing the role, playing Dad's side off of Mom's.

Therapeutic Interventions

- The therapeutic process began to erode Rob's idealization of marriage, which he held even now.
- In pressing Rob to surface his assumptions about his parents' marriage, the therapist was urging him to rework his loyalty binds as well as his split loyalties.
- The therapeutic effort to help Rob wrest himself free from blind loyalty to his parents was rooted in the therapist's advocacy for his sons.
- The therapist helped Carl and Jim surface the injustices of being caught between their parents.
- She helped them surface their feelings and transform them into claims.
- The therapist introduced their stepmother as a factor in the boys' split loyalties; credited the difficulty of Sally's position; and held Rob accountable for allowing Sally to parent in his stead.

- The therapist offered a *merit-based* interpretation of their parents to Carl and Jim to offset the youngsters' *power-based* interpretation.

PARENTS, CHILDREN, AND GRANDPARENTS

Rob and his parents, Ralph, 90, and Lucy, 86; Jean and her mother, Sara, 81; and Carl and Jim attended the session. Jean was acutely aware of her dead father throughout the meeting. Carl began by crediting the fact that his grandparents were willing to be there. Jim seconded his brother's gratitude. The therapist asked Jean and Rob to tell their elderly parents what led to the impasses that took place between them. Jean immediately turned to her relationship with her mother.

JEAN: This is the first time I ever defined myself with my mother present. I have never told her how I was mandated to care for my sister; how I was supposed to be successful, be a good student, and look pretty; how we weren't supposed to talk about successes or looking nice because that wasn't done. One of the only times that I was credited as a success was when you, Ralph [Rob's father], said you were grateful I had the children. I knew my father was grateful, but he never said so. I let silence define me in my family.

ROB: I was the firstborn of three, and I felt that I led the way. My brother was born on my first birthday. I was born on my maternal grandfather's birthday. I never felt it was ever a day for *me*. Mom and Dad always made the decisions for us. It was a very loving sort of relationship. I got to be tall when I was 13, I grew 6 inches in one year. You guys were kind of worried about that. I always felt that I stood out and was much more lonely than my siblings. I had a more serious view of the world, and this somehow can be seen in my son Carl.

The therapist then turned to Jean's mother, Sara.

THERAPIST: How much did you and your husband talk with each other and the kids?

SARA: I'm surprised that she said that we were silent because we used to talk a lot. I never realized I was silent.

THERAPIST: The kind of silence we are talking about is whether people can disclose themselves in order to make decisions together.

SARA: We only made decisions or answered questions when they were asked.

JEAN:	I first remember telling my father about the divorce, but not directly. He used to take care of the children when Rob and I would go to try to work out our problems.
THERAPIST:	Was it difficult to tell your mother?
JEAN:	Yes, it was real difficult. I never had the idea that I was going to end my marriage. It was not a quick or easy decision. I always liked Rob. We didn't have the resources at the time to work out a marriage. But we struggled hard to find them.
THERAPIST:	Did you turn to your parents at any point?
JEAN:	No.
THERAPIST:	Can you say why?
JEAN:	I was afraid to disappoint them.
THERAPIST:	Sara, how did you respond when Jean told you that she and Rob were ending their marriage?
SARA:	That was one of the hardest things that I ever had to face. I knew that Jean would survive, but I worried about the two boys. I couldn't talk to anyone about it. For 16 years I mulled it around in my mind and found out later what it was all about.
THERAPIST:	I wonder Carl, and Jim, if you want to respond?
CARL:	I hear a lot of things that are ringing close to home right now. Being the firstborn, I feel like I have to take care of Jim. I have never been the frivolous one. That tendency has been passed down to me in a big way. Right now I feel I suffer from it.
THERAPIST:	What was it like for you, Rob, to tell your parents that your marriage was ending?
ROB:	It was very difficult. I didn't want to talk to them about it because they would be disappointed. I was always a good boy. My dad said, "One good thing came out of the divorce; we have gotten to know you better." I don't know if you remember, Dad, but I said, "I'm not responsible for your happiness." I saw that he didn't fold up at that, and we continued to talk. We are closer today.
THERAPIST:	Lucy, would you be willing to say how the news hit you?
LUCY:	We just hoped everything would just smooth over, mostly for the boys. I seem to be able to throw off hits like that a little quicker than my husband. We really praise the Lord for Rob's closeness now, but I'm sorry it had to be this way.
THERAPIST:	How did the news affect you, Ralph?
RALPH:	It came upon us like a ton of bricks. Their marriage looked like an ideal thing to me.

Therapeutic Interventions

The therapeutic emphasis here was to help family members transform silent protectiveness and implicit blame into options for fair consideration through direct address.

- The therapist was careful to credit the divorced couple's investments in reworking past injuries between themselves, between themselves and their children, and between themselves and their respective parents.
- Now the therapist was free to incorporate elderly parents, who only now after 16 years had come face to face to address each other in their adult children's presence.
- The therapist's encouragement of direct address helped Rob and Jean differentiate between autonomy and ethical disengagement.
- The therapist's focus helped Rob and Jean begin to move from self-isolating "independence" to ethical reengagement.
- The therapeutic process surfaced the degree to which monologue created stagnation among members of this intergenerational family.
- The therapeutic use of direct address elicited long-standing parental shame and disappointment triggered by filial divorce. It surfaced the merit of family members who were still willing to be present to each other in spite of their disappointments. And it allowed the children to witness the healing consequences of intergenerational dialogue.

IN-LAWS

Up to this point in the session, Jean and Rob had addressed their own parents. Now the therapist turned to the more precarious dynamics of in-law relationships.

THERAPIST:	What happened between you and your former in-laws, Jean, and between you and your former mother-in-law, Rob?
ROB:	I thought that everything could go on as before. I would stop in at my ex-mother-in-law's school and say hello.
THERAPIST:	Did you discuss what had happened?
ROB:	No, I talked to Jean's Aunt Roberta a lot.
SARA:	I didn't have much interaction with Rob the first couple of years. But we never had any animosities. I miss the visiting, and I miss the associations with family. Lucy and Ralph were friends. I feel if you are a good Christian, that you have to have love for a person and that is what I try to have.
JEAN:	I felt blamed for the divorce. I struggled with my own silence and inability to have a side when it came to all of my in-laws. I care a lot about Curt, and I have not had any contact with my nephews and nieces in years. That's a loss for me.
THERAPIST:	Do you experience it as an unfair loss?
JEAN:	I experience it as a loss to which I have contributed.
THERAPIST:	No one reached toward you, and you didn't reach toward them.

JEAN:	Right.
THERAPIST:	Ralph, is there anything you want to say to Jean?
RALPH:	We certainly never shunned her, and there's never been a break between her mother and us. I'm still looking for a golf date and she doesn't come up.

Therapeutic Interventions

- As the session unfolded, 16 years' worth of estranging myths began to crumble under the weight of direct address.
- The therapeutic shift from monologue to dialogue resulted in a variety of consequences:

    —Each family member was exposed to his or her own ambivalence.

    —Moralisms, cloaked in religious language, were transformed into a belated recognition of each in-law's loss.

    —Each family member's felt blame for his or her part in disconnecting was transformed into shy and tentative acknowledgment of each other's merit.

    —Unaddressed grief was transformed into tentative permission for future reconnections.

    —The natural isolation and fragility of the elderly were penetrated by the mere presence and address of their children and grandchildren.
- The therapist tried to help family members distinguish between the inevitable losses of divorce and gratuitous relational injustices— conveyed from generation to generation by the failure to test the latent resources of marital legacies.

VOICES FROM THE NEXT GENERATION

Technically, the exchange between Rob and Jean and their parents and ex-in-laws might have been limited to themselves. But like all of the generations that preceded them, these parents and grandparents were deeply invested in the well-being of the next generation. Ethically, in the therapist's view, children of any age are entitled to be present to a process in which consequences of other people's decision and indecision begin to be redressed.

THERAPIST:	Jim, you sat here and listened to your parents and grandparents. Maybe it is time for them to listen to you.
JIM:	When I hear Grandpa say things like "We just try to go with it," it means a lot to me to hear, to know that I'm part of you. It means a lot to me to hear Grandpa speak out loud.

CARL: One of the things consistent since the divorce is my grandparents' concern, and overconcern at times, for how Jim and I are.

JIM: It feels a little bit constricting, really overbearing. It's almost as if we have to prove in some way that we are okay.

CARL: If we showed emotion or cried all of a sudden, we heard them say, "See what happens when people get divorced? Poor kids."

THERAPIST: You are saying that somehow your life had to redeem your parents' decision?

CARL: I think on some level, yes. Mom, what you said about having to succeed in divorce really struck home for me.

THERAPIST: Maybe the people around you, and each of you, have not been essentially characterized by divorce but by courage and a willingness to bring yourselves to each other. Each of you in this circle is certainly a statement that divorce doesn't have to end in estrangement. It can strengthen people and lead them to a sturdy balance in their own lives. Once it is done, it has to be used either as a framework for resourcing or a framework for disconnection.

CARL: There are ways in which divorce has affected my relationship with my grandparents. This whole concern with how we are doing. Maybe we can try to look beyond just that.

THERAPIST: You seem to be saying that your grandparents parentified you and expected too much of you as well as of your parents.

SARA: They are the only two grandchildren I have. Maybe one of the causes for doing that, especially to Carl, is because he is the oldest. And Jim and I played golf together many years. I bought them their clubs and started them off and loved every minute of it. But I do think that I have been overwhelming with them. If so, I apologize for that.

Therapeutic Interventions

- The therapist was attuned to how loyalty silences the young in front of their elders and so moved to include them whether or not they could respond.
- Therapeutic efforts at inclusion of the young were sanctioned by implicit and explicit parental permission.
- The therapist's dialogic stance opened up a way for grandparents and grandchildren to address each other despite years of estrangement, intended or unintended, between their parents and grandparents.
- Therapeutic efforts to include grandparents in the process of trust building after divorce had several consequences.
  —Jim was able to delineate himself through closer identification with his grandfather.

—Carl was able to protest the burden on his brother and him by virtue of his grandparents' dismay at Jean and Rob's divorce.
—Grandmother was able to acknowledge her part in burdening her grandsons.

- The therapist's capacity to credit each family member alerted some of them to the destructive quality of their overexpectations that blinded them to the fair give-and-take that was actually in process.

Not to be overlooked in this process are the fundamentally redemptive possibilities that were born of three generations of family members who for the first time ever chose to sit in the same room and address each other, and rework the particular costs of a divorce in the family.

SIBLINGS

Rob and his younger brother, Chet, and Jean and her younger sister, Betty, as well as Carl and Jim attended this session. Rob's younger sister, Kim, had been Jean's special friend in high school and had introduced her to Rob. She did not come to the session because she "had issues to work out with Jean that were not appropriate to a public forum." Rob and Jean were in touch with their respective siblings. Carl and Jim maintained a perfunctory contact with their aunts, uncles, and cousins. Carl opened the session by citing the costs of being separated from his father's side of the family.

CARL: It's hard to bring the other half of my life when we go to visit grandparents and aunts and uncles. I think there are some unaddressed issues, specifically with Aunt Kim.

JIM: One set of my family doesn't really know much about the other side anymore, because of the separation—the divorce. It is kind of hard to bring that side of life into the conversation.

THERAPIST: Is it because you don't feel invited, Jim? Or is there some kind of silent agreement at work?

JIM: It seems more like a silent agreement. I get questions. One side asks about the other. But no one would ever call. Say, Chet or Aunt Kim would not call Mom and ask her what is going on. So it sort of puts me in the middle. But at the same time I see what would happen.

THERAPIST: I want to refine a little. It seems to be a matter of cutoffs between the people involved rather than a fear of encountering hostility.

CARL: Yes, it feels like the relationship between the extended families has been romanticized into a good or just very happy or something relationship.

THERAPIST: The words belie the relating. Is that what you're saying?
ROB: I don't know if that is necessarily true. When they see each other at graduations, they still kind of remember.
THERAPIST: But if you and Jean were still married there would probably be a more direct connection.
ROB: Oh yes!
CARL: But when I hear them talking there is a sense of loss. It feels like it is something they would like to talk more about but they don't know how. And as the child of parents who are divorced, I feel in the middle. I don't know exactly where I stand or what is going on. The time before the divorce seems like a mythical period to me.

Therapeutic Interventions

The very structure of the therapy session held significance for everyone involved.

- Siblings distanced from siblings were willing to be present to each other in the midst of clear and current estrangement.
- Siblings-in-law who had been out of contact for 16 years let themselves be included out of past, present, and future motivations. Among them were a past life that had left trust and affection as well as anger and resentment in its wake, and a present life that involved everyone's deepened awareness of the complexity and consequences of marriage, divorce, and remarriage and a concern for impacting the future of their collective children who are cousins.
- Carl and Jim were the clear beneficiaries of their parents' position that they were connected to their aunts, uncles, and cousins, who had been and could still be resources as well as stumbling blocks.
- By definition, the conjoint therapy signaled to Carl and Jim that their loyalties were legitimate. They were entitled to connect with everyone in the family whether or not divorce had taken place.
- The chance to address their aunt and uncle in their parents' presence give Carl and Jim fresh options for demystifying the past and for engaging in the future.

In their efforts to establish a bridge between their siblings and their children, Rob and Jean had to reinvest in their respective siblings, nieces, and nephews themselves. Theirs was a conscious choice to bridge the gap of their own unreworked loyalties and preferences. It was their embodiment of what was important rather than empty exhortation that pierced the stagnation between the generations.

The ongoing impetus for ethical reengagement was propelled by residual trust between sibling and sibling.

JEAN: Betty, I feel like I pursue you more than you pursue me. I felt like I needed to talk to you around things like Maggie's adoption. But I'm not sure where the boundaries are with us.

THERAPIST: Has having Maggie been some kind of bridge between you and Jean, Betty?

BETTY: It has been to some extent. In other ways it has probably created more obstacles. It has connected me to Jean in that now I have a basis of being a mother. I really had no idea what that was like all the years I visited her when Carl and Jim were small. I am only now beginning to analyze relationships with our own mother.

THERAPIST: Are you saying that your mother comes between you?

JEAN: I never thought of it that way.

BETTY: I wouldn't say that. No. She definitely holds you up to a higher standard. I think I have been able to take more freedom than you.

THERAPIST: What about your father? To what degree do your memories of him bond you? And to what degree do they separate you? The way your mother relates to each of you leaves you with the burden of addressing each other about her behavior. That doesn't entirely belong to you.

JEAN: I hear tales that keep getting told. I was Dad's kid and Betty was Mom's kid.

BETTY: Well, this thing about you being Dad's child was news to me. I remember Mom talking about this recently, and I thought, When did that happen? I never felt that. It sort of made me angry. Why was Jean Dad's kid? I felt very close to him.

THERAPIST: Did you challenge your mother, Betty, when she said it?

BETTY: Nooooo!

THERAPIST: Why do you think you didn't challenge her?

BETTY: Sometimes I'm afraid of undercutting the memories she has. I don't want to cross over what is myth and what is not. I suppose on that one I could have challenged her.

THERAPIST: Could either one of you say how Jean and Rob's divorce impacted your relationship?

JEAN: I don't remember talking to you about the divorce. I thought that you felt betrayed by our getting divorced. But I never checked that out with you.

BETTY: Well, it was just real hard. Jean and Rob had gone on to something else. For me it was a loss in the family.

JEAN: Well, it was a loss for me as well, but a different kind of loss.

Rob, I often felt your lack of boundaries with my sister, my aunt, and my mother. At times it was a problem.

THERAPIST: You are saying that Rob should have addressed you and not presumed that your family could remain his?

JEAN: Yes, I think that has changed over the years since you and I talk with each other directly.

Therapeutic Interventions

- The therapy session helped Jean and Betty identify long-held injuries and stagnant patterns between them. The two sisters grew increasingly aware that their lack of connection was predicated on colliding views of their parents.
- Jean's direct address and acknowledgment of their mother freed Betty to relate more fully to Jean.
- The unacknowledged differences in their parents' expectations of them were elicited.
- The differences between them were credited; and they were encouraged to continue to test their respective premises against each other and with their mother.
- The capacity to imagine each other's reality in their family of origin freed the sisters to explore the impact of Jean's divorce on the two of them.
- The pseudomutuality between them was replaced by direct address.
- For the first time, they could grieve their respective losses together.
- The sisters' engagement with each other freed Rob to disclose his own unaddressed loss of Jean's family.
- Betty's loss of Rob was discrete and only now, after 16 years, able to surface. Her mourning for the consequences of the divorce only now could be addressed.
- The therapist helped to identify how Rob's efforts to cling to Jean's family were a way of protecting his family from disappointment. And Jean's cutoff from Rob's family was a replication of how she treated her own.

By this time everyone in the session had less anxiety about articulating their side and more clarity about what that side was. The consequences of divorce had sealed in already-stagnant patterns of relating between ex-mates, their siblings, nieces, and nephews. Now all of them were facing their respective losses in a move toward reengaging.

THERAPIST: At this point I would like to switch the discussion to you Rob.

ROB: As we all know in this room, Chet was my biggest, if not my only, birthday present on my first birthday. We did everything together, but I don't remember that we shared a lot. That was generally true about my whole family. I think of the day that you stayed home from school. You shouldn't have been rummaging around, but you found that Dad was married before. That was one of the most traumatic days that I can recall. Suddenly, we spent several hours talking about whether Mother was our mother.

THERAPIST: Given so much closeness and commonality of interest, how did you lose each other?

CHET: We did a lot of things together. But there was as much difference between us as there was commonality. I would go running around with my buddies, and Rob wouldn't. As time went on, our personalities moved toward one another. There was and is still a very strong bond between Rob and me.

THERAPIST: Have you turned to Rob as a resource, as someone to talk to when you're in pain, or even for purposes of enjoyment?

CHET: Once or twice but not regularly, partly because geographically we are so far apart.

ROB: I tell him things. He is an attorney so I ask him technical questions. My relationship with my sister, Kim, is so strong; she is my primary person that I do that with. He would do anything good for me and I for him, but we don't use each other as resources.

THERAPIST: Have you ever turned to anyone for help, Chet?

CHET: My motivation was not to upset my parents.

THERAPIST: The hard part about how your parents operate is that silence covers a multitude of feelings and opinions. So it is easy to pretend that there is no conflict.

ROB: The problem for me is that I never sensed that I had a feeling I couldn't share. It was just that I didn't have the feeling.

THERAPIST: Maybe I can put it this way, Rob. You may not have had permission to delineate yourself from your parents' point of view.

CHET: I think we both thought then and right now that we might not have agreed with my father but he was right! We never asked him. We assumed that, like it or not, he is right.

THERAPIST: His tone is that he is right.

ROB: I can recall getting angry with Jean. She said, "How can you and your family let your father get away with that?" And I thought, "Who the hell are you, lady?"

THERAPIST: Chet, did you ever call Jean to express your regret about the divorce?

CHET: No, but my wife called Jean several times to talk about me, I think.

THERAPIST:	You didn't feel pulled or free or inclined to?
CHET:	Inclined to, yes. Pulled to, probably not. Free to, pretty much not. When that split occurred, it seemed that it was not proper for me to call Rob's ex-wife and ex-in-laws. So I didn't.
JEAN:	I'm not sure you know of the service you provided me, Chet. I have no brothers. I often felt if I said something to you and you disagreed, you would tell me. That was something I missed with you, Rob. There was a trustworthy quality with Chet.
THERAPIST:	I want to ask you, Chet, about how Rob and Jean's divorce affected your relationship with Carl and Jim.
CHET:	I have not ever really had a chance to establish a serious relationship with either Carl or Jim. They are my nephews and I love them, and I would do anything I could for them.
THERAPIST:	So you don't pursue them, and Carl and Jim have not pursued you?
JIM:	It has been the same kind of relationship throughout the past 20 years. It is not really close. It is a family bond and it is always great to see him. But I never really had a desire to establish a close relationship or friendship.
THERAPIST:	Is he someone who you would turn to with worry about your dad?
JIM:	I would turn more to Kim, only because of the kind of relationship Dad and Kim have.
THERAPIST:	So it seems that your relationship with your uncle, Jim, reflects your dad's relationship with your uncle. And your potential relationship with Kim reflects your dad's relationship with Kim.

Therapeutic Interventions

- The therapist's eliciting tensions between siblings after Rob and Jean's divorce guided them to examine the consequences of their disengagement on their nieces and nephews.
- The therapist's ability to tap into latent resources between adult siblings and ex-siblings-in-law helped Carl and Jim learn of earlier disconnections between and among them.
- The therapeutic effort to help family members disclose the depth of their residual trust offered everyone the option of transforming past estrangements into future reengagement.
- The therapist's persistence in surfacing the triadic base of sibling relationship tempered the splits between siblings and allowed them room to choose for each other.
- The increasing identification of unfinished business between the siblings and their respective parents allowed them to differentiate

between the primary roots of their current stagnation and future possibilities for healing through meeting.

- Therapeutic attempts to surface the consequences of unfinished family business between adults and their parents revealed how filial protectiveness of parents can lead to marital disengagement.
- The safety of the therapy room and the depth of the dialogue not only encouraged siblings to reconnect at a new level of involvement. It also freed ex-in-laws to credit their past and present merit directly to each other.
- The resource of direct address in the session freed Rob to express his regret about past and current difficulty in knowing, much less in disclosing, his ground.
- Rob's ability to acknowledge his felt limits confirmed Jean's efforts to remain loyal to him without staying married to him.
- The therapist helped to identify parallel splits between the generations. The relationship between Carl and Jim as a mirror image of their father's relationship with his brother.

The willingness of siblings and siblings-in-law to engage each other as well as the next generation elicited fairness and meaning from their own past legacies. It provided closure to issues that had been unaddressed in the past. And it released energy for Jean's and Rob's investment in their futures.

PARENT, STEPPARENT, AND STEPCHILDREN

Remarriage can be a fresh attempt to build a life in common, to test anew old longings for love, companionship, and security. It is also a time when old loyalties and new loyalties collide: What old illusions do a couple bring into a new marriage? What new tensions are introduced to old tensions and to whom? What is to be done when concern for two sets of children flies in the face of what the adults want together? What is to be done with the imbalance when one partner has children and the other has none? What is to be done with the imbalance when one partner has ill or aging parents and the other has none? How can a couple make use of a fresh moment in their respective existences to temper flight with facing? How can a couple hold the tension between unmet expectations of past marital context and unrealistic expectations in a current context? How do adults help children differentiate what they owe and deserve from parents from what they owe and deserve from stepparents?

Jean and Tim, and Carl and Jim were present in the fourth session. The level of anxiety during this session was very high. Invisible presences in this room were Jean's former husband and his context and Tim's children and former wife and her context.

THERAPIST:	It seems to me, Tim, there is a particular burden on you here.
TIM:	My feelings at this point are with my own children. I wish they were here. I didn't anticipate it quite as strongly as I'm experiencing it.
THERAPIST:	Can any of you identify a particular stumbling block in these thirteen years? Is there a single thing that stands out as particularly difficult during this process?
JEAN:	In the beginning of my marriage to Tim, I sort of threw the kids at him. I said, "Adjust. Get along. This is the way it is. Lots of families that stay together don't have it this good." And to the kids, "This is where I'm staying. He is a nice man. So adjust!" I abandoned the kids at times. I tried to explain Tim to my kids. My biggest struggle was being in the middle.
TIM:	The struggle for me involved boundaries. One set of boundaries had to do with not being Carl and Jim's father and trying to work out what was and what was not my place in their lives. I had some resentment, at first, over Jean consulting Rob. I don't think I appreciated the importance of doing that. The other boundary was my own kids, even though they were older. One question was how to include them. Another was the complexity of the relationship between their mother and me.
THERAPIST:	Could you be more specific about what it meant to you with your children to have stepsons now?
TIM:	In the new situation with Jean, I was more experientially aware of the deprivation that I had worked on my own kids. I had certain guilt feelings about that, and sometimes my own children, in a joking way would say, "Dad, you have sure mellowed." That was always painful.
THERAPIST:	Carl, a special stumbling block?
CARL:	My stumbling block derived from the fact that you both were stumbling so much as well. There was a different set of dynamics that went on at your house than did at Dad's, and because of that there was a different set of ways to act. It got difficult to keep track or understand or figure out what was supposed to happen or how I was supposed to fit in. I really wanted to accept you into the house, but I was probably feeling a lot of anger. One of the stumbling blocks was a certain kind of split loyalty. There are some qualities that you offer that my dad is not able to give me. And there are certainly some things that he can give me that you can't.
THERAPIST:	To whom, Carl, were you able to take your anger and confusion?

CARL: Probably most with Mom. I think my anger came out more to my dad. A lot of times earlier on I was scared of you and your reaction. When I got to college I could come to you, Tim. Being away helped earlier on.

THERAPIST: You were scared of Tim at what level, Carl?

CARL: I was scared of you yelling and just being big. I was also scared of what the ramifications might mean for the family situation in terms of Mom and Tim's relationship.

THERAPIST: Jim, how about you? What comes to mind as a major stumbling block?

JIM: (on the phone from the West Coast) I think I am still stumbling. I perceive a better relationship with Tim. I understand more where Tim is coming from. I think he understands more about me from my talking. When I took this trip and came back at Christmas, we really started to connect.

THERAPIST: When you say you are still stumbling, does anything come to mind?

JIM: I guess it is still hard for me to talk to Tim about some of the things I would talk to Mom about ...

THERAPIST: Obviously, Jim, there are a bunch of triangles in every family where there are two loyalty systems, where parents have remarried. Is it hard for you to talk to your dad?

JIM: Yes, it is. It is surprising. It was a lot harder when I was at home. But I have talked to him an awful lot since I have been out here.

TIM: I think that one of the by-products of divorcing my children's mother was wanting my children to approve of what I was doing. I think my primary energy early on was really to force Jean onto my children. My kids were older, and they were somewhat able to tell me to get out of the way. I don't think I was as sensitive to their agony. I was less aware of the problems for Carl and Jim than I was of the problems I felt with my kids and the feeling I was losing them by doing what I was doing. I guess I wanted them not only to be a part of my life with Jean but to accept Carl and Jim as their stepbrothers. One of my sons said very kindly, "But they are not my brothers, and I am not ready to do that," and I remember feeling hurt by that. But I think he was absolutely right.

THERAPIST: It has been said a couple of times that Jean made it clear that her primary attachment was to her children. I know of the intensity of your devotion to your children, Tim. Do you see a distinction between the two of you?

TIM: When I raised my kids, we only had Dr. Spock and "parenting" was not a word. Everybody was naturally a parent, and I don't

	think we were as aware of the dynamics of family and how and what happened with kids. So I was aware of what I had done with my children, and then I would see Jean doing something with her kids. I was struck by the difference in the way we had gone at parenting.
THERAPIST:	What issues, in your view, Jean, belonged between you and Tim vis-à-vis your children? What issues belonged between you and Rob?
JEAN:	What comes to mind was my sadness quotient. I felt like talking with Tim, early on, when Carl or Jim were hurt. You, Tim, were there for me as a person, but there wasn't a way for you to have the same feeling about Carl and Jim as Rob did. I could just talk to Rob over the phone about Carl and Jim being hurt and there was a different quality of investment.
THERAPIST:	So you and Rob were ontically tied to each other through the children in a way that you and Tim could not be. In all fairness, Tim had his own children to invest in so there were at least two or three levels at which the ground was common but not in common.
CARL:	Mom, one thing I wanted to say before we end is that, as hard as it has been to do what we have done with Dad and you and with Jim and me and our grandparents and your siblings, I feel closer to you and Tim and more trusting of our relationship now than I was before starting a lot of this stuff.
JEAN:	I don't know what would have happened to us had you, Tim, not given me the space or had I not pressed for the space to do what I needed to do with Rob, Carl, and Jim.
THERAPIST:	That is an important acknowledgment, Jean. It is logical to ask the question, "What has happened to Tim while Jean has gone after the people she has had to go after?" There is a concern for Tim and whether or not he has been treated fairly in the process.
TIM:	I do feel I've been treated fairly. I think I have grown in trust with Jean, though it gets shaken sometimes. I know that it is not that she does something to shake it. It is that I feel shaken. The struggle for trust is my struggle in somehow claiming something for myself. I am learning how to do that, but I'm not very good at it. Intellectually, I can see the value of things and I know what relational justice is. I don't think I can be intimate. The process of being intimate is the process of being intimate with myself as well as with somebody else. That is a tough struggle in terms of my profession [the ministry], in which appearance is often taken as reality. It struck me when Carl was talking about the shadow quality of the divorce. It is very difficult to

talk about those things with the burden of being clergy. His dad is a clergy person too. I think looking down on your own soul is hard work. I think it is part of the relational work that happens. So it is not just trusting Jean, it is trusting myself with Jean.

THERAPIST: And trusting that something can happen between you even if you are on divergent planes.

Therapeutic Interventions

- The therapist knew that she was addressing the interface of three loyalty systems—his, hers, and theirs.
- She proceeded from the baseline that relational justice is most fully catalyzed between members of a triadic context.
- She helped family members to delineate their respective loyalty systems and to fine-tune where their loyalties lay.
- She credited the losses involved in shattering unspoken myths and monologic premises, and moved to help people reconnect without violating their primary loyalties.
- The safety of dialogue in therapy sessions allowed Jean to surface her simplistic expectations in the early days of remarriage. Her courage to disclose the costs of her own naiveté lent courage for direct address to Tim, Carl, and Jim.
- The therapist pressed Tim to move from the monologic constraints of psychological insight to the dialogic imperative of ethical reengagement.
- The therapist's emphasis on loyalty dynamics allowed Carl to surface the burden of his split loyalties and acknowledge his growing bond with Tim.
- The therapist's acknowledgment of Jim's entitlement to find terms on which to live his own life allowed him to disclose his anxiety over addressing family dynamics without the cover of his older brother's protection.
- The therapeutic invitation for dialogue between stepfather and stepsons freed Carl to surface his frustration and the costs involved in everyone's idealization of women in general and his mother in particular.
- In turn, Carl was able to surface his relief and appreciation when Jim was able to refuse their stepfather's claim.

OUTCOMES

The notion of trust building after divorce may seem like an oxymoron. But there is no gainsaying relational ethics. If a civilization finally loses its grip on what the generations owe each other, eventually birth itself will hold no meaning. The path to trust building after divorce is not necessarily less arduous because two people live their lives separated from one another. It is a myth of divorce to presume that two people can get on with their lives with impunity to the consequences for the next generation that take place in the aftermath of each ex-partner's order of existence.

The fact is that Rob and Jean found courage to address each other because of their devotion to their children, their grasp of their own complicity in the failure of their marriage, their awareness of destructive repetitive patterns in their new relationships, and the invisible barriers between them and their respective families caused, in part, by the divorce itself.

The sessions in which family members participated together were essentially catalytic. But the fact is that the resources and outcomes that eventually coalesced were precipitated, on the one hand, by one person's persistent pursuit of meaning through reconnection; and, on the other hand, by the unanticipated receptivity of the people on whom Jean was willing to make her claims.

As always, conviction that informed the therapist's professional ground in her work with members of this context was provided by her personal ground: Meaning is the outcome of reconnecting with people of long-term significance whose contributions and injuries to each other require the dignity of direct address. *Her basic stance was dialogic. Her basic intervention was presence. Her timing was a direct response to what family members seemed willing to test and able to tolerate.* She was clear on what part of the process belonged to these family members, and what belonged to her. At one and the same time, she felt the weight of what was happening to each family member but resisted undue pressure to become a surrogate for dialogue between relating partners. She was the testing ground for a barrage of untested questions, approaches, and presuppositions. But when the moment came to implement mutually developed plans inside or outside the therapy room, she was able to place them on the shoulders to which they belonged.

Confronted by complaints like "Why does it always have to be me?," she was able to replace self-parentification with a series of challenges and choices. "It doesn't have to be you," she might respond. "What would you like instead?" Or, "Does it serve your purposes to act now or are you prepared to let go?" Or, "If you stood in the childrens' shoes, what would you want of your father?" Or, "Given your position as your dad's favorite child, why would you expect your sister to be close to you?" Or, "If you have to be at a function with your ex-in-laws, does it serve your purposes to be silent or to speak? And what do you want to say?" Faced with the quandary of whether to call her current husband or her ex-husband when Jim "disappeared" on his first day of college, Jean, in internal dialogue with the therapist, called Jim's father. She was acting on her own behalf in response to trust-building questions: Am I now entitled to arrive at my own conclusions? What am I willing to do now? Who deserves to hear what I have to say? Who would Jim want to seek him out?

Accessibility was the overarching outcome of these four sessions of therapy built on years of multilateral investment. Carl's and Jim's evolving parity with each other had consequences for them individually, with each other, and with each of their parents as well as with their stepfather. Their recognition of fears in common freed them to tap their resources in common. Their commonality and solidarity challenged the skew in their elders' expectations of Carl as responsible and Jim as indifferent.

Carl and Jim could now be free to engage their uncle. They now felt invited to be cousins to their aunt's adopted child. Carl would come close enough to his paternal grandmother to do dishes together, and to learn that he and his father had a mutual concern about how, at 91, she could no longer get in or out of the tub. Rob and Jean could now discuss financial concerns more easily and respond more readily to concerns in common about their childrens' lives. Rob could even point to Tim's abruptness whenever he had to call Jean and asked if there was anything to do to mitigate the situation. Jean became less blaming of her mother and more willing to respond to her mother's terms such as Christmas at her mother's retirement home. Jean and her sister, Betty, even managed to take a family portrait together and enjoy each other in the process of preparing the picture as a joint gift to their mother. Rob's father included Rob and his grandsons in making a decision to forgo hip surgery and even disclosed his fears of dying and death. Jean's work with her ex-mate freed her to be less instructive to her current mate about what work he might do in his families of origin and generation. Tim responded by acting more freely on his own behalf. Jean came into a clearer realization that marriage could never be a substitute for self; and her presence to Tim was more of a resource between them than her unilateral efforts to please him. Jean's relational work within her own context unexpectedly prodded Tim to attempt direct address with his former wife and their adult children. The repetition of unfinished family business in their offsprings' lives and marriages also motivated Tim to act. The anguish attached to important events like graduations, weddings, and ritual celebrations now began to yield to earned consideration and respect between everyone involved. Trust building between Tim and Jean has increasingly freed them to say what they mean and to claim what each feels is theirs. The consequences of their respective divorces have been assuaged and mitigated.

They still struggle with the consequences of Tim's lack of entitlement with his children since the divorce. His continuing difficulty in telling his adult children what he wants is not only self-isolating to him but also double-binding to them. But Jean abandons her own ground when Tim is disappointed in order to compensate him for the consequences of his guilt feelings and self-incrimination. Still the consequences of their trust-building efforts have fortified their loyalty and devotion to each other, and continue to deliver resources to help them find a way.

If the people in this context were clear about the catalytic merit of therapy, the therapist was equally clear that the dogged pursuit of truth and trust in the service of fairness among members of this context had instructed therapy. Direct address was of course the catalyzing agent among the participants. But over and above everybody's efforts were grace and awe that evolved from their simple willingness to turn from predetermined paths constructed by consequences of injury and mistrust. Their respective and collective willingness to face into the structural and relational meaning that they once held for each other was not only salvific for each of them but made clear a path to resources and meaning for future generations.

It would be easy to argue the privilege of this family context. To be sure education, sophistication, and emotional, spiritual, and ethical resources were all there to be tapped. The material deprivation that drive many families to their knees were never the dominant factors here. But the longing to connect, the internal demand for fairness in context, and the redemptive possibilities attached to the capacity of human beings to embrace their roots and their progeny without debilitating shame or guilt or resentment are humanity's common legacy. No family can tolerate an unrelenting analytical stance. There is no way for family members to remove the beam from the eye of their own complicity in the dissolution of their family's life. But even in the shambles left behind by divorce, adoption, death, and loss of every kind, reconnecting remains an option.

Epilogue

*...And he looked and, behold, the bush burned with fire, and the bush was
not consumed.*

*And He said: "Draw not nigh hither; put off thy shoes from off thy feet, for
the place whereon thou standest is holy ground."*

—Ex. 3:2–5

Parenting from generation to generation is the bedrock of civilization. It varies in content and differs in form but the need for basic nurturing is irreducible and its fulfillment irreplaceable. With this knowledge, healers, in their rightful place stand in the shadow of the flow of eternity. In their role, healers stand in danger of becoming an icon in an age without heroes, a creature of their clients' creation. In their purpose, however, dialogic therapists are iconoclastic as well as faithful to what is set before them. Like healers of old, they have a mandate to help root out and restore, pull down and rebuild, destroy and create, overthrow and reinstate, plow and replant (Jer. 1:4).

The healer's essential task is to point toward meaning and to lend people courage to pursue it. But this is a generation when it has become a privilege rather than a right for children to be in the presence of both of their parents. This is a time when parental neediness, depletion, and preoccupation often render parents into children and children into parents. This is an age when the notion of relational ethics is almost an anomaly, when cynicism and mistrust are more reliable entities than the trustworthiness that gives birth to direct address. In a society increasingly characterized by violence and abandonment of one or another kind, in a world in which people in search of healing are looking for solace instead of repair, how does a therapist witness to reality and still keep from being consumed?

The Rhawn family was seen by a therapist on and off in the course of 20 years. Chaos was the prevalent characteristic of the progeny in this family from the time of their parents' embittered divorce. The therapist never joined the family in parity with other family members but she was a fixture in it and was expected to be there when people chose to use her—as they suffered each others' assaults. Early on in the divorce, Father called in the sheriff to enforce visiting rights with the children. *The therapist was called.* Father and Mother went to court and the judge tried to address the children. "One day you will want your father," he admonished the recalcitrant listeners. The children wept. The mother was distraught. The father felt extruded. *The therapist was called.* The children felt pulled by their parents' unremitting unforgiveness of each other and subtly turned against each other. *The therapist was called.* Each child graduated from high school and from college and wanted to celebrate the event. But no one knew how to have a celebration that allowed for everyone's *inclusion. The therapist was called.* The eldest child developed an eating disorder. The middle child seemed suicidal at one point. The youngest child was guilt stricken and enraged. *The therapist was called.* The father offered money to his son and not his daughters. *The therapist was called.* Eventually it became apparent to Ms. Rhawn that the children deserved to connect with their father as well as with her. But by now the history of estrangement between the divorced parents had extended into a history of estrangement between children and parents, between child and child, between grandchildren and grandparents, and between nieces and nephews and their uncles, aunts, and cousins—all people with a capacity to care. Then a daughter married. Who was to walk her down the aisle? *The therapist was called.* And then, with very little warning, Ms. Rhawn died at 50 years of age. *And the therapist was called.*

Three young adults, 28, 26, and 24 years of age, had now fallen heir to a legacy of estrangement. Their mother was no longer there to act as a buffer. They held their father at bay in keeping with their devotion to how they interpreted their mother's wishes. We don't want to talk to anyone, they all agreed, who didn't really love her. *The therapist was called.*

Now the therapist stood in the shadow of her client's death. The presenting problem was the younger siblings' concern about their older sister's dependency. "I want to be strong for her," said the youngest child, "the way my mother was." "She is afraid to go to work," her younger brother added. "I know it is just 2 weeks since our mother died. I was afraid to go to work but I did it. I want to be there for my sister, but I also want to live my own life." "I feel misunderstood and misrepresented," the eldest child protested. "I am not as weak as everybody thinks. I want your truth not your worry. I don't want you to be Mom."

The therapist redefined the presenting problem. At base the issue was not an overdependent sibling. *It was a new generation's turn to make meaning of their connections.* "What of your father," the therapist finally asked. "Did he come to your mother's funeral?" "He had no guts," one of the children replied. "But did you ask him?" she persisted. "No," they responded. "He kept calling and leaving messages on our answering machine. He wanted us to put our mother in a hospice." "Well, that took some guts," the therapist reflected.

"Maybe it was his way of offering some help." "But he did our mother harm," they objected.

"Your mother did your father harm as well," the therapist went on. "They had equal and opposite legacies," she related. "Your dad was overshadowed by his mother; your mom lived in fear of the chaos wrought by her father. There is a difference between survival and forgiveness. Your mother disliked your father but she tried to make room for him in your lives. She tried not to confuse their bitterness with each other with your right to have two parents. She was a powerful lady who did not know her power. But she never wanted you to be bound into a chronic state of unforgiveness. Your father is now your only living parent. Don't drive him further away on your mother's behalf."

Relief swept the room. Each young person spoke their piece. "I remember," said the eldest, "that my mom said that even if we saw my father three times a year it would still be a relationship." "Yes," said the middle child and only son, "maybe I'll call him after a while." The youngest child was silent but seemed less burdened. The therapist remembered the young woman's anguish as a child of 12 when she decided not to visit her father anymore.

Before these three young people left the therapy session, they registered their thanks. "There were only two people who ever knew my mother," the eldest said. "One was Kelly, the priest, but he represented God too. And then there is you." The session ended. Prodded by each person's memory of their mother, we moved toward each other. Silently, briefly, without precedent we touched and embraced. Tears mingled with tiny threads of meaning. The moment was an epiphany. Essential meaning had been struck. For a moment at least father, mother and child had been rejoined in the image of the original order of existence. Awed by the impact of the young peoples' loss and grief the therapist could have been silenced by the overwhelming weight of the moment. But impelled by conviction and inspirited by grace, she rested in direct address.

In those instants in which epiphany, awe, and grace are known and received, they are palpable confirmations of healing through meeting. Therapists, of course, are never entitled to impose their wills on people who come to them in search of succor and transformation. But therapists are entitled to witness to the holy ground of creation and connection. They are free to point the way to relational justice illumined by the burning bush whose branches are truth and trust. Epiphany, awe, and grace are the ineffable manifestations of healing through meeting. They are the outpouring of a still, small voice now breaking into a passionate cry for uncorrupted connection. They are the saving if unrecognized sacraments of all professional efforts at healing.

Glossary

The purpose of this glossary is to point a way toward the sphere of the between whose complexity and grace are rooted in the mystery of speech-with-meaning. Meaning can be in the word because it is in being (Buber, 1965b).

Covenantal relationship. Covenantal relationship is a redemptive way built into the understructure of existence. It both anticipates and is a consequence of the human longing to connect. It witnesses to reciprocity as a goal of reality. It proceeds on the premise that human beings are born into dynamic partnership, with all of its attendant benefits, burdens, and joys. It is a grounded commitment or living contract that incorporates limits as well as possibilities, shortfalls as well as sufficiencies—without premature movement on anyone's part toward cutoffs and condemnation. Held fast by the connective tissue of blood and merit, covenantal relationship has the power to motivate and in-spirit relating partners even in the midst of chaos, real and perceived injuries, and profound disappointments.

Crediting. The capacity to acknowledge and confirm the merit in another person's ground just because it is his or her ground. Crediting is not to be confused with agreement, but it has the ethical force to mitigate disagreement, demystify motive, and disarm conflict.

Direct address. Words spoken with meaning, direct address is characterized by a willingness to know one's own truth and to risk it in the service of building fairness and trust. The choice to delineate one's truth and to elicit the truth of another can energize, catalyze, and magnify the intrinsic vitality that lies between person and person who are ontically connected or volitionally engaged with each other and their respective contexts.

Elemental triads. Bonds established by birth, blood, relational longevity, and merit between a child and his or her respective parents, and, by inference, between two adults and their offspring, constitute an elemental triad. These ontic roots of relationship, which preempt the question of good and bad, or likes and dislikes, establish an irrevocable connection between members of an elemental triad. The bedrock of a child's capacity for truth and trust in future relationships is anchored in the degree of address and response that can eventually take place, resolve injuries, redistribute burdens and benefits, and rebalance injustices among father, mother, and progeny and their respective legacies.

Ethical despair. A consequence of flight from direct address, ethical despair goes beyond the psychological condition of depression or ordinary sadness. The outcome of chronic ethical disengagement, it entraps people in situationlessness, isolation, and disconnection.

Ethical engagement. Also known as vital association. The well-being of organic forms of life in common that enables people to live in direct relation to and security with each other—including family, friends, community, and work. Its alternatives are destructive cutoffs and crippling isolation (vital dissociation).

Ethical reengagement. The outcome of a person's or persons' decision in an organic context to rejoin, that is, to act on the strength and weight of a connection that is already in place. The choice to reengage can occur in the midst of broken trust, polarization, conflict, and mutual injury. The decision to reengage is usually a timid and wavering movement past old and stagnant impasses toward a coalescence of vital forces. Its ethical character evolves out of the fundamental truth that people in relationship owe and deserve—regardless of contrary feelings.

Ethical imagination. The capacity to picture and test what is owed and what is deserved in a given context—with equitable regard for the self and for the other. Predicated on the imperative of inclusion, it is one of the most demanding of relational movements. Its omission results in untested, one-sided judgments with spiralling negative consequences.

Exoneration. Exoneration is a choice and a process of lifting the load of culpability off the shoulders of a given person whom heretofore we may have blamed (Boszormenyi-Nagy & Krasner, 1986). It is an effort to develop more ethical imagination for a "victimizer's" context, more realistic premises from which to rework stagnation, and more inclusive criteria for long-term healing.

Intrinsic authority. That inborn right to grasp and act on the uniqueness and merit of one's own person. Neither selfish nor selfless per se, intrinsic authority is tested again and again in the struggle to elicit the truth of others without ceding or silencing one's own.

Invisible expectations. Relationship is characterized by spoken and unspoken expectations. Unacknowledged, unstated, and invisible expectations are not in themselves destructive or injurious. The premises underlying long-term resentments and guilt that remain undisclosed and harbored, however, take on pathological characteristics. Chronically stagnant, unaddressed, and untested invisible expectations can generate and sustain corrosive disappointment and blame.

Merit. *Intrinsic merit* is a person's invisible repository of uniqueness, gifts, and graces that are constituent parts of his or her being. *Earned merit* is gained through contributions, care, and direct address offered to another—whether or not they are acknowledged or reciprocated. Merit is an attribute of relationship, coinage through which entitlement is gained and indebtedness is balanced.

Multidirected partiality. A therapeutic attitude, stance, and method, multidirected partiality presumes merit *in* each relating partner and merit earned through contributions given and received *between* them—despite injuries and estrangements. Siding *with* each person's real and perceived suffering and *against* each partner's unmitigated tendencies to blame, therapists use multidirected partiality to acknowledge pain, elicit trust, identify resources, help people assess personal accountability, and establish new balances of burdens and benefits between and among them.

Multilateral contracting. A multilateral contract operates on the simple premise that everyone is involved in a network of relationships, past and present, which holds massive significance for them. That is, every member of a given context is understood to be a legitimate element in a process and is entitled to parity with each other—regardless of imbalances of status and power. Only a sharp recognition of *each* relating partner's parity can authenticate the merit of all participants and free them to risk contracting with the certainty that everyone has a chance at address and response.

Ontic hierarchy. Being itself establishes a hierarchy of human connectedness. Ontically, grandparents, parents, children, and long-term marriages or associations are embedded in a matrix of compelling indebtedness and entitlement—ethically pressed to meet incurred obligation and anticipate specific privilege in a way that is typically singular in nature. Whether or not they like each other, family members share a common context that bonds and binds them in complex balances of give-and-take.

Psychologizing. The use of psychological categories to invalidate the merit in a relating partner's person or stance. An objectification that monologically assigns negative cause or intent to someone else's words, mutual psychologizing is a gratuitous barrier to healing through meeting. Psychologizing always functions as a subtle means of personal disconfirmation and interpersonal disengagement.

Realm of the between. A way of interpreting reality that incorporates ethical dimensions as well as psychological dimensions. Its focus is on person *with* person rather than on the individual or on the group. The realm of the between is characterized by physical, verbal, emotional, material, and spiritual action, intercourse, and exchange in a moment or event impacted by legacy as well as by presence. The grace that brushes this sphere of human existence emerges from a will to connect that catalyzes courage and preserves merit in and between relating partners.

Restoration. A person's effort to repair the breaches that have occurred in that person's relationship with other people, with the express intent of rediscovering options for healing the injured order of existence between them.

Seeming. A facade that permeates our being and distorts our vision of relational possibilities insofar as it obscures who we are or who we want to be. Seeming is a conscious or unconscious effort to appear as other than we are. As a way, it is always determined in degree in one's family of origin. Seeming is the inevitable consequence of a lack of personal ground and failed imagination. It is a submission to a mandate to please, regardless of ethical outcome.

Self-delineation and due consideration. Self-delineation and due consideration are constituent parts of address and response. Viewed dialectically, they are the fundamental movements of dialogue. Truth born of self-disclosure and trust born of acknowledgment, inclusion, and crediting elicit safety and deepen connection. They also reflect the essential tension that exists in the process of two or more people trying to delineate their own ground while offering consideration to their partner's terms and ground. Their alternating impact on each other requires ethical imagination, which helps people receive each other's terms without having to abandon their own.

Situationlessness. A condition of stagnant disconnection. An "extended holiday" from the repugnant and injurious has been likened to schizophrenia or a dreamlike state. The "fugitive flight" out of vital association and the constant rejection of the claims of a given situation undercut trust, eliminate truth, and violate justice. Uninterrupted situationlessness can rip the fabric of organic context into unrecognizable shreds.

Theologizing. The misuse of religious tradition and conviction to moralize dynamic realities. The lifeless maxim to forgive and forget, for example, bypasses the necessary work of turning and facing the mistrust and injustice of a given situation. The attempt to evade the legitimacy of conflict and collision overrides the possibility of reparation, forgiveness, and redemption. The tendency to theologize creates pressure to achieve peace at any price. Dynamic theology recognizes clear and present injustice and presses for fairness as a condition of peace.

REFERENCES

Boszormenyi-Nagy, I., Grunebaum, J., & Ulrich, D. (1991). Contextual family therapy. In A. Gurman & D. P. Kniskern (Eds.), *Handbook of family therapy (2nd ed.)*. New York: Brunner/Mazel.

Boszormenyi-Nagy, I., & Krasner, B. R. (1980). *Trust-based therapy: A contextual approach, American Journal of Psychiatry, 137,* 767–775.

Boszormenyi-Nagy, I., & Krasner, B. R. (1986). *Between give and take: A clinical guide to contextual therapy,* New York: Brunner/Mazel.

Boszormenyi-Nagy, I., & Spark, G. (1973). *Invisible loyalties: Reciprocity in intergenerational family therapy,* New York: Harper and Row.

Buber, M. (1957). *Pointing the way: Selected essays*. (Trans. and ed. M. S. Friedman). New York: Harper and Row.

Buber, M. (1958). *For the sake of heaven*. (Trans. L. Lewisohn). New York: Meridian Books.

Buber, M. (1963). *Israel and the world*. New York: Schocken Books.

Buber, M. (1965a). *Between man and man*. New York: MacMillan.

Buber, M. (1965b.) *The knowledge of man: A philosophy of the interhuman.* (Trans. and ed. M. S. Friedman and R. G. Smith). New York: Harper & Row.

Buber, M. (1969). *A believing humanism: Gleanings,* (Trans. and ed. M. S. Friedman). New York: Simon and Schuster.

Buber, M. (1970). *I and thou.* (Trans. and prologue W. Kaufmann). New York: Scribner's.

Buhl, J. (1992). *Intergenerational inter-gender voices. Shared narratives between men and their mothers: An ethical perspective.* Unpublished dissertation.

Clancy, J. (1991). Unpublished paper.

Cotroneo, M., & Krasner, B. R. (1981). A contextual approach to Jewish Christian dialogue. *Journal of Ecumenical Studies, 18* (1), 41–62, Winter.

Farber, L. H. (1966), *The ways of the will. Essays toward a psychology and psychopathology of the will.* New York: Basic Books.

Friedman, M. S. (1960). *Martin Buber: The life of dialogue.* (Originally published in 1955). New York: Harper Torchbooks.

Friedman, M. S. (1985). *The healing dialogue in psychotherapy.* New York: Jason Aronson.

Friedman, M. S. (1990). Dialogue: Philosophical anthropology and gestalt therapy. *The Gestalt Journal, xiii, 1,* Spring, 7–40.

Friedman, M. S. (1991). *Encounter on a narrow ridge: A life of Martin Buber.* New York: Paragon House.

Friedman, M. S. & Schlipp, P. A. (1967). The Philosophy of Martin Buber. *The Library of Living Philosophers (Vol. xii).* La Salle, IL: Open Court.

Heschel, A. (1949). The mystical element in Judaism. In L. Finklestein (Ed.), *The Jews.* Philadelphia: The Jewish Publication Society of America.

Krasner, B. R. (1981–1982). Religious loyalties in clinical work: A contextual view. *Journal of Jewish Communal Service, LVII* (2), 108–113.

Krasner, B. R. (1983). Towards a trustworthy context in family and community. *Journal of Christian Healing, 5,* 39–44.

Krasner, B. R. (1986). Trustworthiness: The primal family resource. In M. Karpel (Ed.), *Family Resources.* New York: Guilford Press.

Krasner, B. R. (1987). Choosing for trust: Method, process, way. Monograph. King of Prussia: Contextual Media.

Krasner, B. R., & Joyce, A. (1989). Male invisibility: Breaking the silence. *Journal of Christian Healing, 9.*

Krasner, B. R., & McCabe, A. (1987). Adoption: Reworking the burden of split loyalties. (Monograph). King of Prussia: Contextual Media.

Krasner, B. R., & Shapiro, A. (1979). Trustbuilding initiatives in the rabbinic community. *Conservative Judaism, 33*(1).

Menninger, K. A. (1973). *Whatever became of sin.* New York: Hawthorn Books.

Murrow, L. (1991). *Time Magazine,* August 12.

Rilke, R. M. (1981). *Selected poems of Rainer Maria Rilke.* (With commentary and trans. by R. Bly.) New York: Harper and Row.

Rome, S., & Rome, B. (Eds.) (1970). Martin Buber section conducted and with Buber's replies trans. by M. S. Friedman. *In Philosophical Interrogations.* New York: Harper Torchbooks.

Trombone, M. (1994). Classroom discussion.

Uhlig, M. A. (1990, October 7). A boyfriend, a bank fraud and greed imperil Mexico's economic renewal. *The New York Times* p. A3.

INDEX